Non-profit Organizations and Co-production

Non-profit Organizations and Co-production: The Logics Shaping Professional and Citizen Collaboration develops a novel framework for analysing the practices of co-production between citizens and professionals in the non-profit sector. Analysing organizations in three contexts (Sheffield, England; Lyon, France; and Montreal, Quebec, Canada), the book examines the international differences between non-profits, evidenced by the way that they variously blend or assimilate the logics of the market, state, and community, and how this shapes the motivations for and approaches to co-production at the micro level in each context. This book presents a major step forward in comparative non-profit studies and the co-production of public services.

This book will be of interest to researchers, policymakers, practitioners, and graduate/postgraduate students in public administration and management, particularly within Public and Non-profit Management and Organization Studies. The book speaks directly to key contemporary debates in these fields, including the nature of organizational hybridity, public service innovation, and approaches to service user involvement.

Caitlin McMullin is an associate professor in the Department of Politics and Society at Aalborg University, Denmark.

Routledge Studies in the Management of Voluntary and Non-Profit Organizations
Series Editor
Stephen P. Osborne
(University of Edinburgh, UK)

Voluntary and non-profit organizations are playing an increasingly significant role, worldwide, in the provision and management of public services. Drawing together significant and ground breaking research, this series will be essential reading for students of public policy and management as well as the thinking manager. Topics covered include the management of innovation and change, financial management, performance evaluation and management and organizational development and project management.

Also available from Routledge:

Performance Management in Nonprofit Organizations
Global Perspectives
Edited by Zahirul Hoque and Lee Parker

Management Innovations for Health Care Organizations
Adopt, Abandon or Adapt?
Edited by Anders Örtenblad, Carina Abrahamson Löfström, and Rod Sheaff

Financing Nonprofit Organizations
Inigo Garcia-Rodriguez and M. Elena Romero-Merino

Remittances and International Development
The Invisible Force Shaping Community
Sabith Khan and Daisha M. Merritt

Public Sector Volunteer Management
Best Practices and Challenges
Aminata Sillah

Non-profit Organizations and Co-production
The Logics Shaping Professional and Citizen Collaboration
Caitlin McMullin

For more information about this series, please visit: www.routledge.com

Non-profit Organizations and Co-production

The Logics Shaping Professional and Citizen Collaboration

Caitlin McMullin

Routledge
Taylor & Francis Group
NEW YORK AND LONDON

First published 2023
by Routledge
605 Third Avenue, New York, NY 10158

and by Routledge
4 Park Square, Milton Park, Abingdon, Oxon, OX14 4RN

Routledge is an imprint of the Taylor & Francis Group, an informa business

Library of Congress Cataloging-in-Publication Data
Names: McMullin, Caitlin, author.
Title: Non-profit organizations and co-production : the logics shaping practitioner and citizen collaborations / Caitlin McMullin.
Description: 1 Edition. | New York, NY : Routledge, 2023. | Series: Routledge studies in the management of voluntary and non-profit organizations | Includes bibliographical references and index.
Identifiers: LCCN 2022019755 | ISBN 9781032157672 (hardback) | ISBN 9781032157689 (paperback) | ISBN 9781003245605 (ebook)
Subjects: LCSH: Nonprofit organizations—Management—Case studies. | Social service—Citizen participation—Case studies. | Public administration—Citizen participation—Case studies. | Voluntarism
Classification: LCC HD62.6 .M433 2023 | DDC 361.7068/1—dc23/eng/20220425
LC record available at https://lccn.loc.gov/2022019755

ISBN: 978-1-032-15767-2 (hbk)
ISBN: 978-1-032-15768-9 (pbk)
ISBN: 978-1-003-24560-5 (ebk)

DOI: 10.4324/9781003245605

Typeset in Bembo
by Apex CoVantage, LLC

Contents

Tables

Abbreviations

ABIS	Age Better in Sheffield
ACA	Autonomous community action
ACEPP	Association des Collectifs Enfants Parents Professionnels
BSCC	Best Start Communities Count
CAF	Caisse des Allocations Familiales
CDC	Community Development Corporation
DRE	Décider Rosemont Ensemble
NPG	New Public Governance
NPM	New Public Management
NPO	Non-profit organization
SDL	Service Delivery Logic
SML	Social Movement Logic
SSE	Social and Solidarity Economy
SSL	Social Solidarity Logic
TSO	Third Sector Organization

Acknowledgements

This book is the culmination of several years of research and writing while as a PhD student at the University of Birmingham, a postdoc at the University of Montreal, and finally as an associate professor at Aalborg University. I am extremely grateful to the Centre for Interdisciplinary Research on Montreal at McGill University for funding my research in Quebec, which enabled me to extend this study from a two- to a three-context comparative study.

This book would not be what it is without the support of Chris Skelcher and Catherine Needham while working on the England and France portion of the research at the University of Birmingham and Laurence Bherer while working on the Quebec research at the University of Montreal.

I would also like to express my gratitude to my wonderful writing group – Ethan Park, Maeve Curtin, Jade Wong, and Matthew Bakko – for their invaluable feedback and for their moral support during the last year of writing this book. Our monthly discussions have given me more than a few "light bulb" moments that have greatly improved my work.

Victor Pestoff has been incredibly kind, generous with his time, and constructive in helping me develop as a co-production scholar. Thank you for inspiring me to take this research agenda forward.

Thank you to all the participants who agreed to be interviewed for the research. I hope that I have done your work justice and that this book will make a small contribution to helping us understand how to better provide public services and improve communities. *Merci à tous les participants qui ont acceptés d'être interviewés pour la recherche. J'espère que ce livre nous aidera un petit peu à comprendre comment améliorer les services publics et promouvoir la solidarité.*

Finally, I am grateful as always for the support, encouragement, and patience of my wonderful husband, Neil. You make this all a whole lot easier.

1 Introduction

1 Introduction

In the summer of 2019, I sat down to interview the director of the Rosemont Community Development Corporation (CDC Rosemont) in a centre-east neighbourhood of Montreal, Quebec. Montreal is a large city, with a population of 1.7 million people and a rich tapestry of community organizations operating in distinct neighbourhoods. CDC Rosemont is well-known in the city for its approach of bringing together citizens and frontline staff from local non-profit organizations to collaborate in 'action groups' to develop new, innovative projects for the community. In fact, frontline staff from another Montreal neighbourhood had explained how much they admired Rosemont and took inspiration from their co-production approach to their own work.

Unlike in other locations I had studied, Rosemont seemed to have no trouble getting several hundred residents to attend a forum to decide priorities for the neighbourhood, and dozens of residents signed up to become members of action groups. When I asked the director why it was that citizen mobilization was so strong in the neighbourhood and that it seemed to be less of a challenge to get citizens involved in co-production than elsewhere, he responded by asking, "Do you like cheese?" When I (confused) responded yes, he explained:

> Why do you like cheese? Because you tasted it, and you thought it was good. Sure, there are particular tastes. Maybe you don't like bleu cheese. But you like cheese. So it's normal that at a party, you might have a cheese board. That's it – I'd say it's the same thing. . . . Why is Rosemont like this? I don't know. We often say that Rosemont has a DNA of collaboration. The neighbourhood is one that collaborates on a lot of things. It's rare that organizations are in competition against each other.

This response caught me off guard, because the classic assumptions about citizen participation and co-production suggest that it's not as straightforward as this: much of the literature argues that the greatest challenges for

DOI: 10.4324/9781003245605-1

co-production are about changing professional cultures to be more open and about overcoming the barriers to getting citizens involved. But in Rosemont, and indeed in other neighbourhoods in Montreal, it was easy. The flippant question about cheese prompted more questions, underscoring the key puzzle of my research – how can we understand whether, how, and why co-production between non-profit professionals and citizens varies in different contexts?

This question points to two important themes in our understanding of the evolving nature of public management: first, the growing interest in co-production (between professionals and citizens), and second, the role of non-profit organizations in the welfare system. Co-production of public services has become popular in many contexts, and the notion that citizens and professionals working together in public service delivery will both decrease the costs of services as well as make them more effective and democratic has appeal across the political spectrum. Co-production has been promoted to address the multiple intersecting challenges of changing demographics, democratic deficits, and challenges to public finances.

Co-production relates to the collaboration of citizens and professionals (working the public, private, or third sectors) in delivering public services. However, the term has been interpreted in different ways to refer to multiple practices and processes, from those who see co-production as an inherent part of the service production process, to the other end of the spectrum where co-production is conceived as a radical transformation to empower citizens and service users. By some, co-production is also employed to discuss individual relations between public servants or other practitioners and service users, and as collaborations between organizations by others. Despite these inconsistencies, there is tremendous optimism about the potential for co-production.

At the same time, non-profit or third sector organizations have begun to play an increasingly important role in providing public services. While this is often described in relation to a 'hollowing out' of the state, where public services are contracted out to external providers under the auspices of New Public Management principles (Rhodes, 1994), the third sector's role in public service provision is not a new one in many contexts. Under some corporatist welfare regimes, non-profit organizations have long provided services on behalf of the state, while in others, a new wave of public management reforms often referred to as the New Public Governance has prompted new collaborative arrangements and partnerships between governments and third sector organizations (Osborne, 2006).

The two parallel phenomena of co-production and the involvement of third sector organizations in public service provision have received growing academic attention (e.g. Pestoff et al., 2012; Mazzei et al., 2019), but despite research being undertaken across Europe and North America, we still have limited evidence about how and why co-production might be undertaken differently and for different reasons by organizations in diverse contexts. Previous studies have established critical differences between the welfare states (Esping-Andersen, 1990) and third sectors or non-profit regimes

(Salamon & Anheier, 1997) between countries, with even further distinctions made between contexts emanating from the non-profit tradition and those where the social economy is more prevalent (Evers & Laville, 2004). What is left unclear from these typologies is how these third sector organizations deliver services and how they work with service users, or in other words, whether there is a thread between the macro (welfare state), the meso (organizations), and micro level day-to-day practices.

In this book, I examine this phenomenon of co-production, which I define as the involvement of paid non-profit staff and citizens/service users in the delivery of these organizations' services. I focus both on the involvement of traditional 'end users' of services as well as citizens/community members more broadly who are also likely to derive some benefit from the service (as distinguished from traditional volunteering). Co-production means a type of collaboration between different stakeholders as equals, beyond simply consulting service users to involving them in doing things together. In other words, co-production encompasses both co-design and co-delivery between professionals and citizens. Though there is some debate about whether the 'third sector' refers to groups of citizens or simply another type of professional public service provider, I examine non-profits that employ paid staff and deliver key services to the community, making these professionals equivalent to public servants when it comes to co-production.

Although the appeal of co-production has extended across Western Europe, North America, and Australia, when we look across national borders, less is known about how different contexts shape co-production practices. In this book, I explore this question by studying co-production between non-profit professionals and citizens in three contexts – Sheffield, England; Lyon, France; and Montreal, Quebec (Canada). Based on the literature, I had some expectations before undertaking fieldwork in England and France – while there is a dynamic discourse about the involvement of the third sector and citizens in public service provision in England, publications and interviews with French academics led me to believe that French political culture is critically obstructive to the involvement of citizens in public service delivery. I speculated that Quebec, which straddles a cultural and linguistic boundary between England and France, might fall somewhere between the two when it comes to non-profit professional and citizen co-production.

There are strong examples of co-production in all three locations, but they vary markedly in terms of discourse and practice. In three vignettes, we see how different these approaches can look in practice:

* * *

In Sheffield, England, a volunteer and an early-years practitioner set up craft stations and a snack table in anticipation of the arrival of a dozen or so parents and their excited children for a family fun day. The volunteer is a parent herself and had been a participant in the toddler groups for many months before being recruited to become a volunteer group leader. She now works alongside a practitioner to plan activities, manage group budgets, and facilitate the toddler groups. The programme delivers family activities in some of the most deprived neighbourhoods in Sheffield. By engaging parents as volunteer group facilitators, the programme can work towards its aim of supporting and empowering isolated parents whilst working within a context of extremely limited grant funding.

For this programme, this is co-production – service users (or potential service users) who are involved in actively delivering services alongside paid professionals. Parents are involved in service delivery both as a way to help them as individuals, but also as a way to reduce the costs of running the toddler groups and family activities to supplement the capacity of the limited number of paid staff associated with the programme. Alongside this, informal community engagement forms a key aspect of making the programme work – ensuring that local people are directly involved in deciding what services they want and how they want to access them.

In another part of the city, the local library opens for the day. Instead of professional librarians, the front desk is staffed primarily by volunteers from the local community since the library was threatened with closure by the local council. Citizen co-producers reshelve books, run book clubs, and staff the library cafe while one or two paid staff members (who work for the community development organization in charge of the library) train, coordinate, and supervise the volunteer librarians. This, too, is co-production by citizens and non-profit professionals in Sheffield – where engaging citizens in co-production is done pragmatically, to improve services or to prevent important services from being cut.

★ ★ ★

In Lyon, France, an association's most important forum for citizen and professional co-production is underway: the annual general meeting (AGM). In the lobby of the community centre building where the meeting takes place, members of the association are encouraged to write ideas for new projects, services, or other ideas on pieces of paper shaped like light bulbs, which are then hung on banners around the lobby. These will later be collected, collated, and analysed as part of the strategic planning process for the coming four years. Throughout the year, residents are actively encouraged to come to the social centre with ideas for activities or services they would like to run, which they develop with the support of the organization's staff.

Members have gathered for the AGM in part to discuss priorities for the coming year, but also to vote on key issues, including the election of new members of the *conseil d'administration* (board of trustees).

> We're an association of residents. The residents meet once a year for the general assembly, and they elect a board of trustees. There is a board of

> residents who decide the association's major policies, major strategies, etc. . . . We cross paths with residents every day. What is specific to [Avancé] is that in order to participate in the implementation and in order to reflect on things, there are the employees, but there are also a lot of volunteers.
> (Director, Avancé)

Though this form of non-profit governance is common to organizations both across the English Channel as well as across the Atlantic, the formal involvement of citizens as members of these non-profit organizations – particularly through participatory democracy and strategic planning (or 'co-construction' of strategic plans) – is the most significant arena for citizen co-production for non-profit organizations in Lyon. Here, we see fewer concerns about public service austerity, but more complaints about restrictive government policies.

* * *

On the other side of the Atlantic, in a neighbourhood of Montreal, Quebec, a story emerges that is quite different to both Sheffield and Lyon. A group of people sits around a table in the community centre on a snowy evening in December, discussing the details of a new service they are developing for vulnerable people in the neighbourhood. Members of the group include several residents, an employee of the local Integrated Health and Social Services Centre, and frontline staff from three or four local community organizations. On this particular evening, the group is debating how to get the service off the ground – including finding a space and making key decisions about staffing, targeted populations, and activities. While it is one of the professionals who chairs the meeting and takes notes, it is otherwise difficult to discern who at the table is wearing a hat as a 'citizen' or who is an *intervenant* (practitioner or frontline staff).

> It's super important because it's the foundation of Décider Rosemont Ensemble – the foundation is the participation of citizens and professionals/intervenants. It's important, the union of the two, because if it's just citizens, we're looking at something else – it's autonomous citizens, attached to nothing, they could do whatever they want, and that's that. It's not that at all.
> (Community organizer, CDC Rosemont affiliated org 3)

This group is one of many that has emerged through Décider Rosemont Ensemble, a neighbourhood-wide priority and 'community action' development process, where the local community development corporation supports the co-production of numerous new services and projects to support the local community, such as a drop-in service for vulnerable residents, a community restaurant, and new green spaces. But unlike elsewhere, the focus is not on finding ways to involve citizens in the services that non-profits run, but rather on bringing non-profit professionals in to support and co-produce activities that tend to be more led by citizens.

* * *

Each of these instances can be defined as co-production between non-profit professionals and citizens, because both stakeholder groups are actively involved in designing and delivering the services of the organization. Rather than being passive beneficiaries, service users and community members become active agents in service provision. These are, of course, only three isolated anecdotes, but they start to tell a story of contrasts. On paper, the organizations where these co-production practices take place are similar in their structures (non-profits, governed by a board of trustees) and aims (supporting local social/community development), but there are clear differences in their day-to-day practices and approaches to working with citizens. If the opportunities, constraints, and approaches to co-production are dependent on context, we do not yet have a framework or typology to help explain how.

This book seeks to address this issue. To account for differences in language, culture, and administrative and governance traditions between contexts, I develop a framework of institutional logics – or rules, practices, values, beliefs, and ideas – that help us to explain and interpret why co-production differs between contexts. In order to understand why co-production works – or not – we cannot divorce these practices and approaches of collaboration from the barriers and opportunities that are specific to an organization's context. This model can be employed to undertake further comparative research into the service delivery approaches and practices of third sector organizations.

2 Why co-production?

Public administration scholars and practitioners have always sought to understand how public services can be improved – whether improvement means doing more for less, becoming more inclusive and democratic, and/or improving outcomes (e.g. health, education, and poverty reduction). Modern welfare states are also confronted by increasingly complex wicked problems, such as climate change, shifts in international migration and increasingly frequent refugee crises, and the global COVID-19 pandemic. While there is by no means a silver bullet that can solve these challenges, many governments are beginning to take notice of the potential for co-production to make substantial improvements to public services. Engaging citizens in co-production has the potential to transform the welfare state and radically redistribute power from professionals to citizens as experts by experience.

The notion of co-production was developed by Elinor Ostrom and colleagues in the 1970s and 1980s by evaluating why policing was more effective in some neighbourhoods compared to others. They found that crime was reduced when police undertook their beats on foot rather than in patrol cars and therefore were better able to talk to and work directly with residents to protect the safety of the neighbourhood – or engage residents in co-production. Following these pioneering studies, co-production has regained traction with public administration scholars since the early 2010s, particularly because of the waning popularity of New Public Management and the notion of citizens as customers who exercise their power in public services solely through choice or exit. There is, however, a lack of broad consensus about the definition of co-production and what stage of the public service provision process it refers to. Recent works have aimed to clarify this point, distinguishing between co-creation (referring to the involvement of citizens at the strategic level) and co-production, which relates to the involvement of citizens in implementation or delivery (Brandsen & Honingh, 2018).

Co-production has subsequently become an important theme in current public policy and public administration research, with the number of articles on the topic increasing considerably over the past decade. While the interest in co-production has exploded, much of the focus has been theoretical in nature, with an abundance of literature typologizing different types of co-production based on who is involved, what level of the process they are involved and what type of activities they partake in. Using these theories and typologies, researchers have considered the co-production of community development projects, neighbourhood safety (Van Eijk et al., 2017; Van Eijk, 2018), healthcare (Pestoff, 2021), social care (Mortensen & Needham, 2022), fire services (Alford, 2014), and childcare (Pestoff, 2006), among other areas. Through these studies, we have gained a more comprehensive understanding of the opportunities and barriers for individuals (professionals and citizens/service users) to take part in co-production, whether it is because of individual motivations, the design of co-production processes or structures and cultures at the organizational level.

What is lacking from these analyses, however, is a more macro level framework to compare and contrast the opportunities and barriers unique to particular contexts. Given the challenges facing modern welfare states and the urgent need to find new ways of delivering public services that are effective and democratic, we need to better understand how to make co-production work – and this may not be the same in every service area, in every country, or in every city. Much of the evidence we have about co-production thus far has tended to assume a universal understanding of the notion of co-production, and likewise, that the evidenced motivations for and obstacles to engaging in co-production might be understood as generalizable.

3 Why non-profit organizations?

In this book, I focus on non-profit or third sector organizations that provide public services. I use the terms *non-profit* and *third sector* more or less interchangeably to refer to self-governing organizations, independent of the state, that are driven by a values-based approach and some degree of voluntary origins or involvement of volunteers in their operations (Salamon & Anheier, 1992). While non-profits have always provided vital services for communities, including poverty relief, education, and community development, their important role as part of the welfare state has until recently been under-acknowledged. However, since the turn of the 21st century, trends in public management research and practice have shifted towards a recognition of the multitude of actors – in the public, private, and third sectors – that are involved in public policy and public service delivery, which has been coined New Public Governance (NPG) (Osborne, 2006). In particular, with NPG, we see an increasing acknowledgement of the role of the third sector as providers of public services and the role of citizens/service users as co-producers (Pestoff et al., 2012).

Non-profits are perceived to have inherent advantages in delivering public services over both the state and the private sector (Smith & Lipsky, 1993). Because of a legal status that prohibits the distribution of profits, they operate for the benefit of society rather than for shareholders and are thus well poised to participate in the creation of social, environmental, and other types of public value. According to government failure theory, non-profits exist in order to fill gaps in provision and representation that occur as government seeks to offer roughly uniform service provision to appeal to the median voter (Matsunaga et al., 2010). In addition, non-profits are perceived as better understanding local needs and preferences through their community rootedness, thereby overcoming some of the shortcomings of the state, which has become bureaucratic and increasingly distanced from the general population.

When it comes to co-production, previous studies (e.g. Pestoff, 2009) have argued that a 'glass ceiling' exists for citizen involvement by private and public sector providers, but that the third sector is better able to engage citizens in co-production. Frontline staff who work for non-profits typically have more flexible working practices and the ability to work in collaboration with volunteers, making them potentially better placed than their public servant counterparts to engage citizens in co-production of the services that they provide. Indeed, the notions of co-production and social innovation are in large part linked to the third sector, which is seen as being able to combine economic, social, and political goals in novel ways to provide social services (Krlev et al., 2019).

However, though the research base considering the role of third sector organizations in the welfare mix and in co-production is growing, several questions are left open. The 'third sector' is a hugely heterogeneous concept, with considerable variations from one country to another. Many have noted the inherent 'messiness' associated with trying to pin down what constitutes the third sector and have described it as a "chameleon" (Brandsen et al., 2005) or a "loose and baggy monster" (Kendall & Knapp, 1995). While the non-profit studies literature is dominated by an Anglo-Saxon perspective where non-profits are understood as inextricably linked to philanthropy and volunteering, in much of continental Europe, the third sector sees high levels of social welfare spending and the social economy perspective that emphasizes democratic internal governance over not-for-profit status and includes co-operatives, unions, and mutual organizations in the sector (Evers & Laville, 2004). This therefore creates the potential for significant variations in goals, modes of operation, and the relationships with the state that shape organizations' approaches to co-production with citizens.

4 Institutional logics

To study co-production between non-profit professionals and citizens from an international comparative perspective, I draw upon institutional theory, the application of which has been lacking in the study of co-production. Institutional theory allows us to go beyond explanations of co-production as being linked to individuals' motivations and skills (e.g. Van Eijk & Steen, 2014; Mortensen & Needham, 2022) or organizational characteristics (e.g. Pestoff, 2009) to consider the impact of the broader context in which non-profit organizations operate on their day-to-day practices.

Institutional logics refers to the rules, norms of behaviour, and beliefs that structure cognition and inform decision-making within organizations (Lounsbury, 2007). These logics are associated with the primary institutional orders of society, and non-profit organizations are frequently positioned as existing somewhere between the market, state, and community. They are therefore conceived as 'hybrids' that must therefore assimilate, blend, or reject the logics emanating from these different institutional orders (Smith, 2014; Skelcher & Smith, 2015). Taking forward the agenda on institutional logics, hybridity, and non-profit organizations, I apply the institutional logics approach to examine both the formal constraints on organizational decision-making and behaviour (policies, contracts, funding), the informal and normative, and the ideational. In developing this framework for the study of co-production, I further advance the study of the third sector to providing a new means to study the micro level of practices within organizations and how these are impacted by the meso (organizational) level and macro (external context) level.

Institutional logics are composed of three component parts: (1) rules, (2) practices, and (3) values, beliefs, and ideas. Rules relate to formal regulations and constraints. Practices are informal, day-to-day activities, or 'the way things are done around here.' Finally, the third element – values, beliefs, and ideas – refers to the ideational, the immaterial, and the symbolic. These three components of institutional logics are derived in various degree from the state, market, and community institutional orders. While previous studies of third sector organizations as 'hybrids' suggest that these exist in the interstices between the market, state, and community (see e.g. Brandsen et al., 2005), employing a more nuanced institutional logics perspective allows us to interrogate this assumption and delve more deeply into the varied structures, cultures, and practices of organizations in different contexts.

Through this volume, the institutional logics framework of rules, practices, and values, beliefs, and ideas serves as a structure to explore the impacts of the market, the state, and the community on the non-profit organizations. I employ this as a means to examine co-production practices; however, this approach has significant broader applicability for the (comparative) analysis of other third sector practices as well.

5 Research design and methods

Using this framework of institutional logics, the research explores whether, why, and how co-production practices differ between non-profit organizations in different contexts. This research is based upon qualitative data from case studies in three contexts – France, England, and Quebec (Canada) – focusing on multiple organizations in one city in each context (Lyon, Sheffield, and Montreal respectively). Because of the multi-level nature of institutional logics, I employ a 'nested' or 'embedded' case study design (Thomas, 2011) – thus while the unit of analysis is the organization level, these are nested within their city and national contexts. This approach usefully allows me to apply my analytical framework of institutional logics, which likewise operate on the same three levels of analysis (societal, field, and organizational).

The comparative international research design addresses one of the key weaknesses in the literature, namely that we lack a comprehensive evidence base about the factors that differentially shape, enable, and constrain co-production in different countries. International comparative research enables us to derive policy recommendations, develop new insights and/or theories, and assess transferability of policies between societies (Hantrais, 2009). The three contexts were selected to best represent 'most different' cases (Seawright & Gerring, 2008) in order to explore cases that are markedly different in terms of culture or institutions and whether these factors impact co-production practice.

England, France, and Quebec provide notable contrasts for numerous reasons. The United Kingdom and France are frequently typologized as contrasting categories in terms of welfare regimes (Esping-Andersen, 1990), non-profit regimes (Salamon & Anheier, 1997), and dominant public management models (Pollitt & Bouckaert, 2011). While the United Kingdom is seen as a liberal welfare regime and non-profit regime, characterized by low government spending on welfare and a large non-profit sector, France is typologized as corporatist, with large welfare benefits and a similarly large non-profit sector that, by contrast, is heavily subsidized by the state. The research in England and France was undertaken using a strategy of paired comparison between the cases, investigating organizations that are most similar in terms of their size, aims, and activities within two 'most different' case contexts (Tarrow, 2010).

Though the choice of Quebec as a third context may seem aberrant as a province within a broader national context that is regularly typologized alongside the United Kingdom, there are notable differences between Quebec and the rest of Canada that make Quebec a compelling case to contrast to England and France. First, Quebec is in many ways culturally and politically at the interstices between England and France, exhibiting a blend of both the English sense of community along with French notions of participation and co-construction (McMullin, 2019). In addition, while Canada has been one of the stalwarts of the New Public Management, Quebec has long employed an approach of multi-stakeholder partnership and co-construction of public policy that is more in line with accounts of New Public Governance (McMullin, 2021). Given the cultural, historical, and institutional links between Quebec and both England and France, it therefore provides a unique opportunity to explore the contextual contingency of institutional logics within the third sector.

The research focuses primarily on organizations in the community development or community regeneration sub-sector, referring to organizations that focus on improving both the physical places where people live (including better housing, environments, and access to services and transport), as well as supporting and developing the people that live there. Community development, at least on paper, is also by its nature about co-production – as Vanleene and Verschuere (2018) define it, community development relates to the implementation of solutions to community problems through the joint actions between professionals and residents. Community development organizations also provide a range of services (general health and wellbeing, employment support, programmes for families and children, and poverty reduction, among others). I investigated five community development organizations in Sheffield, five organizations in Lyon called 'social centres' (which are similar in terms of purpose and services delivered), and two community development organizations in Montreal. In addition, in Sheffield and Lyon, I examined programmes to reduce loneliness and isolation of older people and programmes for parents/children.

I conducted interviews with key informants (third sector representatives, consultants, and academics) before selecting one city in each context as the focus for the case studies. Sheffield and Lyon were chosen based on suggestions that these were cities with a tradition of a strong third sector/social economy, and where innovative participation/co-production activities were taking place. Although Montreal is a larger city than Sheffield and Lyon (with a population of about 1.7 million, compared to a little over 500,000 in the former two), Montreal offers the unique opportunity of being a French-English bilingual city with a significant third sector, providing the potential to explore the applicability of the institutional logics and co-production model in a context where both French discourses of co-construction and English notions of community development are present. The data were collected through a multi-method approach of interviews, document analysis, and observation, which will be discussed in further detail in Chapter 3.

6 Structure of the book

In the next chapter, I discuss the concept of co-production of public services and the various ways in which this has been conceptualized in the literature. I outline the multiple typologies of co-production that have been developed and establish the operational definition of co-production for the purposes of this research. The chapter also provides a general overview of the empirical evidence on the barriers and enablers to and motivations for individuals to engage in co-production. Chapter 3 introduces the institutional logics approach, which forms the analytical framework for the research. Institutional logics help us to understand and trace the processes of decision-making in an organization and how it is impacted by its institutional context. I operationalize this concept into three key components: (1) rules and regulations, (2) norms, practices, and routines, and (3) values, beliefs, and ideas. I conclude the chapter by briefly discussing the methods used to conduct the empirical research in England, France, and Quebec.

In the following three chapters, I apply my model of institutional logics to study co-production by third sector organizations in three contrasting contexts. To demonstrate the value of the institutional logics approach in typologizing co-production by third sector organizations, this book is based on primary qualitative research undertaken in three cities – Sheffield, Lyon, and Montreal – that contrast in terms of language/culture, relationships between the third sector and the state, and public service arrangements. Despite these differences, the organizations that I study in each context have in common the mission and aims to improve local neighbourhoods and communities. As we will see through a comparative analysis, the institutional logics framework allows us to better understand how these contextual differences shape the approaches of practitioners and citizens in undertaking collaborative work within organizations.

In Chapter 4, I present an analysis of qualitative research undertaken in Sheffield. Sheffield, located in the North of England, has long been recognized as having a history and reputation of co-operative, trade union, and third sector activism. In the UK, the notion of co-production of public services has become a bit of a buzzword, popular with politicians (keen to both cut the costs of public services as well as increase democratic responsiveness). At the same time, the term has a mixed reputation in the third sector, as some professionals have been eager to adopt new public service innovations, while others remain sceptical that the policy push for co-production is simply a cover for austerity. The chapter examines five community development/community regeneration organizations, a project to reduce loneliness and isolation of older people, and a project to start up parent and toddler groups and services for parents.

Chapter 5 moves across the Channel to France, where the research focuses on Lyon. Unlike in England, the term *co-production* has received little attention in France, although the term *co-construction* (which refers more to the involvement of citizens in policymaking) is increasingly on the agenda.

Lyon was selected as a case location because, like Sheffield, it belongs to a region with a recognized tradition of experiments in citizen participation and strong third sector. I examine five organizations called 'social centres,' which are community centres that also have a shared mission of local social development and citizen empowerment. These organizations run a range of neighbourhood activities (language classes, leisure and social activities, political debates) and encourage citizens to put forward their own projects to be developed with professional support. In addition to the social centres, I discuss a parent co-operative and the local affiliate of a national project that aims to address older people's isolation.

In the third empirical chapter (Chapter 6), I present case studies from Montreal. In many ways, Montreal presents a unique intersection between the English and French cases, as a fully English-French bilingual city that has been shaped both by the English Canadian notions of public service delivery and charity as well as the French values of solidarity, mutuality, and citizenship. In practice, the third sector in Montreal represents its own unique combination of logics that mirror neither the Sheffield nor the Lyon experiences. For this chapter, I took a more ethnographic approach to studying projects undertaken by community development organizations in two neighbourhoods of the city. I investigated several 'community action groups,' where non-profit professionals work with citizens to develop new services, and a 'laboratory of collective intelligence.'

Following the empirical analysis, Chapter 7 begins with an interpretation and discussion of the data from the case studies. I return to the institutional logics framework and present a typology of institutional logics and co-production that describes the English, French, and Quebecois cases. I then present a set of propositions about how different combinations of institutional logics within non-profit organizations shape the motivations to engage in co-production, the barriers to doing so, and the types of co-production that are likely to be most compatible with the organizational environment. I connect these models to the theories on public management regimes and the shift to New Public Governance.

Finally, Chapter 8 considers the broader theoretical implications and contributions of the research, some challenges and limitations of the study, and some potential areas for future investigation.

References

Alford, J. (2014). The multiple facets of co-production: Building on the work of Elinor Ostrom. *Public Management Review*, *16*(3), 299–316.

Brandsen, T., & Honingh, M. (2018). Definitions of co-production and co-creation. In T. Brandsen, T. Steen, & B. Verschuere (Eds.), *Co-production and co-creation: Engaging citizens in public services* (pp. 9–17). Routledge.

Brandsen, T., Van de Donk, W., & Putters, K. (2005). Griffins or chameleons? Hybridity as a permanent and inevitable characteristic of the third sector. *International Journal of Public Administration*, *28*(9–10), 749–765.

Esping-Andersen, G. (1990). *The three worlds of welfare capitalism*. Polity Press.
Evers, A., & Laville, J.-L. (2004). Defining the third sector in Europe. In *The third sector in Europe* (pp. 11–42). Edward Elgar Publishing Ltd.
Hantrais, L. (2009). *International comparative research: Theory, methods and practice*. Palgrave Macmillan.
Kendall, J., & Knapp, M. (1995). A loose and baggy monster: Boundaries, definitions and typologies. In J. Davis Smith, C. Rochester, & R. Hedley (Eds.), *An introduction to the voluntary sector*. Routledge.
Krlev, G., Anheier, H. K., & Mildenberger, G. (2019). Introduction: Social innovation – What is it and who makes it? In *Social innovation: Comparative perspectives*. Routledge.
Lounsbury, M. (2007). A tale of two cities: Competing logics and practice variation in the professionalizing of mutual funds. *Academy of Management Journal, 50*(2), 289–307.
Matsunaga, Y., Yamauchi, N., & Okuyama, N. (2010). What determines the size of the nonprofit sector?: A cross-country analysis of the government failure theory. *Voluntas, 21*(2), 180–201. http://doi.org/10.1007/s11266-010-9125-9
Mazzei, M., Teasdale, S., Calò, F., & Roy, M. J. (2019). Co-production and the third sector: Conceptualising different approaches to service user involvement. *Public Management Review, 22*(9), 1265–1283. http://doi.org/10.1080/14719037.2019.1630135.
McMullin, C. (2019). Coproduction and the third sector in France: Governmental traditions and the French conceptualization of participation. *Social Policy and Administration, 53*(2), 295–310.
McMullin, C. (2021). Challenging the necessity of New Public Governance: Co-production by third sector organizations under different models of public management. *Public Administration, 99*(1), 5–22. http://doi.org/10.1111/padm.12672
Mortensen, N. M., & Needham, C. (2022). "I do not want to be one of her favourites". Emotional display and the co-production of frontline care services. *Public Management Review*, 1–22. http://doi.org/10.1080/14719037.2021.2013071
Osborne, S. P. (2006). The New Public Governance. *Public Management Review, 8*(3), 377–387.
Pestoff, V. (2006). Citizens and co-production of welfare services: Childcare in eight European countries. *Public Management Review, 8*(4), 503–519.
Pestoff, V. (2009). Towards a paradigm of democratic participation: Citizen participation and co-production of personal social services in Sweden. *Annals of Public and Cooperative Economics, 80*(2), 197–224.
Pestoff, V. (2021). *Co-production and Japanese healthcare: Work environment, governance, service quality and social values*. Routledge.
Pestoff, V., Brandsen, T., & Verschuere, B. (Eds.). (2012). *New public governance, the third sector and co-production*. Routledge.
Pollitt, C., & Bouckaert, G. (2011). *Public management reform: A comparative analysis: New public management, governance, and the neo-Weberian state* (3rd ed.). Oxford University Press.
Rhodes, R. A. (1994). The hollowing out of the state: The changing nature of the public service in Britain. *The Political Quarterly, 65*(2), 138–151.
Salamon, L. M., & Anheier, H. K. (1992). In search of the non-profit sector. I: The question of definitions. *Voluntas: International Journal of Voluntary and Nonprofit Organizations, 3*(2), 125–151. http://doi.org/10.1007/BF01397770
Salamon, L. M., & Anheier, H. K. (1997). *Defining the nonprofit sector: A cross-national analysis*. Manchester University Press.
Seawright, J., & Gerring, J. (2008). Case selection techniques in case study research: A menu of qualitative and quantitative options. *Political Research Quarterly, 61*(2), 294–308. http://doi.org/10.1177/1065912907313077

Skelcher, C., & Smith, S. R. (2015). Theorizing hybridity: Institutional logics, complex organizations, and actor identities: The case of nonprofits. *Public Administration, 93*(2), 433–448.

Smith, S. R. (2014). Hybridity and nonprofit organizations: The research agenda. *American Behavioral Scientist, 58*(11), 1194–1508.

Smith, S. R., & Lipsky, M. (1993). *Nonprofits for hire: The welfare state in the age of contracting*. Harvard University Press.

Tarrow, S. (2010). The strategy of paired comparison: Toward a theory of practice. *Comparative Political Studies, 43*(2), 230–259.

Thomas, G. (2011). *How to do your case study: A guide for students and researchers*. Sage Publications.

Van Eijk, C. J. A. (2018). Helping Dutch neighborhood watch schemes to survive the rainy season: Studying mutual perceptions on citizens' and professionals' engagement in the co-production of community safety. *Voluntas, 29*, 222–236.

Van Eijk, C. J. A., & Steen, T. P. S. (2014). Why people co-produce: Analysing citizens' perceptions on co-planning engagement in health care services. *Public Management Review, 16*(3), 358–382.

Van Eijk, C. J. A., Steen, T. P. S., & Verschuere, B. (2017). Co-producing safety in the local community: A Q-methodology study on the incentives of Belgian and Dutch members of neighbourhood watch schemes. *Local Government Studies, 43*(3), 323–343.

Vanleene, D., & Verschuere, B. (2018). Co-production in community development. In *Co-production and co-creation: Engaging citizens in public services* (pp. 198–207). Routledge.

2 Co-production and the third sector

Co-production was originally developed as a concept in the late 1970s, but it regained the attention of public management scholars, sociologists, and political scientists in the early 2000s as researchers aimed to understand and often promote more collaborative and cooperative ways of working between public service professionals and public service users. This growth of co-production literature has done little to fine tune conceptual consensus; on the contrary, it seems to have become more contested, with researchers using the term to refer to a wide range of activities and practices. Similarly, the idea of the 'third sector' is one that is challenged by a range of definitions that are shaped by national cultures, historical trajectories, and welfare systems.

In this chapter, I present the two key concepts for this research: co-production of public services and the third sector. Through discussing the conceptual basis of co-production and the range of definitions and typologies of this notion, I come to an operational definition for the purposes of this research. Following the discussion of co-production, I turn to the third sector. I survey the historical antecedents of the sector and the two key streams that have come to dominate research in the field – the non-profit school of thought (Salamon & Anheier, 1997) and the social economy approach (Evers & Laville, 2004). Finally, I discuss the challenges of studying co-production in the context of non-profits that provide public services.

1 Citizen participation

Citizen participation relates to the involvement of citizens in the administrative processes of policymaking and implementation, as compared to political participation, which refers to voting (Callahan, 2007). Many political theorists argue that traditional representative structures are falling short of representing the preferences and interests of citizens, creating a democratic deficit. Greater direct citizen involvement is framed to address this as well as to reform government bodies, which have moved away from their democratic ethos and are seen to be overly dominated by bureaucratic norms.

No discussion of citizen participation is complete without discussing Sherry Arnstein's seminal 1969 article, 'A Ladder of Citizen Participation.' Arnstein

DOI: 10.4324/9781003245605-2

developed a typology of levels at which citizens can be involved in decisions, ranging from non-participation (manipulation and therapy) to citizen power (partnership, delegated power, and then citizen control). Writing in the context of the 1960s social movements when citizens increasingly demanded to be involved in government decision-making, Arnstein argued that citizen participation was necessary to redress the systemic imbalances of power that had come to characterize public policymaking. The article contended that many participation initiatives that fall on the lower rungs of the ladder of participation simply recreate existing power structures between decision-makers and those for whom decisions are being made, thereby implying that the goal of any citizen involvement should be the eighth rung, or full citizen control.

Even though this typology is over 50 years old, the ladder of participation continues to be the mostly widely recognized model of citizen participation and empowerment by academics, policymakers, and practitioners alike. As the field has developed, critiques of this model have revealed some of its weaknesses in providing a comprehensive guide for practitioners aiming to improve citizen participation. First, Arnstein's ladder fails to account for what activities or decisions citizens participate in or how they participate, arguing only that, essentially, more participation is better. This has allowed governments to exploit the normative appeal of the ladder, managing to notionally employ rhetoric around participation at the higher rungs of the ladder, which is in practice no more than a 'tick box exercise.' As Cornwall (2008) argues, full citizen 'control' accorded to meaningless areas (such as deciding the colour of paint in a waiting room) does little to transform entrenched power relations. Similarly, designing the model as a ladder makes a judgement that there are 'better' and 'worse' forms of citizen participation, and it implicitly devalues any of the middle rungs, or forms of participation that do not neatly fit on a typology that is solely about transferring decision-making power.

Many of the subsequent theories and models of participation have worked to address these shortcomings. Proponents of deliberative democracy contend that the means by which decisions are made are a crucial part of achieving meaningful citizen participation and that the actual design of involvement exercises can determine whether the aims of redistribution of power and/or improved public services is realized or whether existing power relationships are simply recreated (Fung & Wright, 2003). Arnstein herself asserts that, with many consultation exercises, "What citizens achieve in all this activity is that they have 'participated in participation'" (Arnstein, 1969, p. 216). Fung and Wright (2003) argue that for participation to be meaningful for participants and lead to real change, there must be a focus on developing new, innovative processes of deliberative and participative democracy.

One of the participative democratic models designed by Fung (2006), a 'Democracy Cube,' is designed to consider three further dimensions – who the participants are (to address exclusion and disenfranchisement), the means by which decisions are reached, and the link between these discussions and real policy change. In the same vein, Lowndes et al. (2006) develop an evaluative framework in order to help organizations design participation initiatives and to assess their effectiveness. The CLEAR framework (which stands for 'can, like, enabled, asked, responsive') suggests that citizens will engage if they can, if they find that participation gives them a sense of identity, if they are enabled to do so, if they are asked for their opinion, and if the organization they engage with is responsive. These models suggest a more nuanced view on what citizens should participate in, and how.

2 Public management reform

Co-production is also situated within the context of macro-level reforms of public management and governance. The period following World War II, during which modern welfare states were established, is classified as a period of 'traditional public administration,' where government strategy was centrally defined and public services were controlled by government hierarchies. Under this paradigm, citizens were conceived as beneficiaries of the state, and the opportunities for participation and voice were limited. In the 1980s, a new paradigm began to take hold, which scholars termed New Public Management (NPM) (Hood, 1991; Dunleavy & Hood, 1994). NPM focused on increasing government efficiency by applying market rationales and business logics to public service management. In many countries, but particularly Australia, New Zealand, the UK, and the US, this paradigm began to dominate public administration discourse throughout the 1980s and 1990s, prompting the privatization of services and new performance measurements. Under NPM, the position of citizens went from being considered beneficiaries to customers who could exercise their rights through choice or exit (Aderbach & Christensen, 2005).

NPM has since fallen somewhat out of favour, with opponents arguing that the emphasis on a market for public services and the role of service user as simply a customer undermines the importance of public services to address equalities issues, for example (Ackerman, 2012). Furthermore, the reliance on choice and exit as recourse for service users has been criticized for the fact that it assumes that citizens have equal access to high-quality public services and the ability to exit the market if they are unhappy (Simmons et al., 2012). A new phase in public management reform is suggested to be emerging, which has been termed New Public Governance (NPG) (Osborne, 2006), networked governance (Hartley, 2005), or New Public Service (Denhardt & Denhardt, 2000). New Public Governance (NPG), the most prevalent of these terms, particularly within the co-production literature, is based on a move in focus from state institutions and the market towards the citizen as driver of decision-making and change.

NPG as a model of public management is based on values of openness and collaboration (as compared to NPM's focus on competition and traditional public administration's focus on bureaucracy) (Pollitt & Bouckaert, 2011). Under this shift, therefore, citizens as well as third sector organizations begin to play an increasingly important role as partners with the state both in making decisions about public services as well as providing them (Pestoff et al., 2012). Networks, partnerships, and collaborations become the key mode of governance, based on a value basis of participatory democracy (Pestoff, 2009) or neo-corporatism (Osborne, 2010; McMullin et al., 2021). The involvement of citizens in co-producing public services thus becomes intrinsically linked to this new NPG regime or paradigm. NPG represents a shift both in terms of values (from business and efficiency towards democratic participation) as well as tools used by government (from contracts and performance measurement towards networks and partnerships).

However, this argument of a global evolution in public management from traditional public administration through New Public Management to New Public Governance ignores some important differences in the political and administrative traditions of different countries. While NPM has been primarily influential in the English-speaking world, other continental European countries with more state-centric traditions have followed a model of reform that has been called the Neo-Weberian State (NWS). NWS bucks the trend of marketization popularized by NPM and instead focuses on modernizing bureaucracies to become more responsive to citizens' needs and preferences, while at the same time reinforcing the centrality of the state (Lynn, 2008; Ongaro, 2009).

The dominant model of public management has important impacts on not only defining approaches to policy implementation and public service delivery, but also on the relationship between the state and civil society, and the tools used to manage these relationships (McMullin, 2021). While NPM positions the third sector as a contractor who must compete against other private sector companies, NPG is based more on open collaboration and partnership between the state and third sector, and NWS sees the third sector as a quasi arm of the state who exist to deliver services (Table 2.1).

Table 2.1 Public management models and relationship with third sector

Model	*Values/ideology*	*Role of state*	*Role of third sector*	*Tools to manage relationship*
New Public Management	Competition, efficiency, performance	Decreased	Contracted to provide services (if price is competitive); activism limited	Contracting out; public-private partnerships
New Public Governance	Openness, collaboration	Facilitator/ moderator	Equal partners in policymaking and service delivery	Partnerships; networks
Neo-Weberian State	Enlightened bureaucracy, increased responsiveness to citizens	Primary actor	Providers of services/arm of state – highly regulated	Regulations; conventions

Source: McMullin (2021a)

3 Facilitation of citizen initiatives

While the citizen participation and governance literatures are primarily concerned with the ways that governments and organizations that provide services on behalf of the state involve citizens, professional/citizen collaborations also occur outside of the realm of professional ownership. The facilitation of citizen initiatives (or civic initiatives) relates to the ways that professionals support citizens to develop and undertake self-organized and community-owned activities (Igalla et al., 2019). While we typically associate co-production with the process of bringing citizens in to contribute to services that they would otherwise passively benefit from, citizen initiatives relate to the opposite scenario, where professionals are brought into the citizens' domain.

According to Igalla et al. (2019, p. 1176), citizen initiatives are "a form of self-organization in which citizens mobilize energy and resources to collectively define and carry out projects aimed at providing public goods or services for their community." Often professionals are invited into this process to create an environment conducive to success, to remove barriers, and to provide resources. Therefore, while professionals may facilitate citizen initiatives and contribute similar actions to co-production, they do not lead the process, and ultimate control remains in the hands of citizens (Ansell & Gash, 2008).

In practice, professionals' roles in facilitating citizen initiatives may be either through indirect actions to create conditions for success or through direct collaboration with citizens (Bakker et al., 2012). In the first area, facilitation relates to setting the rules of the game so that citizens may undertake their action without unnecessary impediments. For example, professionals may support citizens by changing local bylaws (for instance, those regulating the use of public space) or by offering neighbourhood budgets that citizens can use to develop their projects. These facilitation acts are more about regulation than co-production, as they do not require that professionals and citizens work directly together. In their more direct roles, professionals facilitate citizen initiatives by providing advice and training, helping to coordinate citizens, or signposting and undertaking boundary-spanning activities (Mees et al., 2019).

Co-production and the direct actions of professionals to facilitate citizen initiatives have much in common, but the co-production literature has focused almost exclusively on instances where citizens co-design and/or co-deliver traditional public services. In fact, only 9% of co-production studies related to instances of the citizen as initiator and government as supporter or facilitator, according to a systematic literature review by Voorberg and colleagues (2015). When we study co-production within the non-profit sector, this type of co-production becomes more relevant, because flexible and community-based working practices mean the distinction between whether a service is initiated by a public service professional or a citizen/volunteer is often a grey area.

This has implications for the logics that shape co-production practices. If citizens initiate the co-production process, they therefore are more likely to define the rules of the game. In other words, a community logic (focused on solidarity, neighbourliness, and mutuality) is likely to dominate, as compared to a government-financed public service that is influenced by state rationales of provision and the potential for market rationales of efficiency. I will return to the influence of the community logic in the next chapter, where I review the concept of institutional logics and delineate how this will be used to analyse co-production between third sector professionals and citizens.

4 Theorizing co-production

A. Defining the various 'co-'s

Rooted in these traditions, the concept of co-production was developed in the late 1970s to describe the involvement of citizens not only in decision-making (i.e. public participation and involvement) but also in implementation or delivery of public services in collaboration with professionals. Elinor Ostrom and colleagues argued that service users – beyond being simply recipients or beneficiaries of services – could offer their time, expertise, and/or resources to become actively involved in the process of service delivery (Sharp, 1980; Parks et al., 1981; Brudney & England, 1983). Ostrom defined co-production as the "process through which inputs used to produce a good or service are contributed by individuals who are not 'in' the same organization," e.g. between 'regular' service providers (professionals) and citizens (Ostrom, 1996, p. 1073). The notion arose from research on policing, where it was found that community policing was more effective in smaller neighbourhoods than in bigger neighbourhoods, and it was concluded that a key contributing factor was the willingness of local citizens to work with police, report suspicious incidents, and build relationships and trust with local officers (Parks et al., 1981).

There is still a considerable lack of agreement within the literature on a single definition of what is and is not co-production. In one perspective that stems from the services management literature, when contrasted with products, all services are co-produced, in the sense that they cannot exist without the active participation of the service user (Osborne & Strokosch, 2013). For instance, this perspective would argue that education can only take place if the student takes the time to listen to lectures and do their homework (thereby co-producing their education with their teacher and/or parents). In this perspective, co-production is not necessarily voluntary – "If services have inherent coproduction, then free will does not enter into it: to make use of the service is to coproduce" (Brandsen & Honingh, 2015, p. 429).

We can also consider co-production as part of the creation of public value. In other words, some see co-production as being about the contributions that both professionals and citizens make to improving public services and improving their communities, or "making better use of each other's assets, resources and contributions to achieve better outcomes or improved efficiency" (Bovaird et al., 2016, p. 49). This allows for a far broader consideration of the possible activities that comprise the co-production process but also considers the contributions made by citizens and professionals *not* necessarily done in collaboration with one another. For instance, Parrado et al. (2013) cite citizens locking their doors as the co-production of public safety, telling others to pick up litter as co-producing environmental services and changing to a healthy diet as co-production of health. In this sense, these behaviours contribute to the improvement of public outcomes; however, they are done independently of the providers of public services in a way that conflicts with other conceptions of co-production which emphasize the 'co-' aspect as meaning 'together.'

In contrast to the previous two conceptualizations, the approach I take to co-production is based on Bovaird's (2007, p. 847) definition of co-production as "the provision of services through regular, long-term relationships between professionalized service providers (in any sector) and service users or other members of the community, where all parties make substantial resource contributions." According to this definition, co-production therefore requires that professionals and citizens work together to make decisions about services and to implement or deliver them. Bovaird develops a typology to describe different variations of co-production depending upon who is involved and what they are involved in, delineating seven different forms of relationships where "full" user and professional co-production relates to the combination of co-design and co-delivery of services between service users and professionals. This typology demonstrates that there is a spectrum of co-production and varying degrees of participation by service users and service professionals, depending on factors such as resources available, type of service, capacity of service users, etc. Bovaird, however, stipulates that full co-production only occurs when service users or citizens are involved in both planning and delivery of the service.

Beyond a distinction between the involvement of service users in the design or delivery of services, we can also characterize the potential involvement of service users in either core or complementary co-production (Brandsen & Honingh, 2015). Core co-production relates to the involvement of service users in delivering the primary service, while complementary activities are tangential to this but nonetheless important to supporting the core service. For example, childcare would be seen as a core service, while complementary activities may include facilities management and maintenance, supervising field trips, or bookkeeping (Pestoff, 2012).

Taking this forward, others contend that co-production relates to further stages of the service production process – commissioning/planning, design, delivery, and assessment or evaluation (Loeffler & Bovaird, 2016; Brix et al., 2020). This distinction provides nuance to our understanding of the process of service production, and that involving citizens is crucial not only at the point of delivery but also earlier on in the process (i.e. when strategic decisions are made about what type of services and what to prioritize), as well as in evaluating whether the process was successful or not, so that this becomes a constant and iterative process of collaboration. The existence of multiple 'co-' concepts can certainly complicate the research landscape, though, with some terms being used interchangeably or in different ways by different authors. Bringing together some of the major definitions (Pestoff, 2012; Brandsen & Honingh, 2018; Voorberg et al., 2015), the following concepts are relevant for the current study:

- **Co-design:** involvement of citizens in decisions about the content and process of a service;
- **Co-delivery:** involvement of citizens in service implementation or delivery;
- **Co-production:** involvement of citizens in both the design and implementation/delivery of a service;
- **Co-creation:** involvement of citizens in strategic decisions or planning about services, or in the initiation of services.

Two other concepts relate to the role of third sector organizations in public services, but they concern the involvement of organizations, rather than the involvement of citizens *by* organizations:

- **Co-governance:** arrangement where third sector organizations participate in planning/decision-making about public services with the public sector;
- **Co-management:** arrangement where third sector organizations deliver public services in cooperation with the public sector.

These multiple perspectives on co-production can create challenges when assessing the comparability of data from one study to another, which has prompted some to call for one definition to be advocated or adopted across the discipline. However, as Pestoff (2019, p. 160) contends, "The problem may not lay in definitions per se, but rather might be a question of different approaches, models or schools of study that colour our understanding of this phenomenon." Pestoff instead suggests that we can group perspectives into three different 'schools' of co-production: an 'Input-output' model that focuses on the involvement of individuals in policy/service implementation (e.g. Ostrom, 1996), a 'Value-chain' model (e.g. Bovaird, 2007) that recognizes the contribution of citizens at various points in the service process (i.e. commissioning, design, delivery, and evaluation), and a 'Public value creation' (e.g. Osborne, 2018) model that shifts the emphasis on the delivery of public services to the co-creation of value between service users and public service organizations.

B. *Who is co-producing? Clients, customers, service users, citizens, volunteers, and members*

Within this spectrum, another key distinction to draw concerns who is co-producing (i.e. which citizens/service users) and who benefits from this. Here, Brudney and England (1983) distinguish between individual, group, and collective co-production. Individual co-production refers to activities where a service user takes part in the co-production activity and the benefit or impact is limited to that individual alone. By contrast, group co-production is defined as the collaboration of numerous citizens with service professionals to increase the quantity or improve the quality of the services they use. Finally, collective co-production again requires the participation of groups of citizens, but the benefit of the co-production extends to a wider population or society as a whole. Individual co-production tends to be associated with activities that citizens do independently for their own personal benefit, such as the aforementioned example of locking one's doors, but this can also be understood through a lens of personalization, or one-to-one collaborations where patients and service users are encouraged to make choices about services in partnership with a professional (McMullin & Needham, 2018).

The question of who is co-producing is brought further into question by the different terms used by scholars, who refer to *clients*, *customers*, *service users*, *communities*, and *citizens*. Ostrom (1996) argues that the process of co-production changes the role of a passive public service client to that of a citizen who plays an active role in the production of public services. Others (e.g. Alford & Yates, 2016) contend that the client/citizen distinction relates to different types of co-production: co-production with clients relates to those who directly consume/benefit from a service and thereby receive private value, while co-production with citizens creates broader public value. Other studies discuss the involvement of citizens and/or service users in co-production as being more or less equivalent (Loeffler & Bovaird, 2016) or propose that the designation depends on the activity (Mortensen et al., 2021). Co-production is generally presented as distinct from traditional volunteering – where individuals contribute time and efforts to benefit others, while *co-production* refers to voluntary efforts contributed to services that the citizen co-producer uses or benefits from in some way (Verschuere et al., 2012; Pestoff, 2019).

These distinctions are more difficult to draw in practice than in theory, particularly when it comes to certain types of community development services provided by non-profit organizations. Community and local social development services have broad aims to improve the lives of local people, which may include direct interventions for specific service user groups (such as peer support groups for people with addiction problems) but may also have broader aims and less clear target populations. For instance, any individual might conceivably be, or become, a client/service user of a drop-in service for people experiencing loneliness or isolation. A person might therefore contribute to service provision as a 'volunteer,' but the degree to which they 'consume' these services or receive private value is ambiguous.

For this reason, co-production may usefully be considered to take place between paid professionals and service users or other (unpaid) individuals with direct lived experience (who may or may not necessarily receive private value). In this way, co-producers may include members of a target group who engage in representative or peer co-production by helping to leverage their commonalities with a target group to improve a service (Eriksson, 2019; Park, 2020). Within the services delivered by the third sector, this type of co-production is common as the involvement of individuals as members of or representatives of 'the community' are often involved in service delivery to ensure that services are best meeting needs.

Because of these multiple sources of ambiguity regarding the terminology of the 'non-professional' co-producer, in this book I primarily refer to co-production with 'citizens.' While this may be controversial to the extent that *citizen* as a term is meant to be linked to democratic processes, voting, and collective benefit (Alford, 2002), of the possible terms, this is the broadest and most inclusive way of describing the 'non-professionals' who are 'outside' of the organization that delivers the service. *Citizen* then becomes a proxy to simply mean 'people' – people who live in a community and who may potentially use or otherwise benefit from a service. I also at times refer to 'citizens/service users' to reflect the heterogeneous nature of this group when relevant. Employing this language of citizens also is a choice to align to the tradition of research that sees co-production as an effort to improve the democratic, empowering approach to public services, rather than the service management perspective that conceives co-production as an inherent element of the service production process.

C. *Impacts of co-production*

Much of the work on co-production has taken a normative position of promoting the benefits that co-production is purported to offer, centring on two primary arguments: the improvement of democracy and citizenship, and increases in efficiency and better services. However, because most studies focus on processes rather than outcomes, this has meant that the evidence base for co-production is comparatively limited (Bovaird & Loeffler, 2012; Verschuere et al., 2012). As Durose et al. (2017, p. 138) argue, "Most of the theorisation around co-production has been of the who/what/when/how type . . . and it is less common to find accounts of why it is that co-production is expected to produce its espoused benefits."

In the United Kingdom and some countries of continental Europe, there has been a growing trend in policy documents and think tanks to promote arguments for public service professionals and citizens to engage in more co-productive working because of this range of purported benefits (Boyle

& Harris, 2009). Co-production is said to be a solution to the challenges of ageing populations and growing strain on the welfare state in many countries (Pestoff, 2012). One of the qualitative arguments for co-production, influenced by Arnstein's participation ladder, is that the process of partnership between professionals and service users leads to a redistribution of power – from an expert-led model where users are 'done to' to a model where users 'do with' professionals (Dunston et al., 2009).

This redistribution of power also extends to the valuation of alternative types of knowledge. According to Needham (2008), co-production allows for a greater recognition of the expertise of both frontline staff (who may feel marginalized in technocratic service delivery systems) as well as seeing service users as 'experts by experience' rather than simply recipients of services. Through building relationships and trust between service providers and service users, Needham argues that service quality can improve as services become more aligned to citizen preferences. Like other deliberative and collaborative processes, co-production is also said to improve social capital and feelings of community belonging among participants (Evers, 2006). It is seen as a way to combat the democratic deficit and gaps in public accountability, by erasing the gap between the public sector and citizens and allowing citizens to have more direct influence over the services they use (Pestoff, 2008).

From a more financial point of view, several authors have posited that co-production can lead to cost savings (Alford & O'Flynn, 2012; Boyle & Harris, 2009). This is purported to be because of the greater coherence between the service offer and service user preferences, which thereby reduces waste and inefficiencies. However, the impact of co-production on the cost of services is a matter of some debate. Some evidence suggests that taking a more co-productive approach, like any other citizen participation activities, may in fact require greater investment and resources from service providers, at least initially (Irvin & Stansbury, 2004). Recognition of the cost of co-production is, however, relatively scarce within the co-production literature, where the primary narrative insists upon these processes' capacity to reduce costs. Providers may be hesitant to invest in different structures or training for staff to engage in co-production without proof that there will be cost savings in the future as a result. In addition, as Pestoff (2006) suggests, while co-produced services may be cheaper, this is often as a result of shifting work that was previously performed by paid professionals to unpaid service users and volunteers. Thus, this claim is somewhat misleading, and any evidence of cost savings due to co-production needs to be investigated to explain why this might be the case.

As previously discussed, because of the conceptual fuzziness of the term *co-production* and focus on a wide range of dissimilar practices, it is often challenging to produce comparative or generalizable evidence. Furthermore, evidence to support the claims of co-production proponents is difficult to acquire and evaluate because of the nature of the normative claims made about co-production. If we cannot adequately define and delineate what is and is not co-production, what we mean by 'better services,' or a correction to the democratic deficit, we cannot evidence these improvements. In relation to the economic benefits of co-production, or the suggestion that co-production leads to service efficiencies, this is likewise challenging to evidence because the cost savings gained may take place in a different department or service area to where the co-production took place (Bovaird & Loeffler, 2012). Durose et al. (2017) argue that to produce an evidence base for co-production, we need to move away from a traditional understanding of what constitutes sufficient evidence, i.e. quantitative, controlled studies, and towards a recognition that the relational aspect of co-production necessitates a greater appreciation of the specificity of local cases and an approach of theory-based evaluation. Likewise, Brix et al. (2020) contend that co-production can only be evaluated by taking account of the contextual variables in which it is taking place.

D. *Facilitators and obstacles to co-production*

If co-production can create the kind of value that is hypothesized, then the question remains: how and when does co-production happen, and conversely, what prevents it? Previous research has presented us with a range of factors that may facilitate or prevent co-production from taking place, as well as the motivations for individuals to participate in co-production. Loeffler and Bovaird (2021) contend that the barriers to co-production can be categorized as emanating from user characteristics (e.g. age, willingness to co-produce), community characteristics (e.g. levels of trust), organizational characteristics (e.g. resources, skills, organizational culture), and context. It is these first two categories of barriers where the greatest amount of empirical evidence has been produced, while the barriers related to organizational factors, and especially to contextual factors, have been understudied.

Citizens and service users may be motivated to take part in co-production by various considerations, including the possibility to improve the quality of or access to services, as well as more intrinsic motivations such as to gain confidence, skills, or social links (Alford, 2014; Van Eijk & Steen, 2014). On the other hand, several obstacles may prevent citizens from taking part in co-production, such as low confidence, lack of training, and lack of communication (Vanleene et al., 2018; Jaspers & Tuurnas, 2021). Many of the obstacles to citizen co-production are similar to the barriers identified as preventing citizens from taking part in other types of involvement/participation activities. Citizens are also more likely to engage in co-production if participation is deemed salient and important to them, and if they believe that their involvement will make a difference (Van Eijk & Steen, 2016; Van Eijk, 2018).

Norms of professionalism have also proven to be a barrier to effective co-production (Tuurnas, 2015). The skills needed for professionals to deliver services in a traditional manner compared to co-producing them with citizens are not always identical, and professionals thus need to develop competencies in areas such as active listening, leadership, and facilitation (Sicilia et al., 2019). Other studies have similarly suggested that professional culture and risk aversion act as barriers to co-production, as professionals are hesitant to cede power to citizens (Bovaird, 2007; Voorberg et al., 2015), but the barriers to professionals engaging citizens in co-production may vary at different stages of the service – for instance, professional norms for involving citizens in service design vary from the stage of service delivery (Mortensen & Needham, 2022). Van Eijk (2018) further argues that professionals – like citizens – are more likely to participate in co-production if they feel that their efforts are valued and appreciated.

At an organizational level, we have comparatively less evidence about whether, why, and how co-production is undertaken. Some studies have shown that creating new structures to support and take responsibility for co-production is key, and that public managers should promote arrangements that support boundary spanning between the public sector, third sector, and citizens (Sicilia et al., 2019). According to Pestoff (2009), the type of organization providing a public service will enable or constrain citizen participation in service delivery – while a "glass ceiling" exists for both staff and service user participation in services delivered by public and private sector providers, third sector organizations (particularly co-operatives) are better suited to facilitate co-production between staff and citizens. Government bureaucracy and perceived red tape are also barriers to professionals engaging citizens in co-production (McMullin, 2020). Finally, process design also matters, although this element of co-production has received less attention (Durose & Richardson, 2016). Co-production can be encouraged or constrained by when, how, and in what activities participants are invited to participate.

5 The third sector and co-production

Although the co-production of public services is most commonly associated with the services funded and provided by the state, the third sector's role in the 'welfare mix' has become increasingly important, making this sector an ideal arena for further investigation of the workings of co-production. Much of the extant literature on the links between co-production and the third sector focus on inter-organizational dynamics between third sector organizations and the state, rather than at the day-to-day service delivery level between (third sector) professionals and service users. Like the term *co-production*, the notion of the 'third sector' is, however, a matter of debate. In this section, I explore the various conceptualizations of the third sector, non-profits, and the social economy, particularly as these concepts differ across international boundaries.

A. Non-profit organizations

When it comes to defining the 'third sector,' the myriad of terms used creates a great deal of confusion – the *voluntary* and *community sector*, *charities*, *non-profit organizations*, *non-governmental organizations*, *the social economy*, *social enterprise*, *civil society*, and *associations* . . . to name the most common. The third sector has been described as a "loose and baggy monster" (Kendall & Knapp, 1995) that contains a large variety of organizational forms, functions, missions, and purposes. In this book, I primarily employ the terms *non-profit* or *third sector organizations*.

The non-profit perspective of third sector studies has been significantly shaped by work from the United States, most notably the important Johns Hopkins Comparative Nonprofit Sector Project (Salamon et al., 1996). From this viewpoint, *the third sector* refers specifically to organizations that are private, voluntary, and operate on a not-for-profit basis (Anheier, 2014). This means that they are separate from the state and independently governed (i.e. able to control their own activities), involve some degree of voluntary labour to undertake their mission, and are legally prohibited from the distribution of profits to members or shareholders. Being a non-profit does not mean that an organization cannot generate a surplus, but that individuals inside the organization cannot benefit personally. Notably, this legal and categorical non-profit perspective excludes co-operative and mutual organizations.

Non-profit organizations fulfil multiple purposes within society. Frumkin (2002) distinguishes two core areas – an instrumental function and an expressive function. The instrumental function refers to their service delivery role. Linked to the notion of government and market failure, the instrumental function perspective contends that non-profits play a role in ensuring that community needs are met by fulfilling important tasks, activities, and services. Beyond this purely functional purpose, non-profits also serve an expressive role. The expressive role relates to the civil society approach that underpins the notion of the non-profit sector. This means that non-profits also exist to encourage the development of social capital (links between members of a community), to mobilize citizens and encourage civic engagement, and to provide a space where citizens can express their values and faith.

More specifically, non-profit organizations are associated with activities that are mainly unique to this sector. First, charitable giving and philanthropy relate to the donation of personal wealth to the benefit of specific public causes (Anheier, 2014). The concept of charity has its roots with the 1601 Statue of Charitable Uses in the United Kingdom, which defines a charity as being for the public benefit, for the relief of poverty, the advancement of education, or the advancement of religion (Taylor, 2004). Second, volunteering and civic engagement are important activities of the non-profit sector. Volunteers contribute to non-profit organizations as board members as well as in direct provision of services and activities. It is as a result of the 1601 Statue that there has been a similar conception of the third sector across the Anglophone world, which have similar traditions of philanthropy, self-organization, and voluntary action that have shaped sector narratives and practices in similar trajectories (Casey, 2016). While philanthropy is less relevant to the present study, we will return to the concept of volunteering and civic engagement as these relate to co-production.

B. *Welfare regimes and non-profit regimes*

To understand how the third sector varies across borders, several typologies and models are useful. First, Esping-Andersen's (1990) typology of welfare regimes provides a valuable lens through which to explain differences in welfare and public service provision. A welfare regime is understood as the combination of economic, social, and political decisions that provide the basis for a particular type of welfare system. With this perspective, countries are categorized based on the degree of commodification in social policy, social stratification, and employment. Esping-Andersen classifies Western capitalist countries as one of three ideal types: liberal, corporatist or conservative, and social democratic. (Further studies, such as Ferrera, 1996 and Arts & Gelissen, 2002, have suggested four or more ideal types).

This typology provides some theoretical basis for understanding possible differences in institutional logics present at the field and organizational level in different contexts that therefore shape non-profit organizations. Differences between welfare regimes provide an insight into a state's ideology about public service provision, in terms of who is entitled to benefits and services, what services should be funded by the state or provided privately, and what types of organizations should be tasked with providing these services. The welfare regimes approach involves an implicit confirmation of the differential influence of institutional logics within countries categorized under different welfare regimes. For instance, in the 'Southern/Mediterranean' model described by Ferrera (1996), a weak welfare state is partially predicated on the strength of the family and religion logics in the provision of social and welfare services. By contrast, a liberal welfare regime is the only welfare regime of the three categories where we would expect the market logic to play a marked role in the welfare system, while conservative/corporatist welfare regimes are greatly influenced by the state logic, as the government is somewhat paternalistic in making determinations about the extent of welfare provision.

The welfare regimes approach has also been used to build a theory to explain the development of the non-profit sector in various countries, allowing us to further appraise the differences between societal and field level logics between countries. Building upon the argument that the size and scope of the non-profit sector in different countries can be traced to each country's social, political, and economic relationships (the 'social origins' of civil society), Salamon and Anheier (1997, 1998) identify four 'non-profit regimes.' The social origins approach suggests that there are several courses of third sector development that align with countries' class relationships and the relationship between the state and society. Their macro-institutionalist model features four types of non-profit regime – based on the scale of non-profit operations (amount of employment and volunteer time) and sources of funding – liberal, social democratic, corporatist, and statist. Both the liberal and corporatist non-profit regimes are characterized as having large non-profit sectors, but echoing Esping-Andersen's welfare regimes model, the liberal non-profit regime sees comparatively low government spending on social welfare compared to corporatist regimes.

Kenny et al. (2017) build upon these typologies of international third sector differences by proposing a comparative model that comprises not only the position of the third sector as part of the welfare mix, but also the activist or advocacy role that third sector organizations play. Their model characterizes seven ideal types of third sector based on the role of these organizations in promoting citizenship, the relationship between civil society and the state, and their service provision role – dual, welfare state, corporatist, collaborative, associative democracy, quasi-market, and Southern models. These can be differentiated by the values that shape government and sector relationships and the tools used to manage these (e.g. contracts, partnerships, regulations), which bring in more meso level and practical elements to understand why and how third sectors do things differently in different contexts.

These typologies reveal some important characteristics to help us begin to consider the societal level logics that characterize different countries and the organizations that operate within them. We would thus expect these to influence both the field and organizational level logics differently in each context. If, as Verschuere et al. (2012) postulate, a country with a strong third sector may also have a tradition of co-production, then this is likely to be the case in countries characterized by corporatist or liberal welfare regimes. However, this conjecture on its own ignores important differences in the institutional arrangements and logics that govern these complex terrains. For instance, France with a 'corporatist' welfare system and the UK with a 'liberal' welfare system have very different structures of provision and delivery of social services.

C. *Social economy and social enterprise*

One of the key critiques of the non-profit regimes approach is that it is primarily driven by the US-led studies that view non-profits as existing as a result of state and market failures, and distinguish the sector based on legal categorizations (Evers & Laville, 2004). By contrast, in much of continental Europe, the third sector is associated more with the social and solidarity economy approach. Rather than distinguishing the third sector by legal form (i.e. constituted as not-for-profit), the social and solidarity economy is based on a social, historical, and political perspective. The social economy is defined as organizations that aim to democratize the economy and prioritize people and community over profit generation (Moulaert & Ailenei, 2005).

Emphasis is therefore put on the democratic internal operations of social economy organizations and on a desire to reframe the notion of political economy, which is a wholly different notion to that of charities using volunteer efforts to improve the lives of the poor, as per the more dominant stream of the non-profit tradition. The social economy is defined by democratic decision-making within organizations and typically involves more co-operative and collaborative approaches to working (Defourny, 2001). While much of the literature refers to the social and solidarity economy, some theorists suggest that the solidarity economy is distinct, with a stronger emphasis on using services and voluntary work to improve social cohesion (Espagne, 2002). The term *solidarity* is used frequently by associations to describe both the mission and values of the organization as well as to describe types of services and actions undertaken.

The social economy perspective is the dominant view of the third sector in countries with a long tradition of co-operatives and mutuals, such as France, Spain, and Italy, as well as the province of Quebec in Canada (McMullin, 2021b). These organizations were created in order to improve the lives of disadvantaged citizens through principles of redistribution and solidarity rather than charity and volunteering that we see under the non-profit tradition (Moulaert & Ailenei, 2005). In contrast to continental Europe, where social economy describes all mutuals, co-operatives, and non-profit associations, in Quebec some non-profit associations ("autonomous community organizations") reject participation in the market and thus distance themselves from the other non-profits and co-operatives that form the social economy (McMullin et al., 2021).

Linked to the notion of social economy, but not identical, is that of social enterprise, or businesses that blend goals of economic profit and social benefit (Sepulveda, 2015). Newer waves that promote the idea of social enterprise build upon social economy values, but without necessarily requiring the collective ownership aspect of co-operatives and mutuals. *Social enterprise* is a broader and more contested term, in part because of the wide range of legal forms that social enterprises can take, some of which may make these organizations fairly indistinguishable from traditional for-profit companies. Here we see broad divergences between European and North American (aside from Quebec) approaches – with the former driven by the previously discussed social economy values of solidarity and cooperativism, while the latter emerged through commercialization pressures on non-profit organizations that began to employ market activities to fill budget deficits (Defourny & Nyssens, 2010). In the US as well, social enterprise is frequently linked to the notion of social entrepreneurs, or individuals who innovate for the purposes of improving the community (Thompson, 2002). This therefore contrasts somewhat with the European focus on collectivism.

6 Different perspectives on the third sector and co-production: some points of clarification

The notions of 'co-production' and the 'third sector' are becoming increasingly interlinked in the literature, particularly in discussions around New Public Governance (as discussed earlier in the chapter), which posits that we are moving towards a new model of public management where citizens and third sector organizations play an increasingly important role as partners with the state (Pestoff et al., 2012). However, when we begin to discuss how the notions of the third sector and co-production relate to one another, a lack of clarity in uses of these terms and units of analysis emerges across the literature. According to Bovaird's definition (2007, p. 847), co-production relates to "the provision of services through regular, long-term relationships between professionalized service providers (*in any sector*) and service users or other members of the community, where all parties make substantial resource contributions" (Emphasis mine). Later, he also groups together "users, volunteers and community groups as coproducers" (p. 847).

Thus, when considering non-profits and co-production, this definition can be read in one of two ways, depending on how one understands "professionalized service providers" and "members of the community." The ambiguous nature of the third sector means that two opposing perspectives are prevalent: first, a 'third sector as groups of citizens' approach, and second, a 'third sector as professional organizations' approach.

A. *Third sector as groups of citizens co-producing with the state*

First, some theorists conceive of the third sector as the second group of stakeholders, or as members of the community who co-produce public services with the state. Alford, for instance, explicitly defines co-production as the "involvement of citizens, clients, consumers, volunteers and/or *community organizations* in producing public services as well as consuming or otherwise benefiting from them" (1998, p. 128, emphasis mine). This perspective is based on an understanding of the third sector as associations or voluntary organizations comprised of independent citizens, or people acting as volunteers who co-produce public services with the state. Ibsen (2021), for instance, argues that focusing on the collaboration between associations and public institutions is a new way of conceiving 'community co-production' or 'collective co-production,' particularly in the Scandinavian context where the public sector maintains primary responsibility for public services. The term *co-production* has likewise been used in the UK context to evaluate the varying types of relationships between the voluntary and community sector and the state (Osborne & McLaughlin, 2004).

There are several ways in which this perspective clashes with many of the prevalent theories in relation to co-production. First, studying the 'co-production between community groups and the state' means that the distinction between co-production and other types of inter-organizational collaborations, such as co-management and co-governance, is less clear from this perspective (Mazzei et al., 2020; Pestoff et al., 2012). This places the unit of analysis on the organizational level rather than the dynamics between individuals at the delivery level. Furthermore, co-production is typically associated with user empowerment and a move from citizens as passive beneficiaries or consumers of public services to becoming active participants in service provision (Pestoff, 2012). As community organizations were not previously 'consumers' of public services, it is unclear how these approaches can harmonize.

Finally, when considering the range of organizations that comprise the third sector and their increasing role as part of the welfare state, this angle becomes ambiguous. This notion of the third sector as community groups, or independent bodies that rely primarily or entirely on the volunteer efforts (Kendall & Knapp, 1995), misconstrues the contemporary reality of the sector, which has become increasingly professionalized and 'business-like' (Maier et al., 2016). As a result, even organizations that may originally have had grassroots origins have become contractors of the state and have consequently imported more bureaucracy and business practices (Carey et al., 2009). This brings into question the extent to which these organizations are in fact especially different to public organizations when it comes to their role in delivering public services.

B. *Third sector as professional service providers who engage citizens/service users in co-production*

In the second perspective, the third sector instead forms part of the group of "professionalized service providers," which reverses the focus and instead conceives of frontline practitioners employed by third sector organizations as equivalent to public servants who engage citizens/service users in co-production. Indeed, Bovaird indicates that his definition of co-production refines Joshi and Moore's earlier conception, which Bovaird argues is too narrow in "confining itself to co-production with state agencies" (2007, p. 847). According to Pestoff (2019), when public services are provided by public agencies, civil servants act as the professionals, while third sector employees are the professionals when services are contracted out to TSOs. From this perspective, we maintain the focus upon the relational dynamics between practitioners and citizens/service users, rather than between organizations.

This second perspective builds upon our understanding that third sector organizations, by being 'community-based' are closer to the populations they serve and therefore have advantages in engaging service users in co-production that public and private sector providers may struggle to do (Smith & Grønbjerg, 2006; Pestoff, 2009). However, the 'third sector as groups of citizens' approach has often impacted the 'third sector as service providers' approach, in that third sector organizations are often presumed to provide a reliable representation of service users, which forestalls a critical analysis of the degree to which non-profit professionals actually engage service users in co-production (Mazzei et al., 2020).

Clarifying this distinction – i.e. whether third sector organizations are categorized as professional organizations that provide services on behalf of the state or as groups of citizens (and therefore acting as proxies for service users) – is crucial because it determines our unit of analysis when we discuss co-production and the third sector. In this study, I base my understanding of co-production by non-profit organizations on the second – third sector organizations as professional service providers – perspective.

There are still some important points to clarify. First, while we take this approach to mean that third sector employees are professionals while citizens are the people with whom they co-produce, the question of whether the services they are co-producing are 'public' services is a matter of some debate. Pestoff (2018) argues that while third sector organizations provide a range of services, it is only those that explicitly fulfil public policy aims and that receive public support that can be considered as co-produced. On the other hand, public services can also be taken to mean any services provided with the aim of addressing social or economic issues, regardless of whether they are provided by the public, private, or non-profit sector (Osborne, 2020, p. 20).

In contexts such as the United Kingdom, the social and community services provided by third sector organizations are often, but not always, funded by the state, in part due to long periods of government austerity. However, understanding co-production as occurring between (third sector) professionals and the individuals who use their services (regardless how the service is financed) is consistent with the discourse within the third sector in the United Kingdom.[1] While I take this broader view of the type of services that can be co-produced, beyond only publicly funded services, the nature of public service continues to be a matter of some debate (particularly in France, which will be discussed in Chapter 5), and many have criticized the decreasing role of the state in public service provision as threatening the accountability and legitimacy of the welfare state.

Another key distinguishing feature when considering co-production and the third sector is that the type of third sector organization to a certain extent defines the type of relationship it has with citizens and therefore what co-production means in practice. As Mazzei et al. (2020) discuss, there is a significant difference between charitable organizations that are controlled by a board of volunteer trustees and "governed for the benefit of beneficiaries" (p. 4) and associations or membership organizations that are governed by members. Membership organizations are their members, and therefore mutual aid co-production is a fundamental part of organizational purpose. Charitable organizations, on the other hand, are founded on the notion of charitable giving (to the deserving poor), which requires a significant change in narrative to move towards a more equal partnership model like co-production.

7 Conclusions

Co-production has become one of the key areas of focus for public administration scholars, with the potential to address some of the urgent challenges facing the welfare state in the 21st century. Though the attention to this phenomenon has increased dramatically, the lack of agreement about a clear definition has meant that researchers have used the same terminology to refer to a range of varying activities and levels of analysis. This volume is based upon a widely accepted definition of co-production as relating to the involvement of citizens/service users in both designing and delivering services alongside professionals.

The third sector provides a compelling arena to develop this research agenda because of the important role that non-profits play in the provision of welfare services and the potential benefits they may have in working in close collaboration with citizens. Perhaps the biggest hurdle to the study of co-production in the non-profit sector is the lack of agreement or shared understanding about whether the third sector constitutes professional service delivery organizations that co-produce with citizens, or alternatively, groups of citizens who co-produce with the state. With a focus on non-profit organizations that employ multiple paid members of staff and deliver services based on contracts and grants from the state (and other funders), I take the former position that non-profit professionals are analogous to their public servant counterparts.

We must also take account of the wide variety in non-profit sectors between contexts and how differences in size, funding, purpose, and relationship with the state are likely to shape how the staff who work for these organizations engage citizens in co-production. Despite the proliferation of co-production studies, international comparative research, particularly from an institutional theory perspective, has been underdeveloped. In the next chapter, we therefore move to a discussion of the institutional logics framework as a means to better engage in contextually sensitive analysis of co-production between non-profit professionals and citizens.

Note

1. See e.g. https://knowhow.ncvo.org.uk/organisation/collaboration/coproduction-and-service-user-involvement.

References

Ackerman, J. (2012). From co-production to co-governance. In *New public governance, the third sector and co-production* (pp. 101–126). Routledge.

Aderbach, J., & Christensen, T. (2005). Citizens and consumers: An NPM dilemma. *Public Management Review*, 7(2), 225–246.

Alford, J. (1998). A public management road less travelled: Clients as co-producers of public services. *Australian Journal of Public Administration*, *57*(4), 128–137.

Alford, J. (2002). Defining the client in the public sector: A social-exchange perspective. *Public Administration Review*, *62*(3), 337–346.

Alford, J. (2014). The multiple facets of co-production: Building on the work of Elinor Ostrom. *Public Management Review*, *16*(3), 299–316.

Alford, J., & O'Flynn, J. (2012). *Rethinking public service delivery: Managing with external providers*. Macmillan International Higher Education.

Alford, J., & Yates, S. (2016). Co-production of public services in Australia: The roles of government organisations and co-producers. *Australian Journal of Public Administration, 75*(2), 159–175. https://doi.org/10.1111/1467-8500.12157

Anheier, H. (2014). Policy issues and developments. In *Nonprofit organizations: Theory, management, policy* (2nd ed., pp. 493–523). Routledge.

Ansell, C., & Gash, A. (2008). Collaborative governance in theory and practice. *Journal of Public Administration Research and Theory, 18*(4), 543–571. https://doi.org/10.1093/jopart/mum032

Arnstein, S. (1969). A ladder of citizen participation. *Journal of the American Institute of Planners, 35*(4), 216–224.

Arts, W., & Gelissen, J. (2002). Three worlds of welfare capitalism or more? A state-of-the-art report. *Journal of European Social Policy, 12*(2), 137–158. https://doi.org/10.1177/0952872002012002114

Bakker, J., Denters, B., Vrielink, M. O., & Klok, P.-J. (2012). Citizens' initiatives: How local governments fill their facilitative role. *Local Government Studies, 38*(4), 395–414. https://doi.org/10.1080/03003930.2012.698240

Bovaird, T. (2007). Beyond engagement and participation: User and community coproduction of public services. *Public Administration Review, 67*(5), 846–860.

Bovaird, T., & Loeffler, E. (2012). From engagement to co-production: The contribution of users and communities to outcomes and public value. *Voluntas, 23*(4), 1119–1138.

Bovaird, T., Stoker, G., Jones, T., Loeffler, E., & Pinilla Roncancio, M. (2016). Activating collective co-production of public services: Influencing citizens to participate in complex governance mechanisms in the UK. *International Review of Administrative Sciences, 82*(1), 47–68. https://doi.org/10.1177/0020852314566009

Boyle, D., & Harris, M. (2009). *The challenge of co-production: How equal partnerships between professionals and the public are crucial to improving public services*. New Economics Foundation.

Brandsen, T., & Honingh, M. (2015). Distinguishing different types of coproduction: A conceptual analysis based on the classical definitions. *Public Administration Review, 76*(3), 427–435.

Brandsen, T., & Honingh, M. (2018). Definitions of co-production and co-creation. In T. Brandsen, T. Steen, & B. Verschuere (Eds.), *Co-production and co-creation: Engaging citizens in public services* (pp. 9–17). Routledge.

Brix, J., Krogstrup, H. K., & Mortensen, N. M. (2020). Evaluating the outcomes of co-production in local government. *Local Government Studies, 46*(2), 169–185. https://doi.org/10.1080/03003930.2019.1702530

Brudney, J. L., & England, R. E. (1983). Toward a definition of the coproduction concept. *Public Administration Review, 43*(1), 59–65.

Callahan, K. (2007). Citizen participation: Models and methods. *International Journal of Public Administration, 30*(11), 1179–1196. https://doi.org/10.1080/01900690701225366

Carey, G., Braunack-Mayer, A., & Barraket, J. (2009). Spaces of care in the third sector: Understanding the effects of professionalization. *Health, 13*(6), 629–646.

Casey, J. (2016). Comparing nonprofit sectors around the world: What do we know and how do we know it? *Journal of Nonprofit Education and Leadership, 6*(3), 187–223.

Cornwall, A. (2008). Unpacking "participation": Models, meanings and practices. *Community Development Journal, 43*(3), 269–283. https://doi.org/10.1093/cdj/bsn010

Defourny, J. (2001). From third sector to social enterprise. In C. Borzaga & J. Defourny (Eds.), *The emergence of social enterprise* (pp. 1–28). Routledge.

Defourny, J., & Nyssens, M. (2010). Conceptions of social enterprise and social entrepreneurship in Europe and the United States: Convergences and divergences. *Journal of Social Entrepreneurship, 1*(1), 32–53. https://doi.org/10.1080/19420670903442053

Denhardt, R., & Denhardt, J. (2000). The new public service: Serving rather than steering. *Public Administration Review, 60*(6), 549–559.

Dunleavy, P., & Hood, C. (1994). From old public administration to new public management. *Public Money & Management, 14*(3), 9–16.

Dunston, R., Lee, A., Boud, D., Brodie, P., & Chiarella, M. (2009). Co-production and health system reform – From re-imagining to re-making. *Australian Journal of Public Administration, 68*(1), 39–52.

Durose, C., Needham, C., Mangan, C., & Rees, J. (2017). Generating "good enough" evidence for co-production. *Evidence & Policy, 13*(1), 135–151.

Durose, C., & Richardson, L. (2016). *Designing public policy for co-production: Theory, practice and change.* Policy Press.

Eriksson, E. M. (2019). Representative co-production: Broadening the scope of the public service logic. *Public Management Review, 21*(2), 291–314. https://doi.org/10.1080/14719037.2018.1487575

Espagne, F. (2002). Sur l'économie sociale et solidaire. *Revue Internationale de l'économie Sociale, 81*(286), 13–22.

Esping-Andersen, G. (1990). *The three worlds of welfare capitalism.* Polity Press.

Evers, A. (2006). Complementary and conflicting: The different meaning of "user involvement" in social services. In A. L. Matthies (Ed.), *Nordic civil society organisations and the future of welfare services: A model for Europe?* (pp. 255–276). Nordic Council.

Evers, A., & Laville, J.-L. (2004). Defining the third sector in Europe. In *The third sector in Europe* (pp. 11–42). Edward Elgar Publishing Ltd.

Ferrera, M. (1996). The "Southern model" of welfare in social Europe. *Journal of European Social Policy, 6*(1), 17–37.

Frumkin, P. (2002). *On being nonprofit: A conceptual policy primer.* Harvard University Press.

Fung, A. (2006). Varieties of participation in complex governance. *Public Administration Review, 66*, 66–75.

Fung, A., & Wright, E. O. (2003). *Deepening democracy: Institutional innovations in empowered participatory democracy.* Verso.

Hartley, J. (2005). Innovation in governance and public services: Past and present. *Public Money & Management, 25*(1), 27–34.

Hood, C. (1991). A public management for all seasons? *Public Administration, 69*(1), 3–19.

Ibsen, B. (2021). Introduction. In *Voluntary and public sector collaboration in Scandinavia: New approaches to co-production* (pp. 1–20). Palgrave Macmillan.

Igalla, M., Edelenbos, J., & van Meerkerk, I. (2019). Citizens in action, what do they accomplish? A systematic literature review of citizen initiatives, their main characteristics, outcomes, and factors. *Voluntas, 30*(5), 1176–1194. https://doi.org/10.1007/s11266-019-00129-0

Irvin, R. A., & Stansbury, J. (2004). Citizen participation in decision making: Is it worth the effort? *Public Administration Review, 64*(1), 55–65. https://doi.org/10.1111/j.1540-6210.2004.00346.x

Jaspers, S., & Tuurnas, S. (2021). An exploration of citizens' professionalism in coproducing social care services. *Public Administration* [Preprint]. https://doi.org/10.1111/padm.12821

Kendall, J., & Knapp, M. (1995). A loose and baggy monster: Boundaries, definitions and typologies. In J. Davis Smith, C. Rochester, & R. Hedley (Eds.), *An introduction to the voluntary sector.* Routledge.

Kenny, S., Taylor, M., Onyx, J., & Mayo, M. (2017). The third sector in context. In *Challenging the third sector: Global prospects for active citizenship* (pp. 53–76). Policy Press.

Loeffler, E., & Bovaird, T. (2016). User and community co-production of public services: What does the evidence tell us? *International Journal of Public Administration, 39*(13), 1006–1019. https://doi.org/10.1080/01900692.2016.1250559

Loeffler, E., & Bovaird, T. (2021). User and community co-production of public value. In *The Palgrave handbook of co-production of public services and outcomes* (pp. 31–57). Palgrave Macmillan.

Lowndes, V., Pratchett, L., & Stoker, G. (2006). Diagnosing and remedying the failings of official participation schemes: The CLEAR framework. *Social Policy and Society, 5*(2), 281–291.

Lynn, L. (2008). What is a Neo-Weberian State? Reflections on a concept and its implications. *NISPAcee Journal of Public Administration and Policy, 1*(2), 17–30.

Maier, F., Meyer, M., & Steinbereithner, M. (2016). Nonprofit organizations becoming business-like: A systematic review. *Nonprofit and Voluntary Sector Quarterly, 45*(1), 64–86.

Mazzei, M., Teasdale, S., Calo, F., & Roy, M. J. (2020). Co-production and the third sector: Conceptualising different approaches to service user involvement. *Public Management Review, 22*(9), 1265–1283. https://doi.org/10.1080/14719037.2019.1630135

McMullin, C. (2020). Co-production of public services: Institutional barriers to the involvement of citizens in policy implementation. In H. Sullivan, H. Dickinson, & H. Henderson (Eds.), *The Palgrave handbook of the public servant* (pp. 1–17). Springer International Publishing. https://doi.org/10.1007/978-3-030-03008-7_26-1

McMullin, C. (2021a). Challenging the necessity of New Public Governance: Co-production by third sector organizations under different models of public management. *Public Administration, 99*(1), 5–22. https://doi.org/10.1111/padm.12672

McMullin, C. (2021b). *Financial mechanisms for innovative social and solidarity economy ecosystems: The case of Quebec.* International Labour Organization. www.ilo.org/global/topics/cooperatives/sse/WCMS_829908/lang-en/index.htm

McMullin, C., & Needham, C. (2018). Co-production and healthcare. In T. Brandsen, T. Steen, & B. Verschuere (Eds.), *Co-production and co-creation: Engaging citizens in public service delivery* (pp. 151–160). Routledge.

McMullin, C., Roy, M. J., & Curtin, M. (2021). Institutional logics as a framework for understanding third sector development: An analysis of Quebec and Scotland. *Policy & Politics, 49*(4), 615–632. https://doi.org/10.1332/030557321X16239357875918

Mees, H. L. P., Uittenbroek, C. J., Hegger, D. L. T., & Driessen, P. P. J. (2019). From citizen participation to government participation: An exploration of the roles of local governments in community initiatives for climate change adaptation in the Netherlands. *Environmental Policy and Governance, 29*(3), 198–208. https://doi.org/10.1002/eet.1847

Mortensen, N. M., Brix, J., & Krogstrup, H. K. (2021). Reshaping the hybrid role of public servants: Identifying the opportunity space for co-production and the enabling skills required by professional co-producers. In H. Sullivan, H. Dickinson, & H. Henderson (Eds.), *The Palgrave handbook of the public servant* (pp. 1–17). Springer International Publishing. https://doi.org/10.1007/978-3-030-03008-7_17-1

Mortensen, N. M., & Needham, C. (2022). "I do not want to be one of her favourites". Emotional display and the co-production of frontline care services. *Public Management Review*, 1–22. https://doi.org/10.1080/14719037.2021.2013071

Moulaert, F., & Ailenei, O. (2005). Social economy, third sector and solidarity relations: A conceptual synthesis from history to present. *Urban Studies, 42*(11), 2037–2053.

Needham, C. (2008). Realising the potential of co-production: Negotiating improvements in public services. *Social Policy and Society*, 7(2), 221–231.

Ongaro, E. (2009). Administrative traditions and models of reform: Napoleonic countries between global paradigms and the neo-Weberian state. In *Public management reform and modernization: Trajectories of administrative change in Italy, France, Greece, Portugal and Spain* (pp. 247–280). Edward Elgar Publishing Ltd.

Osborne, S. P. (2006). The New Public Governance. *Public Management Review*, *8*(3), 377–387.

Osborne, S. P. (2010). *The New Public Governance? Emerging perspectives on the theory and practice of public governance*. Routledge.

Osborne, S. P. (2018). From public service-dominant logic to public service logic: Are public service organizations capable of co-production and value co-creation? *Public Management Review*, *20*(2), 225–231. https://doi.org/10.1080/14719037.2017.1350461

Osborne, S. P. (2020). *Public service logic: Creating value for public service users, citizens, and society through public service delivery*. Routledge. https://doi.org/10.4324/9781003009153

Osborne, S. P., & McLaughlin, K. (2004). The cross-cutting review of the voluntary sector: Where next for local government – voluntary sector relationships? *Regional Studies*, *38*(5), 571–580.

Osborne, S. P., & Strokosch, K. (2013). It takes two to tango? Understanding the co-production of public services by integrating the services management and public administration perspectives. *British Journal of Management*, *24*(S1), S31–S47.

Ostrom, E. (1996). Crossing the great divide: Coproduction, synergy, and development. *World Development*, *24*(6), 1073–1087.

Park, S. (Ethan). (2020). Representative bureaucracy through staff with lived experience: Peer coproduction in the field of substance use disorder treatment. *The American Review of Public Administration*, *50*(8), 880–897. https://doi.org/10.1177/0275074020930414

Parks, R. B., Baker, P. C., Kiser, L., Oakerson, R., Ostrom, E., Ostrom, V., Percy, S. L., Vandivort, M. B., Whitaker, G. P., & Wilson, R. (1981). Consumers as coproducers of public services: Some economic and institutional considerations. *Policy Studies Journal*, *9*(7), 1001–1011.

Parrado, S., Ryzin, G. G. V., Bovaird, T., & Löffler, E. (2013). Correlates of co-production: Evidence from a five-nation survey of citizens. *International Public Management Journal*, *16*(1), 85–112.

Pestoff, V. (2006). Citizens and co-production of welfare services: Childcare in eight European countries. *Public Management Review*, *8*(4), 503–519.

Pestoff, V. (2008). *A democratic architecture for the Welfare state*. Routledge.

Pestoff, V. (2009). Towards a paradigm of democratic participation: Citizen participation and co-production of personal social services in Sweden. *Annals of Public and Cooperative Economics*, *80*(2), 197–224.

Pestoff, V. (2012). Co-production and third sector social services in Europe: Some crucial conceptual issues. In *New Public Governance, the third sector, and co-production* (pp. 13–34). Routledge.

Pestoff, V. (2018). Co-production at the crossroads of public administration regimes. In T. Brandsen, T. Steen, & B. Verschuere (Eds.), *Co-production and co-creation: Engaging citizens in public services* (pp. 27–36). Routledge.

Pestoff, V. (2019). *Co-production and public service management: Citizenship, governance and public service management*. Routledge. https://doi.org/10.4324/9781351059671

Pestoff, V., Brandsen, T., & Verschuere, B. (Eds.). (2012). *New Public Governance, the third sector and co-production*. Routledge.

Pollitt, C., & Bouckaert, G. (2011). *Public management reform: A comparative analysis: New public management, governance, and the neo-Weberian state* (3rd ed.). Oxford University Press.

Salamon, L. M., & Anheier, H. K. (1997). *Defining the nonprofit sector: A cross-national analysis*. Manchester University Press.

Salamon, L. M., & Anheier, H. K. (1998). Social origins of civil society: Explaining the nonprofit sector cross-nationally. *Voluntas, 9*(3), 213–248.

Sepulveda, L. (2015). Social enterprise – A new phenomenon in the field of economic and social welfare? *Social Policy & Administration, 49*(7), 842–861. https://doi.org/10.1111/spol.12106

Sharp, E. B. (1980). Toward a new understanding of urban services and citizen participation: The coproduction concept. *Midwest Review of Public Administration, 14*(2), 105–118.

Sicilia, M., Sancino, A., Nabatchi, T., & Guarini, E. (2019). Facilitating co-production in public services: Management implications from a systematic literature review. *Public Money & Management, 39*(4), 233–240. https://doi.org/10.1080/09540962.2019.1592904

Simmons, R., Birchall, J., & Prout, A. (2012). User involvement in public services: "Choice about voice". *Public Policy and Administration, 27*(1), 3–29.

Smith, S. R., & Grønbjerg, K. A. (2006). Scope and theory of government-nonprofit relations. In *The nonprofit sector: A research handbook* (pp. 221–242). Yale University Press.

Taylor, M. (2004). The welfare mix in the United Kingdom. In A. Evers & J.-L. Laville (Eds.), *The third sector in Europe* (pp. 122–143). Edward Elgar Publishing.

Thompson, J. L. (2002). The world of the social entrepreneur. *International Journal of Public Sector Management, 15*(5), 412–431. https://doi.org/10.1108/09513550210435746

Tuurnas, S. (2015). Learning to co-produce? The perspective of public service professionals. *International Journal of Public Sector Management, 28*(7), 583–598.

Van Eijk, C. J. A. (2018). Helping Dutch neighborhood watch schemes to survive the rainy season: Studying mutual perceptions on citizens' and professionals' engagement in the co-production of community safety. *Voluntas, 29*, 222–236.

Van Eijk, C. J. A., & Steen, T. P. S. (2014). Why people co-produce: Analysing citizens' perceptions on co-planning engagement in health care services. *Public Management Review, 16*(3), 358–382.

Van Eijk, C. J. A., & Steen, T. P. S. (2016). Why engage in co-production of public services? Mixing theory and empirical evidence. *International Review of Administrative Sciences, 82*(1), 28–46. https://doi.org/10.1177/0020852314566007

Vanleene, D., Voets, J., & Verschuere, B. (2018). The co-production of a community: Engaging citizens in derelict neighbourhoods. *Voluntas, 29*(1), 201–221.

Verschuere, B., Brandsen, T., & Pestoff, V. (2012). Co-production: The state of the art in research and the future agenda. *Voluntas, 23*(4), 1083–1101.

Voorberg, W. H., Bekkers, V. J. J. M., & Tummers, L. G. (2015). A systematic review of co-creation and co-production: Embarking on the social innovation journey. *Public Management Review, 17*(9), 1333–1357.

3 Hybridity, institutional logics, and the third sector

As the literature on co-production has grown, so too has the call for a greater application of institutional theory to the study of co-production in different contexts. In this chapter, I develop a framework of institutional logics that facilitates the comparative analysis of co-production by non-profit practitioners that is sensitive to their unique contextual opportunities and constraints. The chapter discusses the notions of institutional logics and hybridity, and the key characteristics of each of the primary 'institutional orders' of society. It then proceeds to outline the operationalization of this concept into an analytical framework of: (1) rules, (2) practices, and (3) values, beliefs. and ideas. Finally, I explain how this framework forms the basis for data collection and data analysis.

1 Institutional logics

Third sector organizations are commonly understood as existing somewhere at the intersection between the market, the state, and the community, but the diversity of organizational forms, functions and modes of behaviour blurs these boundaries. Organizations of the third sector are thus increasingly conceived of as 'hybrids' of these spheres, blending and adapting to different task, legitimacy, or resource environments (Vickers et al., 2017; McMullin & Skelcher, 2018). Brandsen et al. (2015, p. 758) argue that "hybridity [is] an inevitable and permanent characteristic" of the third sector because of the increasing fluidity of boundaries between the market, state, and civil society, thus making it difficult to unambiguously define the non-profit sector. However, much of the non-profit literature tends to discuss the notion of hybridity as a purely descriptive characteristic of the sector; for example, in analysing organizations that introduce market activities to complement their social welfare dimension (e.g., Billis, 2010; Hasenfeld & Gidron, 2005).

Skelcher and Smith (2015) argue that this notion of hybridity is itself variable and that non-profit organizations may be driven by different approaches to managing and reconciling various pressures. We can therefore employ an approach of institutional logics to remove the taken-for-granted assumptions about how government, the market, and civil society shape non-profit

DOI: 10.4324/9781003245605-3

organizations' activities. *Institutional logics* refers to the cultural beliefs, norms of behaviour, and rules that structure cognition and inform decision-making within organizations (Lounsbury, 2007). Institutional logics are conceived as socially constructed and historically contingent, and are both material, in terms of organizational structures and practices, as well as symbolic, relating to assumptions, beliefs, and identities within organizations (Thornton et al., 2012). In other words, an institutional logic is "the way a particular social world works" (Thornton & Ocasio, 2008, p. 101).

Institutional logics are conceived as existing linked to the main 'institutional orders' of society, or family, religion, state, market, profession, corporation, and community (Friedland & Alford, 1991; Thornton et al., 2012). Each of these institutional orders is characterized by a particular mix of values, assumptions, and structures that form its dominant logic or operating principles. This perspective suggests that individuals and organizations will be variously impacted and driven by different logics depending on the institutional order in which they operate and that conflicts arise when particular demands or situations clash with the dominant institutional logic. For instance, as Friedland and Alford describe, whilst elected bodies can make decisions by popular vote or consensus, they struggle to acknowledge or address claims of expertise or special privilege because these conflict with the dominant democratic values.

For the third sector, the primary institutional orders that influence organizations are the market, the state, and the community (McMullin, 2020). Professional logics may also be in play in service sectors with a high degree of specialization (e.g. healthcare), while religious logics feed into the activities of faith-based organizations. For the purpose of this study, I focus on the state, market, and community.

A. State

Within this institutional order, legitimacy is determined by democratic participation, the source of authority is bureaucracy and hierarchy, and membership is defined by citizenship. Interestingly, Friedland and Alford (1991) distinguish between a bureaucratic state logic (characterized by regulation and bureaucratic hierarchy) and a democratic logic (defined by an emphasis on participation and popular sovereignty in society), which we might expound to assume that there is an inherent contradiction within government bodies between sources of authority and legitimacy. Greenwood and colleagues (2010) investigate the role of the state logic (in addition to a family and market logic) on business approaches to downsizing in Spain but recognize that two distinct historical periods in Spanish history produced two different approaches to the role of the state – one highly centralist and one decentralized, celebrating regional community differences. This study highlights the complexity inherent in studying institutions and the importance in recognizing that logics are historically and contextually contingent.

Thornton and colleagues' (2012) typology notes that the basis of strategy of the state is to increase 'community good,' a point that highlights the inherent blurriness of boundaries between the level of community and that of the nation-state.

B. *Market*

The market as institutional order is theorized to be about maximizing share price or generating surpluses that can be distributed to owners or shareholders. The characteristics attributed to a market or commercial logic by Thornton (2002) include a mission of building a competitive position, a focus on resource competition, and a strategy of acquisition and growth. The main practice and aim of this institution is to sell goods and services. This logic then is clearly associated with the business world. However, as Friedland and Alford claim, "Capitalist firms cannot exchange unpriced human activities that may be rational for an organization or useful to individuals" (Friedland & Alford, 1991, p. 249). In relation to public services, the market logic is associated with the strategies of NPM, such as contracting out services, performance management and evaluation, and a view of service users as 'customers' (Vickers et al., 2017). In many studies of institutional logics, particularly in the case of 'hybrid' organizations, it is therefore this market or commercial logic that most commonly comes into conflict with another competing logic – such as a therapeutic (Spitzmueller, 2016), social welfare (Pache & Santos, 2013), family and regional state (Greenwood et al., 2010), or editorial logic (Thornton, 2002). In terms of values, the market logic is associated with ideas of efficiency and profitability, frequently manifested in for-profit organizational structures with hierarchical control.

C. *Community*

Thornton and colleagues (2012) introduced the idea of a 'community' institutional order to address a gap they felt existed in Friedland and Alford's original typology of ideal typical institutional orders. "Communities embody local understandings, norms, and rules that serve as touchstones for legitimating mental models upon which individuals and organizations draw to create common definitions of a situation" (Thornton et al., 2012, p. 52). 'Community' is defined by Brint (2001) as a group of people with shared geography, activities, or beliefs who are joined by some loyalty or common set of values. The community logic, therefore, differs from other logics in drawing its legitimacy from an emphasis on trust, reciprocity, and solidarity. The idea of community is based on a shared sense of membership in a group beyond the family, which may or may not be geographically contingent. Charities and associations naturally would be expected to be strongly influenced by this logic, as both their legal forms and stated norms/missions require adherence to a community benefit orientation. Narratives within this institutional order are framed in terms of reciprocity, charity, and neighbourliness.

D. *Profession*

The logic of professions revolves around the valuing of personal expertise within occupations. Here, the transmission of the institution is through relationships between practitioners or professionals and the valuing of particular forms of experience and expertise over others. Unlike the corporation, the primary source of legitimacy within the professions is with individuals and the relationships between them, as opposed to at the organizational level within bureaucratic hierarchies (Thornton, 2002). Rules of the professions are established by professional associations, and practices are transmitted through informal codes of behaviour. For example, legitimacy of medical professionals stems from their exclusive level of expertise, such as the narrative in the UK about promoting the NHS (National Health Service) ethos (Vickers et al., 2017). Similarly, in Thornton's studies, the professional logic within publishing was demonstrated through personal reputations of editors, relational networks between editors and authors, and professional reputation gained through the publication of successful books (Thornton & Ocasio, 1999; Thornton, 2004).

E. *Other logics – Family, corporation, religion*

Of less direct importance to the study of multi-issue/general interest third sector organizations are the institutional orders of the family, religion, and corporation. The family logic is based upon the traditional nuclear family, which engenders values and norms of unconditional loyalty and, traditionally, patriarchal domination. Family reputation and honour are seen as important values that drive behaviour and actions. In addition, Thornton and colleagues (2012) distinguish the corporation from that of the market as a distinct institutional order in being centred on the reputation and performance of the firm as a unit of focus. Legitimacy within this institutional order is bestowed by the board of directors (as opposed to shareholders in the case of the market), and bureaucracy and hierarchy are defining characteristics. For the study of organizations incorporated as a non-profit, this is therefore not applicable. Finally, the logic of religion as an institutional order is rooted in the values of faith and absolute moral principles as guiding forces for all activities, and membership is based on a congregation. Religious logics will therefore play a role in shaping the values and practices of faith-based organizations.

2 Operationalizing the institutional logics framework

Identifying the driving institutional logic or logics of an organization has in some previous literature been approached as though the logic is self-evident through the application of quantitative indicators. For instance, Lounsbury (2007) takes a quantitative approach by creating dummy variables to represent institutional logics to analyse a large-scale dataset. Thornton (2002) similarly presents a quantitative analysis of her data, but the two ideal types of institutional logic were identified through applying institutional logics theory to the analysis of case studies.

I take a more nuanced and qualitative approach to employing an institutional logics framework by operationalizing Thornton and Ocasio's definition of "the socially constructed, historical patterns of *material practices, assumptions, values, beliefs*, and *rules* by which individuals produce and reproduce their material subsistence, organize time and space, and provide meaning to their social reality" (1999, p. 804, emphasis mine). This definition includes three key elements: (1) rules, (2) material practices, and (3) assumptions, values, and beliefs. Lounsbury (2007, p. 289) similarly refers to institutional logics as comprising "broader cultural beliefs and rules," while Friedland and Alford (1991, p. 248) note the "set of material practices and symbolic constructions."

These definitions have in common a focus on the three key aspects of institutions, which Scott (2014) suggests consist of regulative, normative, and cultural-cognitive elements. *Regulative pillar* refers to the rules that regularize behaviour, such as laws and sanctions. The normative pillar encompasses values, norms, and beliefs, or ideas about preferred and desired outcomes and how things 'should' be done, based on a logic of appropriateness and social obligation. Finally, the *cognitive-cultural pillar of institutions* refers to the framing of issues, or the "shared conceptions that constitute the nature of social reality" (Scott, 2014, p. 67). This pillar describes the 'taken for granted' behaviours and understandings that shape common beliefs and drivers for action. Lowndes and Roberts (2013) build upon these notions and develop a typology for studying institutions through identifying and describing three modes of institutional constraint: rules, practices, and narratives. When these elements are conceived in terms of their incorporation into and impact on behaviour, cognition, and decision-making, we understand them as institutional logics.

Building upon these tripartite definitions of institutions and institutional logics, I operationalize this concept as an analytical framework consisting of: (1) rules, (2) practices, and (3) values, beliefs, and ideas. These elements can be defined and identified as follows.

A. *Regulative elements: rules*

Rules encompass the regulations, procedures, and laws that enable and constrain actors (Scott, 2014). Rules are formal and recorded, and they create the boundaries and structures of institutions. They are enacted and enforced through systems of reward and punishment (Lowndes & Roberts, 2013). Rules are perhaps the most explicit and straightforward: individuals know (or are supposed to know) what the rules are because they are written and/or agreed upon. However, rules are not sacrosanct and must be interpreted by individuals, and conformity is not guaranteed (Scott, 2014). It is for this reason that rules and regulations cannot provide the basis for institutional logics on their own – humans are not robots or computers that act solely in accordance with the instructions they are given. While rules may exist on paper, there are a multitude of other factors that drive behaviour and organizational decision-making. In relation to co-production, we would therefore expect that rules provide a basis upon which organizations feel either urged to engage in co-production or constrained in their ability or capacity to do so.

In practice, the rules that impact third sector organizations can be categorized into two groups: external rules and organizational rules. External rules include national and local laws and policies, regulations, and legal frameworks that one most readily associates with this concept. In addition, because third sector organizations in many countries are bound by the constraints associated with their funding, I interpret rules to include the requirements of contracts, grants, and other funding arrangements. The guidelines, expectations, and targets of funders appear to inhabit a middle ground between rules and practices – these are sometimes formally recorded (such as in contracts) but sometimes enable and constrain organizations' behaviours through implicit expectations.

Organizational rules refer to internal recorded procedures. As with contracts and funding, the line between formal rules and practices is not always straightforward. Nevertheless, in my analysis in Chapters 4, 5, and 6, I attempt to identify the instances where respondents have spoken about internal rules or policies that appear to be formally recorded. The process of identifying and analysing rules is undertaken by focusing both on the analysis of formal written documents, where rules are recorded (such as reports, strategic plans, and bid documents) as well as interviews, where individuals describe these rules, their interpretations of them, and the degree to which they are perceived to impact behaviour.

B. Normative elements: practices

The second element of institutional logics is the normative, meaning the informal behaviours, day-to-day activities, and routines that are expected of actors but not to the extent of being recorded or codified. Whether variously designated as practices or informal rules, each conceptualization of institutional logics recognizes the importance of these day-to-day acts in explaining the way that actors understand and behave within their context. At their core, practices are simply "arrays of human activity" (Schatzki, 2001 p. 11). Practices are demonstrated rather than recorded, and they produce and uphold norms of behaviour. Studying practices prioritizes the recognition of agency within institutional studies, in the sense that institutions are not just official structures but are also shaped by human behaviours and actions. Norms represent the accepted ways that individuals do things within an organization, as well as how they do them.

The study of the normative element of institutional logics is informed by social theory, based on the works of Foucault, Giddens, and Bourdieu, but this approach is applied more broadly to other schools of thought, such as philosophy, cultural theory, and science and technology studies (Schatzki, 2001). Practices are also used within critical discourse analysis, where discourse is itself conceptualized as a type of practice, and studying discursive practices as the way that discourses play out in reality (Reckwitz, 2002). This is an important point to consider in understanding the interplay between practices and the way that actors describe these through stories – as Lowndes and Roberts (2013, p. 53) argue, "Practices often form the basis of narrative; [and] narrative accounts can present prevalent practices in a positive or negative light." Practices are about appreciating actions, routines, and behaviours in social life, and studying these thus helps us to understand the everyday lived experiences of actors.

For the purposes of this study, two categories of practices are considered. First, and most importantly, I study approaches to co-production themselves as practices. Co-production is a way of describing a particular way of doing things – designing and delivering services, running programmes, etc. The interactions between professionals and service users as they collaborate in service design and delivery thus constitute a form of practice. Second, norms and practices explain not only what co-production is undertaken, but the other informal 'rules-in-use' (Ostrom, 2007) that shape individuals' behaviour. In the realm of public participation, for example, these rules-in-use may include actions such as encouraging citizens to get involved or the choice of channels of communication (e.g. use of social media). Identifying these necessitates asking actors 'how things are done around here' (Lowndes et al., 2006). These more general norms and rules-in-use provide an important basis for supporting certain types of co-production practices over others.

C. Cultural-cognitive aspects: values, beliefs, and ideas

The final component of the institutional logics approach involves the non-material aspects – variously denoted as "assumptions, values and beliefs" (Thornton et al., 2012), "cultural beliefs" (Lounsbury, 2007), or "symbolic constructions" (Friedland & Alford, 1991). These represent the ways that practices and rules are expressed and made meaningful by actors. While rules can be analysed by examining records, and norms identified through observation of behaviour, the symbolic cultural-cognitive aspect of institutional logics is based on people's understandings, beliefs, and interpretations. As such, this can only be identified through how people describe their own feelings, experiences, and motivations, which is done through narrative analysis.

Narratives are defined by Lowndes and Roberts (2013) as the spoken expression of ideas and the way that practices are justified by actors in order to create shared understandings. Narratives consist of stories that individuals tell in order to understand and frame organizational life and communicate information necessary for decision-making (Feldman et al., 2004). There are two primary ways of looking at narratives that involve different units of analysis – we can look at the overarching structure of the story or narrative, or focus on the words used within these stories (Gee, 1986). While narrative analysis focuses on the former, critical discourse analysis studies the latter. For this study, I draw upon elements of both methods to analyse actors' use of language and stories to reveal their beliefs and motivations (but borrow from critical discourse analysis rather than employing it as a methodology).

Coming back to the analytical framework of institutional logics and the way this can be used to understand co-production, this type of narrative analysis can reveal the ways in which actors are motivated and driven by the pressures or values associated with the community, state, and market logics. In other words, how actors interpret things – such as roles, structures, and ideas – can help us better understand what they do. Similarly important in the analysis of cultural-cognitive or symbolic elements is discourse. Fairclough (1995) describes discourse as a form of social practice, meaning that discourse analysis relates to a consideration of the relationship between spoken text and socio-cultural practice. Language and discourse are important components of action and can be used to generate meanings and enact particular strategies, but discursive strategies are contextually sensitive (Hardy et al., 2000). The way that we talk about actions and strategies and the language we use also have political implications. This means that discourses used in different contexts are likely to vary and will contribute to constructing a picture of the different logics embedded in each.

3 Impact of institutional logics

Institutional logics provide us with insight into the activities and behaviours of individuals and organizations. As Thornton and colleagues (2012, p. 12) explain: "Institutional logics represent frames of reference that condition actors' choices for sense-making, the vocabulary they use to motivate their action, and their sense of self and identity." Institutional logics shape decision-making and other actions of individuals within organizations in four key areas: determining which sources of power are legitimate, drawing the attention of decision-makers towards particular issues and problems as priorities and shaping the 'rules of the game,' delimiting which potential solutions are appropriate to problems and issues that arise, and finally by affecting how well organizations adapt and change over time (Thornton, 2004). Numerous studies have used this concept as an analytical framework to explain a range of different phenomena and behaviours within organizations.

Studies have thus sought to analyse how institutional logics shape various behaviours and practices within organizations. Thornton (2002, 2004), for instance, investigated how a shift from a professional to a market dominant institutional logic impacted restructuring processes within the higher education publishing sector. Her evidence suggests that over time, a shift in the industry from the dominance of a traditional editorial logic towards a market logic impacted governance structures and growth strategies within publishing companies. Thornton argues that institutional logics are important because they focus decision makers' attention on issues that correspond to the overarching dominant institutional logic. Implicit in Thornton's argument is the existence of one overarching prevailing logic which drives identities, structures, and strategies within companies.

However, there is an increasing trend to see organizations as being characterized by a multiplicity of logics, which may be competing, complementary, or compartmentalized (Skelcher & Smith, 2015). For example, Lounsbury (2007) demonstrates the varying impact of competing logics on organizational cultures and practices in mutual funds in Boston and New York. Lounsbury suggests that whilst many studies on institutional logics increasingly recognize the existence of multiple logics in a particular field, the tendency has been to assume that one logic will be dominant and that this will promote 'isomorphic' responses (DiMaggio & Powell, 1983). This emphasis on isomorphism provides weak explanations for organizational change and differences through time and across organizations, as several studies demonstrate that logics are contextually and historically contingent, thereby producing different impacts in different settings and at different points in time (Greenwood et al., 2010).

Institutional logics as an analytical framework has increasingly been applied to the study of decision-making and behaviour within hybrid organizations, of which co-production is a component. For instance, Vickers et al. (2017) employ an institutional logics analytical framework in order to explain social innovation within social enterprises, characterized as hybrids of the state, community, and market logics. They demonstrate that co-production with service users was one type of innovation identified in these organizations, which was facilitated by the co-existence of state, market, and civil society logics. However, this study simply identified the existence of co-production practice as an innovation and did not interrogate different types of co-production or the way in which co-production practices occurred. Although there is an increasing literature on the hybridity of third sector organizations, and some theorization about how co-production fits into this picture, this is typically in relation to how co-production forms part of a new form of more citizen-centred governance systems (Pestoff, 2014). There has been little scholarship investigating how this hybridity, or managing of multiple competing logics, dictates co-production practice.

Understanding the underlying logics of organizations can offer key insights into co-production and the differences in practices between different organizations, regions, or countries. Co-production is inherently a relational process, driven both by normative aims of decreasing the democratic deficit and improving community cohesion and citizen empowerment, as well as more instrumental aims of increasing efficiency and improving outcomes for service users. The relative importance of these aims and strategies may be determined at the individual, organizational, or broader field level. The institutional logics approach provides us with an analytical framework in order to compare and analyse both concrete and discursive differences in co-production (McMullin, 2020). We can therefore employ this approach to address an important gap in the co-production literature – recognizing that co-production practices are not solely based on the individual motivations of actors involved but are also dependent upon and shaped by the logics of a particular sector and particular organization. This thus allows us to better interpret differences between the approach that third sector organizations take to citizen involvement and co-production in different countries.

4 Identifying rules, practices, values, beliefs, and ideas

Because of the different nature of the regulative, normative, and cultural-cognitive elements that comprise institutional logics, multiple methods of data collection were necessary for this study. As Lowndes and Roberts (2013) explain, because rules are formally recorded, they can be identified by analysing documents. Practices by their nature are expressed through day-to-day actions and should therefore be seen or observed. Values, beliefs, and ideas are expressed through narratives, and thus are exposed through speech (i.e. interviews) and writing. Taking this as a departure, the research in this volume is based on a qualitative methods approach, involving interviews, observations, and document analysis to provide a richness of data and to triangulate the findings.

A. Values, beliefs, and ideas: narratives and semi-structured interviews

For each case study, I conducted interviews with senior staff members (e.g. chief executives, senior managers), frontline staff members (i.e. paid employees responsible for providing services with job titles such as community development worker, project lead/manager/coordinator, and development worker), volunteers, and board members. I also conducted interviews with numerous local stakeholders about the more general context for co-production and relationships between the third sector and government in each city, including third sector network representatives, commissioners, and several interviewees from other third sector organizations. As singular interviewees from an organization, these did not become full case studies for the research, but they provided a richer illustration of each context and helped to support the broader applicability of the case study findings. Because the research focused on the organizational dynamics and conditions for co-production, I focused primarily on interviewing staff members rather than citizen co-producers. A full anonymised list of interviewees can be found in the Appendices.

Prior to commencing fieldwork, a broad interview question guide was devised in English. This was composed of 18 general topics with indicative questions, along with some clarifying/probing questions and prompts. Questions were grouped into four main sections – overview (of the organization, its history, and services) and overview of co-production/participation, funding, governance and decision-making, and barriers and enablers to participation. As the fieldwork progressed and I developed the analytical framework for the research, I likewise adapted the interview guide to probe more deeply on ideas, motivations, and values associated with co-production with less of an emphasis on funding and policy arrangements.

Interviews lasted on average between 30 and 60 minutes, and with the consent of respondents, all interviews were audio recorded to preserve the distinct narratives and use of language of participants. I transcribed the majority of the recordings myself using an intelligent verbatim approach, which adapts the oral to a written form by correcting minor grammatical errors, and cleaning up repetitions and utterances (McMullin, 2021). This approach is the most appropriate for thematic and narrative analysis. Undertaking the transcription myself rather than outsourcing this task also allowed for a deeper familiarity with the data.

B. Norms, practices, and routines: observations

One of the challenges in studying practices is that these are often 'under-the-radar' – the routines that organization members often do not notice because they are 'the way we do things.' As such, practices may not be fully acknowledged or known to interviewees because they are taken for granted. Thus, while we may acquire some understanding of practices through interviews, it is better to employ direct observation and ethnographic approaches. For the research in Lyon and Sheffield, while I primarily collected data from interviews, I also observed meetings, service delivery activities, and events as much as possible to observe when and how professionals and citizens worked together to deliver services.

In the case of Montreal, a research design centred more on participant observation from an organizational ethnography approach was employed. This is because the community development sector is much more fragmented with programmes and services developed in partnerships between multiple organizations, which meant that it was more difficult to focus on the services delivered by discrete organizations. Furthermore, the timing of the research allowed me the opportunity to follow the progress of several community development initiatives that were being created at that time. As a participant observer, I was afforded a unique insight into the experience of a citizen co-producer of community development projects.

C. *Rules and policies: document analysis*

Finally, I also conducted thematic content analysis of organizational documents (e.g. operational plans, annual reports, bid documents, and evaluations), publications, and website text. Analysing documents gave me access to the official stories told by organizations about their activities, approaches, and outcomes, as well as the rules or formal policies that enable and constrain the organizations. Document analysis was especially important in the instances where I was only able to interview a limited number of respondents for a case study organization (either because of the size of the organization or because of scheduling problems), which therefore afforded me insight into the organization's rules, as well as values and ideas, and whether/how co-production formed part of these.

As the research focus is at the level of the organization, every attempt was made to compile an illustration of the practices, ideas, and beliefs of the organization, which necessitated the collection and cross-validation of various viewpoints from professionals. Organizational documents such as mission statements, plans, and reports provided a more objective reporting of these variables, which are less tempered by one individual's experience or perceptions. Drawing upon documents as another source of data also allowed me to assess whether there were any conflicts or contradictions between formally recorded rules and day-to-day practices, as described by interviewees or observed by the researcher (Lowndes & Roberts, 2013; Ostrom, 2007).

5 Data analysis

Unlike other studies that use a framework of institutional logics, I chose not to assume a priori knowledge of the logics that exist within the case study organizations based on, for example, quantitative variables or the introduction of a government policy as the trigger for a new institutional logic (Reay & Hinings, 2009). Based on the typologies discussed in Chapter 2 that differentiate welfare regimes, non-profit regimes, and conceptualization of the third sector, we might expect there to be different combinations of logics that drive non-profit organizations in these three contexts, but this needs to be explored through an interpretive approach to theory-building.

The data for the research were analysed in a several-stage abductive approach to analysis. This means that while I started the process with a broad idea of the theory to guide the analysis, I also continuously interrogated the data and allowed for new themes and ideas to emerge and coalesce (Timmermans & Tavory, 2012). Taking this approach, which is more pragmatic and adaptive than formal grounded theory methods (Glaser & Strauss, 2017), data collection was not a separate process to theory development but took place simultaneously and iteratively. The framework of institutional logics was developing through the process of conducting, coding, and analysing interviews in England and France, and this framework was then applied in the subsequent research in Quebec.

A. Stage 1: Values, barriers, and participation methods

For the first stage of analysis, I drew inspiration from the grounded theory method of open coding and coded data with descriptive nodes, simultaneously grouping and re-categorizing emerging nodes into developing themes. After some grouping and regrouping of nodes, the primary parent nodes that emerged were around 'values associated with co-production,' 'barriers and enablers to co-production,' and 'participation and co-production methods.' Each of these parent nodes housed approximately 10–20 child nodes, some of which contained one or two third-level nodes. Some nodes did not fit neatly into these three parent nodes, but it felt important to recognize them, so they were retained as their own top-level nodes. The most important of these was 'terminology/definitions,' with child nodes focusing on 'community,' 'customer or client,' and most importantly, 'reactions to and definitions of the word *co-production*.'

Given the abductive design to the research, I began coding while I was still in the midst of fieldwork in England and France, to begin to understand emerging themes and build theory as the research progressed. This simultaneous data collection and analysis allowed me to tweak my interview question guide to better target the issues I wanted to probe on. When I undertook fieldwork in Quebec, I similarly conducted interviews and analysis simultaneously, and I added second- and third-level nodes to the primary nodes of values, barriers, and methods as they arose from the data (at this stage significant new top-level nodes emerged that differentiated the Quebec data from that of England and France).

B. Stage 2: Rules, practices, and values/beliefs

In the second stage of coding, I draw upon my analytical framework of rules, practices, and the narratives that act as a proxy for values, beliefs, and ideas in order to code for institutional logics (Lowndes & Roberts, 2013). Passages were coded according to the definitions of these three elements as described in Section 2. In speaking candidly, interviewees do not neatly disentangle rules, practices, and values/beliefs, and there were many instances where a passage could be indicated as two or all three of these elements. This frequently arose, for example, in describing a particular participation activity (practice) and in explaining why it was done in such a way, or what benefit it had (beliefs/motivations). In these examples, I double- or triple-coded for rules, practices, and/or values/beliefs.

C. Stage 3: Comparison and analysis

Finally, the coded content was then thoroughly interrogated to identify emerging themes and ideas relating to each element of institutional logics, whether these instances were evidence of the market, state, and/or community logics, and how co-production fit within these. Focusing on rules, practices, and values/beliefs/ideas successively allowed me to clearly formulate a picture of how the case study organizations undertook co-production and the reasons (both objective and subjective, non-material, or perceived) for doing things one way or another.

6 Conclusions

Undertaking international comparative research of co-production between non-profit professionals and citizens necessitates a new way to analyse the opportunities and constraints that non-profit organizations face in different contexts. The institutional logics approach is uniquely adaptive for investigating these differences between political, institutional, and cultural contexts and how these may in turn impact practices such as co-production. This framework of analysis has the advantage of allowing the researcher to evaluate not only what actors do at the individual or organizational level but also identifying the broader field and societal level influences on the ways that actors are enabled and constrained to take particular courses of action.

This study takes a multi-method approach to data collection, using interviews, observations, and document analysis, and an abductive, iterative approach to data analysis allowed for a rigorous approach to interpretive theory-building. In the next section of the book, we begin an analysis of the data from the case studies in Sheffield, Lyon, and Montreal.

References

Billis, D. (2010). *Hybrid organizations and the third sector: Challenges for practice, theory and policy*. Palgrave Macmillan.

Brandsen, T., & Honingh, M. (2015). Distinguishing different types of coproduction: A conceptual analysis based on the classical definitions. *Public Administration Review, 76*(3), 427–435.

Brint, S. (2001). Gemeinschaft revisited: A critique and reconstruction of the community concept. *Sociological Theory, 19*(1), 1–23.

DiMaggio, P. J., & Powell, W. W. (1983). The iron cage revisited: Institutional isomorphism and collective rationality in organizational fields. *American Sociological Review, 48*(2), 147–160. https://doi.org/10.2307/2095101

Fairclough, N. (1995). *Critical discourse analysis: The critical study of language*. Longman.

Feldman, M., Skoldberg, K., Brown, R. N., & Horner, D. (2004). Making sense of stories: A rhetorical approach to narrative analysis. *Journal of Public Administration Research and Theory, 14*(2), 147–170.

Friedland, R., & Alford, R. (1991). Bringing society back in: Symbols, practices and institutional contradictions. In *The new institutionalism in organizational analysis* (2nd ed.). University of Chicago Press.

Gee, J. P. (1986). Units of production of narrative discourse. *Discourse Processes, 9*(4), 391–422.

Glaser, B. G., & Strauss, A. L. (2017). *Discovery of grounded theory: Strategies for qualitative research*. Routledge.

Greenwood, R., Díaz, A. M., Li, S. X., & Lorente, J. C. (2010). The multiplicity of institutional logics and the heterogeneity of organizational responses. *Organization Science, 21*(2), 521–539.

Hardy, C., Palmer, I., & Phillips, N. (2000). Discourse as a strategic resource. *Human Relations, 53*(9), 1227–1248.

Hasenfeld, Y., & Gidron, B. (2005). Understanding multi-purpose hybrid voluntary organizations: The contributions of theories on civil society, social movements and nonprofit organizations. *Journal of Civil Society, 1*(2), 97–112. https://doi.org/10.1080/17448680500337350

Lounsbury, M. (2007). A tale of two cities: Competing logics and practice variation in the professionalizing of mutual funds. *Academy of Management Journal, 50*(2), 289–307.

Lowndes, V., Pratchett, L., & Stoker, G. (2006). Local political participation: The impact of rules-in-use. *Public Administration, 84*(3), 539–561.

Lowndes, V., & Roberts, M. (2013). *Why institutions matter: The new institutionalism in political science*. Macmillan International Higher Education.

McMullin, C. (2020). Co-production of public services: Institutional barriers to the involvement of citizens in policy implementation. In H. Sullivan, H. Dickinson, & H. Henderson (Eds.), *The Palgrave handbook of the public servant* (pp. 1–17). Springer International Publishing. https://doi.org/10.1007/978-3-030-03008-7_26-1

McMullin, C. (2021). Transcription and qualitative methods: Implications for third sector research. *Voluntas* [Preprint]. https://doi.org/10.1007/s11266-021-00400-3

McMullin, C., & Skelcher, C. (2018). The impact of societal-level institutional logics on hybridity: Evidence from nonprofit organizations in England and France. *Voluntas, 29*(5), 911–924. http://doi.org/10.1007/s11266-018-9996-8

Ostrom, E. (2007). Institutional rational choice: An assessment of the institutional analysis and development framework. In P. A. Sabatier (Ed.), *Theories of the policy process* (2nd ed., pp. 21–64). Westview Press.

Pache, A.-C., & Santos, F. (2013). Inside the hybrid organization: Selective coupling as a response to competing institutional logics. *Academy of Management Journal, 56*(4), 972–1001.

Pestoff, V. (2014). Collective action and the sustainability of co-production. *Public Management Review, 16*(3), 383–401.

Reay, T., & Hinings, C. R. (2009). Managing the rivalry of competing institutional logics. *Organization Studies, 30*(6), 629–652. https://doi.org/10.1177/0170840609104803

Reckwitz, A. (2002). Toward a theory of social practices: A development in culturalist theorizing. *European Journal of Social Theory, 5*(2), 243–263.

Schatzki, T. R. (2001). Introduction: Practice theory. In T. R. Schatzki, K. Knorr Cetina, & E. von Savigny (Eds.), *The practice turn in contemporary theory* (pp. 10–23). Routledge.

Scott, W. R. (2014). *Institutions and organizations: Ideas, interests, and identities* (4th ed.). Sage Publications.

Skelcher, C., & Smith, S. R. (2015). Theorizing hybridity: Institutional logics, complex organizations, and actor identities: The case of nonprofits. *Public Administration, 93*(2), 433–448.

Spitzmueller, M. C. (2016). Negotiating competing institutional logics at the street level: An ethnography of a community mental health organization. *Social Service Review, 90*(1), 35–82.

Thornton, P. H. (2002). The rise of the corporation in a craft industry: Conflict and conformity in institutional logics. *Academy of Management Journal, 45*(1), 81–101.

Thornton, P. H. (2004). *Markets from culture: Institutional logics and organizational decisions in higher education publishing*. Stanford University Press.

Thornton, P. H., & Ocasio, W. (1999). Institutional logics and the historical contingency of power in organizations: Executive succession in the higher education publishing industry, 1958–1990. *American Journal of Sociology*, *105*(3), 801–843. https://doi.org/10.1086/210361

Thornton, P. H., & Ocasio, W. (2008). Institutional logics. In R. Greenwood, C. Oliver, K. Sahlin, & R. Suddaby (Eds.), *Handbook of organizational institutionalism* (pp. 99–129). Sage.

Thornton, P. H., Ocasio, W., & Lounsbury, M. (2012). *The institutional logics perspective: A new approach to culture, structure, and process*. Oxford University Press.

Timmermans, S., & Tavory, I. (2012). Theory construction in qualitative research: From grounded theory to abductive analysis. *Sociological Inquiry*, *30*(3), 167–186.

Vickers, I., Lyon, F., Sepulveda, L., & McMullin, C. (2017). Public service innovation and multiple institutional logics: The case of hybrid social enterprise providers of health and wellbeing. *Research Policy*, *46*(10), 1755–1768.

4 Service Delivery Logic and pragmatic co-production in Sheffield

In the UK, co-production has captured the attention of policymakers and practitioners, particularly since the publication of several influential think-tank reports in the early 2000s that advocated co-production to address the many challenges facing public services. The problem with many such policy ideas is that there is not always a direct link between policy and practice, and buzzwords eventually fall out of favour. In this chapter, I explore the co-production in Sheffield between citizens and non-profit professionals working for five community regeneration/community development organizations, as well as a programme to reduce loneliness and isolation of older people, and a parent and toddler group project. First, I provide an overview of the context, including the third sector in England generally and in Sheffield more specifically. I then employ the institutional logics framework to demonstrate the influence of the state, community, and market logics in shaping the co-production practices of these organizations. Finally, I provide a synthesis of the analysis and a model of institutional logics and co-production in the Sheffield third sector.

1 Context: the third sector in Sheffield

At the national level, the United Kingdom is classified as a liberal welfare regime by Esping-Andersen (1990) and as a liberal non-profit regime by Salamon and Anheier (1998). This means a low level of welfare provision that focuses on providing for only the neediest, and comparatively low government spending on social welfare and a large non-profit sector. While others posit that the UK is situated somewhere between the liberal and corporatist ideal types of welfare regime (e.g. Taylor, 2004), as the government adopted the tools and ideology of New Public Management since the 1980s and shifted towards privatizing welfare, the regime moved away from the continental European welfare state tradition and became more in line with a liberal regime. We might expect the UK to therefore have a distinct role for the market logic in the welfare system.

In England,[1] the voluntary and community sector has a long tradition of delivering social services independent of the state. The third sector can also

DOI: 10.4324/9781003245605-4

be characterized by two narrative streams or traditions – philanthropy and charitable giving, and mutualism (Taylor, 2004). The concept of charity has its roots with the 1601 Statute of Charitable Uses, which defines a charity as being for the public benefit, for the relief of poverty, the advancement of education, or the advancement of religion. This 400-year-old statue continues to play an important role in shaping both the rules that structure the sector as well as its narratives – the third sector is often referred to in the UK as the 'charity' or 'voluntary and community' sector.

Another defining feature of the English third sector is mutualism. The first consumer co-operative, the Rochdale Equitable Pioneers Society, was formed in 1844 and paved the way for the subsequent formation of mutual aid and friendly societies, which aimed to help the poor to pool resources for sickness and old age, savings, or other common purposes. Like the Charity Act, the legal status that came into place as a framework for mutuals (the Industrial and Provident Society laws in the 1880s) is still in place today. Over the past few decades, this driver of community benefit and reinvesting profits into service provision and communities has also led to the development of social enterprises, which embrace both these drivers of philanthropy/charity and mutualism.

The city of Sheffield is in the North of England and has a population of over 500,000 people. A city with a history of co-operative, trade union, and third sector activism, Sheffield also has historically had a city council with a reputation of left-wing activism, at one time nicknamed the 'Socialist Republic of South Yorkshire.' In 2014, the Sheffield City Region Combined Authority was established, which has responsibility for some regional economic development and transportation issues. The City Region also involves the cooperation of the city councils that comprise the area (Barnsley, Doncaster, Rotherham, and Sheffield) as well as the Local Enterprise Partnership, which is a private sector-led vehicle for local economic growth and job creation.

2 Case study organizations and research methods

To select organizations to act as case studies, I interviewed senior staff members from local third sector network organizations who acted as key informants and gatekeepers to the case study organizations. I investigated five key organizations – anonymized throughout this book as Develop, Enterprise, Leisure, Aspire, and Recreation – which range in size from 14 to 78 full-time equivalent paid staff. These organizations operate in the community regeneration/community development sector, meaning that they offer a range of services that aim to improve the quality of life and general community well-being for specific neighbourhoods of the city.[2] These services include libraries, employment support, leisure activities, social activities and support for older people and for people with mental health difficulties, and public health initiatives. Develop, Enterprise,

Leisure, and Aspire own property (commercial workspace, libraries, support services, and community shops), while Recreation manages a building owned by the local council.

In addition to the community development organizations, I analysed two programmes – Age Better in Sheffield (ABIS) and Best Start Communities Count (BSCC).[3] Age Better is a national programme funded by the National Lottery to create 14 partnerships across England to deliver services and interventions to address loneliness and isolation of people over age 50. The contract for ABIS was held by a housing association in Sheffield that subcontracted projects to other organizations across the city. The programme ran from 2015 until 2021, with legacy work continuing with funding from Sheffield City Council.

The second programme, Best Start Communities Count, aims to support families with young children and reduce isolation by providing family activities, services for parents, and weekly toddler groups. The programme started with a three-year grant from the National Lottery in 2015 to target three disadvantaged neighbourhoods of the city and was initially run by a consortium of community organizations. In 2018, the project was moved to one of the city's community development organizations when the initial consortium was disbanded. It also received a new grant at that stage to further extend the programme for another three years and expand to more neighbourhoods of the city.

For the five community development organizations and two projects, in 2015–2016 I conducted interviews with a total of 26 individuals, which included 16 professionals (directors, frontline staff) and two volunteer board members (from ABIS), as well as eight individuals from associated third sector organizations and local network organizations. As part of a follow-up project in 2019, I returned to ABIS and BSCC and conducted a further 18 interviews (six of which were with individuals I had interviewed for the original research).[4] This approach enabled me to both understand the initial design and intention of the programmes as well as analyse how approaches to co-production had evolved over time.

In addition, I analysed organizational documents, including bid documents, strategic plans, evaluations and reports, and website text. Because practices involve daily, informal behaviour, identifying them from documents and interviews alone is somewhat problematic, as this relies on an analysis of formal recorded material in the first case, and the recall and interpretation of individuals in the second case. Interview and document data were therefore triangulated with some observations, including a community forum meeting associated with Develop and the annual general meetings for Aspire and Recreation. I also observed several service delivery activities that were suggested by interviewees as good examples of co-production, including two mental health 'social cafes' for Enterprise and a family craft day for BSCC (where I spoke informally to practitioners).

3 Institutional logics, co-production, and the third sector in Sheffield

In line with my analytical framework of institutional logics, I present the analysis through a lens of rules; norms; and values, beliefs, and ideas. I discuss the seven case studies concurrently to effectively draw out the common themes as well as to compare organizations and programmes.

A. Rules

As we saw in Chapter 3, rules are formally recognized constraints on behaviour that exist primarily in the forms of laws, policies, and regulations. I categorize rules in two ways: (1) externally imposed rules and policies, and (2) internal (organizational) rules. External rules include these traditional constraints (laws, etc.) as well as contract and grant specifications, which are often recorded but are sometimes implicit rather than explicit. The second type of rules are internal organizational rules and policies, such as formal conventions and operating procedures. I distinguish between external and internal rules because this provides a clearer delineation of the institutional order(s) that influence the creation and enforcement of rules.

Externally imposed rules/policies

When it comes to external rules or policies, the organizations in Sheffield were primarily impacted by the contracts that they receive from government or other funding organizations (such as foundations and the National Lottery Community Fund, which is a major funder in the UK) to support their activities. Funding requirements have provided an important basis of the rules that constrain the Sheffield case studies since their formation in the 1990s, when all five community development organizations became recipients of large regeneration grants from the national government Single Regeneration Budget (SRB) and European Union Objective 1. The rules that these grants imposed demonstrate the influence of the state, community, and market logics, which came into conflict in several instances described by interviewees, constraining organizations' ability to co-produce in certain ways.

> They said for example, you can spend money up to this point, this geographical point, but not a centimetre beyond that. So you'd get, on a particular street, you might have houses 1–20 that were included in the geographical area that was entitled to Objective 1 money. But then house #21 was outside so they weren't allowed to benefit.
>
> (Director [2015], Aspire)

In this example, we see a conflict that ensues between the state logic – which favours redistribution and overall improvement of neighbourhoods –

and the community logic, which in this case reveals a more holistic and community-centred approach to defining boundaries for the distribution of regeneration money. After several years, these regeneration grants came to an end, and the Sheffield organizations were forced to adopt more business-like behaviour in order to remain sustainable and viable as organizations. This resulted in the introduction of the market logic, which primarily can be seen through their changes in practices and discourse, but also to rules in the sense that organizations began to seek other contracts and sources of funding. This led to a degree of instability and challenge to the identities of organizational staff, who had to adjust from being local community activists working together for the betterment of their neighbourhoods to professionals who deliver services and must be concerned about economic viability.

The rules imposed by contracts and funders continue to play an important role in defining the logics of the Sheffield organizations. The balancing of the state, market, and community logics that characterize these rules can, however, conflict with some of the more community-driven narratives.

> When you've got a contract, you've got a very tight specification. Sometimes, they don't just tell you what outcomes they want, they tell you how they want you to deliver it. Sometimes that can be at odds with our ethos. So we have got quite clever at delivering the outputs that they want but doing it in our way, because I don't think there's a single contract that we've delivered where we've not over delivered on the outputs.
> (Director, Develop, interview 1)

This example shows how a conflict between external rules and an organization's values can affect the organization's practices. The Director of Develop suggested that adhering to the organization's values has required them to be somewhat creative in their practices – adapting their 'rules-in-use' because of the incompatibility with the 'rules-in-form' (Ostrom, 2007). They went on to explain that the organization had clashed with the local authority about its approach to delivering a family support service – the council expected outcomes to be achieved within six weeks, which Develop believed to be an unreasonably short time scale. To take a more collaborative and personalized approach, the organization reconciled this by signing service users off the programme at the end of six weeks and then right back onto the programme. "In the end, I think we won the argument that actually – it had to be led by the family's needs and you just had to keep identifying the outcomes and the progress made" (Director, Develop, interview 1).

This issue of contract rules creating impediments to co-production practices was also expressed by the directors of Enterprise, Leisure, and Recreation. The director of Enterprise, like the director of Develop, suggested that the organization often simply ignores the rules in order to engage in co-production. He discussed examples of staff being empowered to provide long-term, personalized support to vulnerable clients to ensure their successful mental health recovery or entrance into the workforce, despite the restrictions on contracts they receive to provide mental health and employment support. For Recreation, however, the short-term and restrictive nature of the contracts and grants they rely on has forced them to adapt their practices to constantly be looking towards the next source of funding, prohibiting them from developing more co-productive practices.

This difference in the impact of rules can be explained by the fact that Enterprise and Develop are two of the largest community development organizations in Sheffield, benefitting from widespread name recognition and influence with the local authority, whereas Recreation does not own any of its own assets and depends heavily upon short-term contracts for survival. The two larger organizations, having assimilated the market logic into their practices (by generating some income through trading) are thus often able to ignore the targets and timescales imposed by contracts and do things according to their ethos of community development or personalized attention. When it comes to co-production, rules often conflict with norms of behaviour, and larger organizations are afforded more flexibility in determining their own narratives and practices that may contravene external rules.

On the other hand, while many contracts (particularly from the local authority and National Health Service) present constraints on co-production practices, other sources of funding actually *require* co-production. This was found to be the case with grants from the Lottery (the funder for ABIS and BSCC), which is perceived to favour projects that take an approach of co-production. The National Lottery Community Fund,[5] which is a non-departmental public body, distributes grants to charities and community organizations across the UK from money raised through the National Lottery. It has become a significant funder of the third sector, focusing on supporting programmes that improve the communities deemed most in need.

> Grant funding from people like the Department of Health, Public Health England, so national grant funders, Big Lottery, people like that are a lot hotter on it [co-production], get it and ask for it in their bids. Where we're looking at other kinds of funding, so typically local authority, longer term contracts for things like a floating support service rather than a grant funded new project. . . . There may occasionally be a question on probably personalization, not co-production.
>
> (Senior staff 1, ABIS)

The fluidity of co-production as a notion means co-production as a rule is problematic – it is difficult to define what qualifies as co-production, and therefore what does not qualify is equally challenging to pinpoint. Rules are sanctioned by "coercive action through formal rewards and punishments" (Lowndes & Roberts, 2013, p. 53), but unless actors can define the terms and perimeters of a rule, it is unenforceable. ABIS has therefore codified this rule through the creation of stringent quantifiable reporting mechanisms as a proxy measure of co-production, such as the number of older people involved in activities, number of residents engaged with, etc.

While the primary external rules that shape the Sheffield organizations come from contracts and grants, the logic driving the creation of BSCC is also derived from government policy. Although the programme is funded by the Lottery, government policy and the decrease in provision of children's services has been the main driver for the project to be established.

> A lot of the reason why we've done what we've done is in these three areas, all three areas had a Sure Start.[6] And all that provision has gone. Nothing has remained. . . . So we are starting from scratch, and it's taken us absolutely months and months and months and years to get them to trust that what we're doing, we're doing with a view to keeping and sustaining and making sure that communities, they won't need us, they'll be able to take this on and run it.
>
> (Programme manager, BSCC, interview 1)

Austerity measures in England have meant that many third sector organizations have attempted to fill gaps where public services were previously provided. The fact that the space for parents' groups and children's activities was left relatively open in these communities has meant that BSCC has more flexibility to determine its own rules, rather than having to negotiate the political landscape. It has used this to its advantage in designing and promoting a model of early years' service that promotes partnership with and empowerment of local parents. Receiving funding from the Lottery also legitimized the programme in the eyes of the local council, which began looking at how it could duplicate the community partnership model across the city. Here again, external rules demonstrate a strategic negotiation of the state logic (public policy), the community logic (favouring local solutions to social problems), and the market logic (which requires a demonstrable return on investment – in this case, social targets).

Internal rules

While the rules discussed thus far originate from funders and government (and primarily reflect the logics of the state and the market), other rules are determined by third sector organizations themselves. These refer to the formal guidelines, procedures, and policies that the organization prescribes in bid documents, strategic plans, etc. For the most part, the interviewees in Sheffield did not describe many internal rules, with their organizations generally allowing a degree of flexibility and informality to determine the way they do things, guided by the community logic.

Although these organizations are officially governed as charities by volunteer elected boards of trustees (residents and/or representatives of local voluntary and community groups), staff and directors did not tend to discuss the role of boards. Despite this official rule of having a board of local people to hold the organization to account, official governance mechanisms appear to assume a limited role regarding the involvement of local people in co-production. Board members are seen more as advisors and representatives to give voice to communities rather than as the key decision-makers of the organization. Governance procedures in general represented a low priority for the community development organizations, with little participation of service users and community members.

I attended the AGMs of Aspire and Recreation, and enquired about the AGM of Enterprise but was told that it was "just a business meeting" (personal email with Director of Enterprise). At the two I attended, a relatively small number of people were present (about 20 at Aspire, and fewer than 10 at Recreation), most of whom were representatives of local community groups and city-wide charities. Aspire's AGM was preceded by a meal, and the meeting included presentations about various activities and a volunteer award ceremony. For the other community development organizations, the AGM is held as a matter of protocol rather than as a proactive tool to co-produce the organization's strategy with members. The formal norms of internal democracy, voting, and representation of citizens in organizational governance simply do not form part of the practices of the community development organizations. As the director of Leisure explained,

> We had our AGM a couple of weeks ago. We're very different from [local network] in that our members are members of the local community. If you have an AGM at 6:30 in the evening because you want your trustees to be there because they're working during the day, you're not going to get 100 people from the community turning up to an AGM because . . . what's the incentive?
>
> (Director [2016], Leisure)

A far more significant emphasis on internal rules was demonstrated by ABIS. This programme, which sub-contracts projects to other third sector organizations in the city, requires that all sub-contractors take an approach of co-production – projects are expected to involve older people at every stage, by which they mean co-designed, co-delivered, and often co-evaluated. While some organizations did this through intensive and creative co-design workshops (for example, a tea party for older people where they were asked, "If you were the king or queen of Sheffield, how would you change the city to make it better for older people?"), others' attempts at co-design appeared to be more consistent with traditional consultation approaches.

This rule can sometimes come into conflict with the more informal and flexible day-to-day routines or practices that some third sector organizations favour. For example, the director of one of the community development case studies, which was sub-contracted to deliver an intervention for ABIS, complained that ABIS specified that all services/projects needed to be completely co-produced, but at the same time expected organizations to outline exactly what the service would look like *before* beginning any co-design with citizens, leaving them in a catch-22 situation. Sub-contractors were also required to undertake co-design and co-delivery activities in a specific way that can be evidenced for ABIS.

> So what was quite an organic sort of process just then suddenly felt that there was a lot of structure put on the top saying, "Okay, but you need to do this for co-production, this, so you need to have workshops and do this," which people wouldn't engage with. . . . It's like, you know, does that really warrant a workshop and all of this recording? So I think it was just more the different approaches in terms of what was realistic for us as organizations in terms of capturing that data and the formal way that they wanted it delivered.
>
> (ABIS project coordinator, Enterprise, interview 2)

The extent to which ABIS requires recording, measurement, and evaluation of all their projects can be seen as a reflection of the market logic. As third sector organizations in the UK have increasingly been shaped by the ideology of New Public Management, which promotes the application of business logics/practices to service provision, organizations are encouraged to engage in performance management to demonstrate the effectiveness and outcomes of their interventions. Similarly, another interviewee expressed frustration at the recording and evaluation procedures required because he felt that these quantitative measures failed to accurately capture the genuine extent of the benefits experienced by participants. Both arguments suggest that this prescribed approach to co-production comes into conflict with more fluid, community-oriented practices.

For both ABIS and BSCC, the internal rules of the programmes are also centred around a model of governance that engages citizens (older people and parents, respectively) in decision-making. BSCC is run by three community partnerships, each of which includes parents, local council staff, local community organization representatives, and other professionals from the health and social services sector. The community partnership structure of decision-making prioritizes the needs and preferences of the parents involved, advocating an approach of co-design or co-decision. ABIS involves a similar co-governance structure, whereby a 'core partnership' comprised of older people alongside representatives from various public bodies and third sector organizations makes important strategic decisions about the programme, including commissioning each of the individual interventions.

> Having older people on the core partnership brings different things as well. And on paper, I think the model is very, very interesting, and it's interesting to see it grow. I would say my reflection of working with it

> is two things – the current core partners who aren't there representing an organization, almost all of them are professional people who have been professionals in their previous life. So if you shut your eyes and you didn't know it was an older person, they behave and bring things to the table like a professional from another organization. So I worry a little bit that they're not really representative of older people.
>
> (Board member 1, ABIS)

As this board member (a staff member of the local council) explains, the ABIS model of co-governance has, on the one hand, brought in experiences of older people that would typically be lacking at a strategic level. On the other hand, the skills and interests needed to participate in board meetings has meant that the older people who choose to get involved as core partners are more likely to be retired professionals who may not be especially representative of the population of isolated older people of the city.

B. Norms and practices

While rules – formal, written policies, guidelines, and regulations – discussed in the previous section are important elements in shaping co-production, the institutional logics perspective maintains that individuals and organizations are also constrained by more informal 'rules of the game.' Norms or practices refer to the 'way things are done here' that are transmitted by a shared understanding of actors but are not formally recorded. In Sheffield, these can be categorized into four broad themes: community engagement, personalization, group co-facilitation, and enforced citizen co-production.

Community engagement

In Sheffield, 'community engagement' forms an important part of the practices of community development organizations. This is often vaguely defined by actors, but it tends to refer to building relationships and maintaining a dialogue with service users and residents about the design and delivery of services.

> Maybe it's the kind of embedded, the thing about the relationship with the clients is embedded in the nature of the relationship we try to develop with the client from the start. Rather than being a kind of formalized, bureaucratic process of filling in forms and all that kind of stuff, it's about the dynamics of the relationship between staff and clients.
>
> (Director, Enterprise, interview 1)

> The simplest, easiest bit of life I guess is the informal – people chat. So any of our service users, they talk to staff, they talk to other service users. . . . We have staff working with different groups of people, and

> doing a lot of work with local residents, service users, there's that informal that happens a lot.
>
> (Director [2015], Leisure)

An emphasis on the practices of community engagement naturally stems from the community logic. This is described more frequently in terms of community development, or "making contact with individuals, supporting groups of people to set up their own activities, and basically consulting with local people, engaging with local people" (Director, Develop, interview 1). In responses to questions about day-to-day activities, each of the five directors and three of the staff members described an ambiguous strategy of "listening and gathering people's views" (Programme officer 2, Leisure) and "working with local people" (Community development officer, Develop) without delineating the exact process for realizing this, which suggests that these actions fall under the category of practices rather than rules.

These community engagement norms are influenced by the principles of community organizing – such as active listening, relationship building, and empowerment of the disempowered (Speer & Hughey, 1995). While community organizing might most naturally be indicative of the community logic (i.e. relationship building and empowering people to effect social change in their local area), the community development organizations in Sheffield were shown to strategically assimilate this with the state logic as well because of their partial reliance on government funding. This includes the national government's Community Organisers programme, which funded the training and placement of community organizers into neighbourhoods.

> In terms of pure community development work, [after a neighbourhood management pilot project] we lost all the capacity. So when Community Organising (sic) came along, it became an opportunity for us. We got on board with that programme. It was all run through DCLG [Department of Communities and Local Government]. Again, small amounts of money to do stuff, but we managed to maintain that programme for three years. . . . We had three people doing community organising in the area.
>
> (Director, Recreation)

The paradoxical nature of the Community Organisers programme was that despite its focus on relationship building and empowering people to effect social change in their area, it was introduced and controlled by the national government. As such, the state logic of centralization and bureaucracy is evident in the top-down design and evaluation of this programme.

Community engagement was similarly an important norm influencing BSCC's approach to co-production, which takes a consciously informal approach to establishing relationships with parents, highlighting the centrality of the community logic in defining practices. Staff members described this approach to informal community engagement as speaking to residents (or "with communities") as well as encouraging local people to take part in activities.

> I've gone and walked just around the community and talked to parents in the street, on the park, outside school. I've gone and chatted with them. They must think, "Oh, there's a crazy woman coming towards me with a big smile," and I've got my ID and I'm like, "I'm not selling anything or whatever, I'm just telling you about a group."
>
> (Community development officer, BSCC, interview 1)

> Programme manager: We engaged with 600 families before we started the three areas. And we continually engage obviously since that, since the start of the programme in September, our target is to engage 300 adults a year, who report that they feel isolated.
>
> Interviewer: When you say 'engage' with over 300, what do you mean by 'engage'?
>
> Programme manager: They attend sessions that we run.
>
> (Programme manager, BSCC, interview 1)

The community logic, which "connotes the collective relationship between people that emphasize the interpersonal and particularistic" (Thornton et al., 2012, p. 52) is the clear driver for these practices, which are informal and flexible, focusing on proximity and local connections. In this area, the state and market logic bear little impact on how staff go about their daily work and achieve programme aims.

Because of the degree of informality of community engagement, these practices are particularly difficult to clearly establish through interview data alone. In addition, it is important to note that many of the interviews (11 out of 25 staff members) were with organization directors or senior staff who may not themselves be privy to the day-to-day norms of behaviour of their frontline staff. I was able to attend a few services that were suggested as good examples of co-production and observed this type of informal listening and engagement between staff and attendees, but the extent to which community engagement translates to real decision-making power is often unclear. As articulated in the previous quotes, the engagement or involvement that occurs is often informal, ad hoc, and managed by professionals, often framed more as 'responding to needs' rather than collaborating with service users on an equal footing.

Individual co-production: personalization and peer support

The norms associated with the involvement of service users in service design and delivery frequently focused on personalization, or an approach of putting the individual at the centre of the services that aim to benefit them. This translates into a preponderance of individual co-production approaches, where the individual service user is involved in improving their own service and/or outcome, as opposed to group or collective approaches that involve a range of people for the benefit of their specific group or broader community, respectively (Nabatchi et al., 2017). Linked to this one-on-one focus is the prevalence of peer support or mentorship approaches, where people with lived experience provide direct support to someone facing similar challenges (e.g. loneliness or mental health struggles).

This norm of personalization as a way of approaching involvement/co-production was common across the ABIS programme. Co-production is framed by staff members as "taking a person-centred approach" (Senior staff 1, ABIS), which translates into practices that emphasize the individual collaboration between professionals, volunteers, and/or isolated older people. For example, one of the original interventions of the programme was a peer mentorship project, where older people who have previously experienced loneliness and isolation are paired with individuals who are currently feeling isolated or "at risk of social isolation" because they have "a big life event coming up or it could be something's happened, like the death of a loved one or retirement or end of carer responsibilities" (ABIS project coordinator, Enterprise, interview 1). The volunteer peer mentors acted in a befriending role, lending an ear and providing informal advice.

> They [volunteers] will be able to sort of work with them to sort of draw in their own experiences of social isolation, so how they got out of it, what helped them, so it might be sort of just being there to listen, offer advice. But ideally, it would be to kind of go out and develop support networks for them, get them a bit more involved in activities, so give them the confidence and the skills that they need to be able to kind of get out there and start being able to do things on their own a bit more.
> (ABIS project coordinator, Enterprise, interview 1)

These peer mentorship approaches also had the mutually reinforcing benefits of involving people with lived experience as volunteers/mentors – one coordinator in charge of the programme indicated that many previous 'mentees' went onto become volunteers themselves, further expanding social capital and reducing social isolation of more older people. Professionals continued to play an important support and facilitation role throughout.

This one-to-one or personalized approach taken in the programme's mentorship and befriending projects is echoed in the efforts to co-design interventions. A document outlining a 'co-production action plan' (which ABIS requires – as a rule – its sub-contracted organizations to produce for each intervention) demonstrates a clearly delineated approach to how individuals will be involved in various processes of the project, and which individuals will be targeted. One staff member explained that this approach to co-design goes so far as to seek out individuals in their homes.

> Then to reach the most isolated, we've done work on a one-to-one basis. So I went and saw an old lady who's had to have a hip replacement. . . . So it's people like her that Age Better really needs to work with, so by actually travelling to her house, we wouldn't have been able to get her opinion and her experience. So by going to see her, we've made sure that she's included in the co-design of Age Better.
>
> (Frontline staff 1, ABIS)

This type of personalized approach is a reflection of the changing landscape of public services in the UK, where personalization constitutes a 'valence' issue, where all parties agree that services should be tailored for each individual service user (Needham, 2011). The move towards personalization of public services indicates both the influence of a market logic of public service procurement and design, where providers are encouraged to treat service users more as customers, as well as the state logic, conceptualizing service users as citizens and designing services to produce better outcomes for them. This is also evidenced through the frequent use of individual service users' stories of success or recovery as highlighted in vignettes and case studies in evaluation reports. Personalization reflects a more business-oriented approach to service provision, driven by the market logic – because decisions are based more on business performance or efficiency, personalizing services to 'client' or 'customer' needs, which means that co-production is not undertaken if it is viewed to be too time or resource intensive.

Co-facilitation of group activities

Another common practice among the Sheffield organizations was the involvement of citizens in co-facilitating group activities or services alongside paid staff members. For BSCC, this approach was the foundation of the programme, with parent volunteers trained to run parent and toddler groups (e.g. setting rooms up, leading craft activities and games, communicating with parent participants on Facebook) with the support of an early years practitioner.

> We provide them [parent volunteers] with policy packs. We talk them through our policies and procedures so that we know that everything, the structure is there, and the infrastructure is there. And also, then to work with them to develop the group, to structure it in some way. But we don't want our groups overly structured because again, it is very, very light touch, but also to help them work out how to sustain that group after the Lottery programme's finished.
>
> (Programme manager, BSCC, interview 1)

While the early years practitioners contribute their specialist knowledge in young children's social and educational development, parent volunteers co-facilitate the groups to determine which activities or additional resources are needed (e.g. inviting health specialists or financial advisors for advice sessions). The parent volunteers also provide important links to minority ethnic communities, such as a Muslim volunteer who was instrumental in helping the programme to gain the trust and participation of her community. Staff members were conscious of balancing the need to rely on volunteers to guarantee the running of the programme, with an effort not to overburden them with too much responsibility by ensuring that staff members were always available for support.

Several of the interventions of ABIS similarly employed an approach of professional/volunteer group co-facilitation. For example, two of the services included social groups for lonely and isolated older people, and a group offering budgeting and money management advice to those in difficult financial circumstances. Like BSCC, this practice of co-production was seen to both be beneficial for the service, by including peers/people with lived experience to help improve the service, as well as valuable to the volunteer co-facilitators, who gained confidence and experience by helping to provide the service.

> We found that groupwork worked best and then the volunteers could sort of take a bit of a lead role; they might help with the group, make cups of tea, sort of initiate conversations or card games or things like that. But really, they were sort of receiving just as much support from staff and through having conversations with other people there and just actually being out in that social setting, being around other people.
>
> (ABIS project coordinator, Enterprise, interview 2)

This type of practice for citizen co-producers was also employed by Enterprise's mental health social cafes, which offer a low-stress environment for people experiencing mental health challenges to socialize and gain confidence. Frequent participants at the social cafes were encouraged to become volunteers who support the running of the groups by welcoming new participants, providing signposting to specific services (e.g. housing, mental health), determining the agenda, and organizing activities. This practice is based on a recovery model of mental health, based on empowerment and peer support.

Co-delivery or co-facilitation of group services extends the approach of personalization and individual co-production to include a broader range of citizens in services that benefit their group. Like the previously discussed practices, here we also see an assimilation of several institutional logics – the community logic of mutuality and reciprocity is combined with the state logic of public service. The market logic is less present in these practices, aside from when these are linked to budget or performance management.

Enforced citizen/service user provision of services

One increasingly important area of co-production in the Sheffield third sector is the notion of 'enforced' co-production or citizen delivery of public services that would otherwise be cut by the state. Enforced citizen co-production relates to an arrangement where professional support is entirely withdrawn and citizens are left to deliver services on their own (or with very limited support), rather than citizens being brought in to co-deliver services. This practice is described variously as transforming citizens into 'responsibilized agents' (Fotaki, 2011) or 'enforced co-producers' (Pestoff, 2019). By contrast to other practices of co-production, where non-profit professionals voluntarily engage citizens in service delivery, in these instances the non-profit takes over a service that would otherwise be cut by the state and engages citizen volunteers to provide the service through necessity.

This type of enforced co-production has become more common in Sheffield over the past decade because of widespread cuts to public services and the entrance of third sector organizations to fill the gaps. Many public libraries have been threatened with closure, but because of local petitions and protests, some have been kept open through volunteer efforts. At the time of the research, Develop, Recreation, and Enterprise were each responsible for running a local (previously public) library, and several more have been transferred to community provision in the subsequent years.

> City council has pulled out of our library nine months ago. Left us with it on a volunteer run basis, literally left us with it. We certainly didn't want that. We're where we are with it. Some of the libraries in the city, particularly in the more affluent areas, have got an awful lot of volunteers, they've got ex-librarians, they've got people with real expertise in that area. And they're going for it. We've found it much more difficult. We have got a good cohort of volunteers volunteering. We find they need support. We would love to relinquish the library. I know that sounds like, what do we want to offload? But we can't do everything.
>
> (Director [2015], Leisure)

Enforced citizen provision of services becomes problematic because of the removal of professional expertise as well as sufficient resources to train and support citizen volunteers to be able to competently provide the service. Another interviewee from Leisure explained that the local council offered inconsistent training for new library volunteers, so two of the volunteers are now in charge of all training as well. Non-profit professionals continue to play a role in supporting the citizens to co-deliver library services, but all the organizations that run a community library indicated this was a challenge because of the lack of time and resources.

To a lesser extent, the practices of BSCC represent another example of enforced co-production, or more accurately 'transitional co-production,' where co-production between practitioners and citizens represents a stage before withdrawing professional support and requiring full citizen provision. Involving parents in co-delivery was chosen as an approach in part because the programme simply does not have sufficient financial resources (via a grant from the Lottery) to employ enough early years practitioners to run the parent/toddler groups without volunteer support. The initial intention was that after training and a period of co-facilitation of the toddler groups, the groups would become self-sustaining with only volunteer time and management. However, as explained in follow-up interviews three years later, it became clear that enforced citizen provision of these services was unrealistic.

> So the idea was in the first project, that they would become sustainable and commence running in their own right. No, they weren't. Partly for many, many reasons – either we got some great volunteers, and they went and got a job, or we'd got volunteers that were very needy and needed the hand-holding and that hand-holding would never stop. And up and down with volunteers leaving, children grow up, volunteers' focus changes to something else.
>
> (Programme manager, BSCC, interview 2)

Because of the volunteers' need for support, as well as the risk of failure involved in transferring to enforced citizen service provision, the BSCC programme continued with an approach of citizen and practitioner co-facilitation of the toddler groups. In terms of the logics at play, enforced co-production illustrates the prevalence of the community logic coming in to fill the gaps with the exit of the state logic in particular service areas. The state logic that emphasizes redistribution and universal access to all citizens effectively becomes hollowed out, and the community logic is mobilized to ensure that local people do not get left behind. The market logic is only present insofar as services are forced to reckon with miniscule budgets and therefore seek to employ co-production as a norm/practice because it is seen as a cheaper and more efficient means of delivering services.

C. *Values, beliefs, and ideas*

The final component of the institutional logics that drive and shape co-production between non-profit practitioners and citizens/services users is the nonmaterial, symbolic, or belief-based elements that I identify through analysing actors' narratives. While rules provide codified constraints on behaviour, and norms indicate the informal expected ways of doing things, actors are also impacted by their values, beliefs, ideas, and the stories told within organizations. Understanding these values helps us to better understand what drives each organization to engage in co-production – or not.

Organizational identity and history

In response to a broad opening question asking respondents to tell me about their organization and what they do, directors of the community development organizations all responded by relaying their history and how they developed in order to manage and deliver regeneration contracts. They each described being founded from either a local community forum or informal group of activists who came together and created organizations to take advantage of the regeneration money. Even though these funding streams have ended, these establishment stories – being community-led organizations that aimed to harness local activism to improve the community – continue to contain important narratives that help to define current values, strategies, and priorities.

> We were originally set up to manage a regeneration programme. It was SRB [Single Regeneration Budget]. It was a bid that was put together by local community activists with support from the council. . . . Really, that was the starting point. We became more than an accountable body for money, and we started to look at delivering the community development programme ourselves, because there was no other organization that was really fit for purpose to do that. That's what we've become. We've become a community development organization that actually delivers services and we've filled the gaps.
>
> (Director, Develop, interview 1)

In this foundation story, several themes emerge that contribute to explaining Develop's approach to involvement and co-production. First, the interviewee explains that the organization was founded because of community activism and an agreement with the local council, establishing an early integration of the community and state logics into organizational identity. This activist and local council collaboration also shows how co-production is essentially part of the way that Develop conceptualizes its approach to community development. In other words, the organization was founded because of co-production between citizens and the council, and the organization now sees its role as continuing to take this approach in its expanded role as an independent service provider. Interestingly, all five of the community development organizations to some extent share this type of organizational identity based on a similar trajectory – from grassroots organizing to delivering large-scale government funded regeneration programmes, with growth and professionalization over the subsequent decades.

While BSCC is not directly comparable to the organization case studies because it is a programme rather than an independent organization, there are some parallels in its foundation story and identity. The programme was originally designed to be a £50 million early childhood development programme funded by the Big Lottery, but after a six-month period of community engagement and development of the bid, it was rejected. However, because the bid scored highly on a community engagement component, it was instead awarded a smaller grant to focus specifically on targeting parents' isolation in disadvantaged neighbourhoods. This establishment story, like the community development organizations, has supported a programme identity based on community engagement, or as one interview explained, "Without community engagement there's very little point in doing anything for under threes. You need communities on board" (Programme manager, BSCC, interview 1).

Social enterprise

For some of the organizations in Sheffield, the guiding set of values that drove their practices were centred around being a social enterprise. A social enterprise ethos, where the focus is on using business activity to achieve social or community ends, suggests the embeddedness of the community, state, and market logics (Defourny, 2001; Nyssens, 2006). This was evidenced most strongly in the discussions with interviewees from Enterprise and Leisure. Interviewees from these organizations described models of being responsive to client demand, and delivering outcomes for service users or clients, with little direct mention of the importance of participation or citizenship.

> Sometimes I describe it [the organization] as a charitable social enterprise to make it clear there's a charity, but we're also a business. The one thing I think that we all kind of collectively learned, we are a registered charity but we're not a charity in that we don't give money away. It has to stack up as a business. We need to be as smart and entrepreneurial as anybody else.
> (Director, Enterprise, interview 1)

Thus the market logic is leveraged to further the social aims, i.e. the community logic. This social enterprise ethos also incites a particular approach to co-production, whereby increased involvement of service users in design and delivery forms part of an approach to social innovation, and co-production is valued as a means to achieve organizational aims (such as improved communities or improved outcomes for individuals). This extends to the language used to describe service users – while most of the Sheffield community development organizations spoke about 'local people,' 'residents,' or 'service users,' some ABIS staff and the director of Enterprise spoke about 'clients,' which the latter explained was an intentional decision to see people more as customers rather than beneficiaries of services. This illustrates another way that institutional logics define co-production practices, because the terms that are used to describe citizens convey implicit value propositions and status assumptions (McLaughlin, 2009).

Community development

While I have grouped together the five case study organizations under the heading of 'community development organizations,' this was not a term universally used across the cases (with some self-identifying, for instance on their websites, as a 'community enterprise' or 'community regeneration charity'). Community development as a group of values was, however, something that characterized many of the values described by practitioners across the Sheffield organizations. These values of empowerment, social justice, equality, and being community-led are core to three of the community development organizations (Develop, Aspire, and Recreation) as well as BSCC.

The community development values that underscore community engagement practices are supported by theory from Paolo Freire (1970/2000) and Saul Alinsky (1971/1989), with the idea of valuing the contribution of individuals and, as one interviewee described, "It's about challenging inequalities, tackling injustice. It's about working with people, not doing things to them" (Director, Develop, interview 1). The focus of these narratives is exclusively defined by the community logic, valuing trust, reciprocity, and cooperation as main priorities. These community development narratives explain in part the values that support *why* actors choose to take a particular approach to co-production.

This was an area of organizational values and identity that had shifted for some of the organizations between the initial and follow-up fieldwork. While Develop had always made community development central to its identity (according to the interviewees and organizational documents), this discourse had entered the lexicon of Enterprise and Leisure three years later as well. They had also begun efforts to translate this value into practice by hiring specific community development staff members and investing in community partnerships.

> We've gone back and done a fundamental review of what our mission, values, objectives and activities are. . . . We've got four strategic objectives, two of which – one is about improving people's economic wellbeing, and the other one is improving people's health and wellbeing. We're in the process of merging those two together, so we have one people objective, which is about improving people's economic wellbeing and health and wellbeing, and created a new objective which is about community development.
>
> (Director, Enterprise, interview 2)

Likewise, Leisure updated its core values to include 'asset-based' in its annual reporting, indicating that this refers to identifying strengths in the community and empowering local people to address local needs. This growing focus on community development principles was also reflected in project descriptions, and it potentially represents a backlash against the market and a reaffirmation of the community.

Pragmatism

In many instances, the values associated with co-production within the Sheffield case studies were more pragmatic rather than aspirational and value driven. Because all the cases were constrained by their funding situation (i.e. rules), co-production was seen as an instrumental way to improve services, improve communities, or continue to run services that would otherwise be unaffordable or unsustainable (i.e. via practices). This is often as a reaction to the conflicting demands of the market logic and community logic – in other words, co-production is part of the way that practitioners typically do things, because they must reconcile the need to demonstrate performance and measurable outcomes while staying true to a community-centred ethos.

In Enterprise, for example, clients' views are seen as important to consider at the level of specific services to ensure that the organization is providing what they want, but they are less involved in broader strategic or organizational decisions. Co-production is therefore part of the supply and demand process of service provision, using involvement to ensure that services meet needs. This pragmatic view of co-production assimilates market and state logics, with a view to use co-production instrumentally to improve services, with comparatively less emphasis on a social justice or active citizenship framing.

> If there's something that the public and community need, you can't just decide what it's going to be. You've got to have their involvement in it and then to sustain it, you've got to have their help to run it. So that's like us with our activities and things. Activities come out of consultation and health statistics and all sorts. This is what's needed, right, we'll do this. Then they help really to sustain it by coming and paying. They're helping to run it. They've had their input and they're helping to keep it going.
>
> (Project manager, Aspire)

For BSCC, the primary ideas and motivations expressed by interviewees overall were apolitical with little discussion of what values motivate a focus on parent participation or co-production. The primary narratives focused on an explanation of day-to-day practices, rather than the values and beliefs that underpin these. The logic of BSCC is therefore dictated by pragmatism – with a focus on meeting needs, achieving goals, and filling gaps in service provision in identified communities. As part of this, community engagement and co-production were discussed as a means to this end.

> We'd said that our programme was designed out of the community engagement and what came out of that, they [funder] said that that is very unique across the country of what they've seen. It's quite a unique way and so it's a unique programme. . . . This is what a lot of organizations don't get. They know that that's common sense, but they then have their own ideas of, "Well, we think this is what you need," and go in and do it. It doesn't work. That's been proven with the children's centres, with what they've said.
>
> (Community development officer, BSCC, interview 1)

Similarly, other respondents discussed taking a "test and learn" approach, particularly interviewees from ABIS, who framed co-production as being part of an ongoing process to try new things to see what is effective. Taking an approach of co-production means recognizing that not everything will work, accepting this, and learning from mistakes to better design programmes in the future. Interviewees described this ethos as allowing them a greater degree of freedom to do things differently. Co-production in this approach is framed as providing 'better' services that deliver what people what, rather than what professionals think they need.

Narratives and discourses of co-production

Since the early 2000s, co-production has become a bit of a buzzword in the UK, with numerous networks, research centres, and events dedicated to promoting it as a value to support public service reform. However, the term has not been met with universal enthusiasm within the third sector. In fact, interviewees from only one of the case studies (ABIS) independently employed the word *co-production* to describe their work. While all senior staff members of the community development organizations were comfortable with the term, most frontline staff were either unfamiliar with it or indicated that it would not be a term they would confidently use to describe their work.[7]

> Okay . . . I think we do co-produce. I just really hate that word. (Laughs) It's nothing personal. It's because I think it is so . . . it's sexy at the moment, but I think people use it and abuse it. I don't think . . . a lot of organizations talk about co-production, but actually, they don't do it.
>
> (Director, Develop, interview 1)

> I'm quite happy with it, totally understand co-design, co-production, yeah, with it. I think it's a bit of a thing about labels and jargon, what's fashionable, though, because to me, it doesn't feel much different to what we've been doing forever and a day. But it's like this week, you put this label on it.
>
> (Director [2015], Leisure)

The scepticism expressed about co-production as a term, illustrated in these two quotes, takes two forms – first, the opinion that there is a disconnect between the rhetoric and practice of co-production in other organizations, or in other words, a gentle accusation that other organizations employ the narrative but not the practice. Conversely, as the former director of Leisure expresses, there is also the suggestion that co-production has been a part of organizational practices 'forever,' but that it is just a new buzzword. The commonality between these two narratives is a recognition of the current normative appeal of the term *co-production*, but a feeling that it does not accurately correspond to practices (either because it is talked about but not done, or paradoxically because co-production is framed as a new practice that is, in fact, longstanding).

By contrast, ABIS interviewees universally described their approach as being 'co-designed, co-delivered, and co-evaluated' (both in the initial and follow-up fieldwork). This indicates that this word and notion have clearly been mainstreamed through organizational discourses, rather than remaining within the rhetoric of directors and senior staff, a common criticism of other organizations. The entire identity and purpose of the programme is grounded in an idea that every aspect of it will be co-produced with older people who have themselves experienced loneliness and isolation.

> The main reason that we've got someone specifically for this job known as co-production coordinator is because, I'm sure [staff member] has explained to you, but when we put the funding in for Age Better, we went with a massive co-production angle. So we said everything we do is going to be co-designed, co-delivered, co-evaluated, because of this. It's going to be better. We're going to do it better than anyone else can do it. So that's one of the main reasons, if not the main reason, that we received the funding from the Big Lottery.
>
> (Frontline staff 1, ABIS)

Co-production is so central to the narrative and values of ABIS that several jobs have been created with *co-production* in their title, as described by this staff member. However, this attention to co-production as a concept created some tensions with sub-contracted organizations, as we saw in relation to the internal rules imposed by ABIS in requiring co-production. Values may conflict with or contradict the preferred language of an organization or its day-to-day practices. Whilst the stories told by ABIS staff are overwhelmingly centred around the importance of co-production, there is some scepticism by other actors about what this means and whether the practices live up to the rhetoric. This theme of a divergence between the vocabulary of co-production and how professionals understood their work arose across Sheffield but came into particular focus as ABIS was the only case to readily use the term *co-production* to describe their approach.

4 Assimilation of the market, state, and community: a Service Delivery Logic

In most instances, the Sheffield organizations exhibit an assimilation of three logics – the market, state, and community – by strategically adapting and modifying elements of these. As Skelcher and Smith (2015) posit, assimilation of plural logics may occur in response to the infliction of a new logic upon a non-profit organization from external stakeholders, where an organization adapts some of the demands of the new logic to the existing logic(s). In Sheffield, the organizations respond to the changes and pressures of the introduction of a market logic by strategically incorporating elements into their narratives and practices but aim to remain true to the values and beliefs of the incumbent (primarily community) logic. This type of logic assimilation is consistent with the widespread argument that third sector organizations represent hybrids of the market, state, and community (Brandsen et al., 2005; Vickers et al., 2017). In the case of the Sheffield organizations, I call this assimilation a 'Service Delivery Logic', which shapes the way that organizations engage in co-production.

One of the most significant influences on the logics of the third sector in Sheffield (and indeed across the UK) are New Public Management ideologies and practices, which since the 1990s have compelled organizations to assimilate the market logic associated with performance management and business-like practices with the previously dominant state/community logics (Lapsley, 2008; McMullin, 2021). This was most clearly evident in organizations' rules. The community development organizations (which have been in existence since the late 1990s) told stories that show how the market logic has become increasingly influential in shaping funding arrangements over time, and these organizations have had to adapt to these new rules by modifying their practices as well as adjusting their values and narratives. This translates into taking a more business-like approach to financing organizational activities (e.g. renting out office spaces and delivering training for a fee) as opposed to relying solely on government grants. Organizations have also adopted more 'corporate speak' in narratives to satisfy funders.

In terms of both practices and values, the Sheffield organizations show attempts to negotiate or balance the aim to prioritize the community logic with the demands and constraints of the state and market logics. The overarching narrative identified across the organizations was a mission to 'improve communities' in some way. For ABIS, this was about tackling the problem of older people's isolation; for BSCC, supporting local parents; and for the community development organizations, this was framed more broadly (given the range of activities and services they deliver) in narratives such as 'tackling local issues' and 'facilitating community regeneration/community development.' In practice, organizations operationalize these aims through delivering services, which highlights the unifying theme across the Sheffield organizations – an emphasis on service delivery. These third sector organizations conceptualize their fundamental role as about provision, meeting needs and filling gaps.

> I always talk about it in terms of market failure, because public services were not delivering what local people needed and the private sector wouldn't operate in our area because there was no money to be made, because it was one of the poorest communities. So we've sort of filled that vacuum, really.
>
> (Director, Develop, interview 1)

This illustrates one of the ways that the Sheffield organizations assimilate elements of the market, state, and community logics – by using business skills and expertise and identifying gaps in service provision (which illustrates a more market-based understanding of public services), third sector organizations leverage their position (being 'community-based') and resources (generally non-monetary, such as knowledge, expertise, and social capital) in order to deliver services that provide public and community benefit. This also highlights how the third sector has evolved in England away from a more politicized community and social movement basis because of the increased contracting out of services to the third sector.

The day-to-day routines of the Sheffield organizations tend to be described as informal and flexible. Norms and accepted ways of working are influenced by the community logic as well as the Anglo-Saxon administrative traditions (i.e. pluralism, negotiation of multiple interests, and a conceptualization of the public interest or common good as an aggregate of the individual interests of all citizens) (Bevir et al., 2003). This notion is rendered into practice by third sector organizations by emphasizing relationship building between staff and community members through community engagement and efforts to bring diverse community voices into decisions about services and how they should be offered.

This Service Delivery Logic is thus defined by a combination of a dominant narrative that stresses the values of community engagement and improving communities, with the need to deliver public services that meet the requirements of the government (state logic), meet other funders' contract requirements, and remain viable as a business (market logic). As a result, the Sheffield cases tend to define themselves by what they deliver. This is not to say that these organizations are not value orientated, but rather that their ethos provides an instrumental basis for their practices and approaches to co-production.

5 Community logic and total withdrawal of the state logic: a Communitarian Logic and enforced co-production

One of the important things to note about the Service Delivery Logic is that though the state logic is assimilated with the market and community, it has become extremely weak as a result of government austerity. In some instances, the state logic is almost absent as government has cut funding for services provided by non-profit organizations. I contend that this related, but more extreme, version of the Service Delivery Logic where organizations are forced to assimilate a community and market logic with an absence of the state logic can be termed a Communitarian Logic. The Communitarian Logic is characterized by an exacerbation of several of the challenges encountered under the Service Delivery Logic, and it results in 'enforced' co-production, or enforced service provision by citizens.

The notion of a Communitarian Logic is based on Pestoff (2019), who argues that a 'communitarian' public administration regime is characterized by government retaining policymaking power but transferring responsibility for service provision to communities. This regime is best characterized by the Big Society agenda and the 2011 Localism Act of the British Coalition Government from 2010 to 2015, which ostensibly aimed to transfer powers to communities by making it easier for communities to 'take over' public services that they felt they could deliver better than public organizations. While the rhetoric behind these programmes was around empowerment and collective action, the absence of government financial support for community initiatives created a mismatch between policy and practice – the Big Society agenda was roundly criticized as being a cover for public sector cuts and for overemphasizing individual responsibility over political and democratic involvement (Kisby, 2010).

Public service cuts mean that many of the services provided by non-profit organizations are now funded by a range of non-state sources, including foundations and income from trading. At the time of the research (2015–2016 and 2019), government funding of non-profits had been consistently in decline (although the COVID-19 pandemic in 2020 reversed this trend in some cases, at least temporarily). The services provided by non-profits can be seen to be in the public or community benefit, but the lack of public sector support means that it is debatable whether these are 'public services' per se or simply alternative community services. Indeed, many of the organizations receive funding from the National Lottery Community Fund – technically a quasi-public organization but funded by proceeds from the Lottery rather than tax revenue. Because people in poverty are more likely to play, the Lottery essentially taxes the poor, representing the opposite of the state logic of redistribution (Beckert & Lutter, 2013). This withdrawal of the state logic results in a preponderance of the community logic, with volunteering, philanthropy, and charity as organizations' guiding values basis.

This has several implications for co-production. With waning financial and policy support for public services, third sector organizations step in to ensure continuity of service provision. The lack of sufficient funding means that service users and volunteers become enforced service providers rather than voluntary co-producers. When funding for services is acquired from other sources (e.g. foundations, the Lottery, etc.), professionals may still engage citizens in co-production, but co-production is more ad hoc and citizens are more likely to be obligated to play a significant role in core service provision. This means that they benefit considerably less from the expertise, resources, and facilitation that professionals offer in voluntary co-production.

The Communitarian Logic was most clearly evidenced in relation to the BSCC programme and the volunteer-run libraries of Develop, Recreation, and Enterprise. BSCC came into being to compensate for the withdrawal of sufficient support services for parents and families in Sheffield. Relying upon a series of time-limited grants from the Lottery, the programme initially intended to up-skill parents so that they could deliver services on their own without the need for professional facilitation, which would transfer responsibility entirely to citizens as enforced service providers. However, as the programme progressed the practices of co-production between citizens and professionals continued due to the needs identified by professionals, revealing the vulnerability of expecting citizens to fulfil a role that should be filled by professionals.

Likewise, the example of volunteer-run libraries clearly exhibits the Communitarian Logic, with volunteers taking over management and operations of public libraries that were threatened with closure by the local government. Similarly, other examples of non-profits taking over operation of public buildings fall into this category (e.g. Recreation, which manages a publicly owned former school that operates as an office building and community centre). These practices are characterized by community ownership and delivery that depends heavily upon citizen/volunteer efforts with extremely limited professional input because of the lack of government support. Co-production is driven by necessity and survival rather than more positive aims of empowerment or community improvement.

6 Implications for co-production: Service Delivery Logic and pragmatic co-production

The assimilation of the state, community, and market logics into a Service Delivery Logic has several implications for whether organizations co-produce with citizens or not and what form co-production takes. While several good examples of co-production were found in the Sheffield case studies, in some instances the rhetoric of co-production may be more developed than co-production practices. This Service Delivery Logic shapes co-production in several ways:

A. Co-production is inseparable from rules related to contracts and funding.

The biggest constraint on the Sheffield organizations' practices arose from contract requirements. This is partly attributable to the way that a market logic to public service contracting has been introduced in Sheffield, which has created obstacles for third sector organizations. For many interviewees, key areas of concern were the issues of bidding for contracts (marketization of services) and cuts to public services. As the government's approach to austerity has, to an extent, informed a business-like logic that urges service delivery organizations to increase efficiency, third sector organizations are struggling to maintain their level of staffing and service offering, constraining their capacity to engage in more intensive involvement activities like co-production.

Co-production is paradoxically conceptualized as a practice that requires large amounts of resource and professional time and capacity, while at the same time being promoted to make services more cost effective (or to sustain services that would otherwise be cut). This duality of narratives results in a degree of scepticism towards co-production as a practice, with some professionals expressing concern about being expected to do 'more with less' as cuts to public services have made funding to third sector organizations increasingly precarious.

B. *Co-production practices are employed as an instrumental means to improve service delivery.*

The assimilation of the market, state, and community logics produces a shared identity around which the Sheffield third sector organizations coalesce, which focuses on the primary purpose of delivering services. This in turn defines how they conceptualize and operationalize co-production, which is typically framed pragmatically as a way to improve the design and delivery of public services. Through the practices and values of the Sheffield third sector, we see limited attention to the democratic aspect of co-production (e.g. citizenship, empowerment, equality) and more focus on the effectiveness aspects (e.g. improving outcomes, meeting needs). At times, co-production (or community engagement more generally) is conceptualized as being part of the unique selling point of why organizations are more effective at delivering services than, for example, the public or private sectors.

For example, several of the community development organizations argue that they are best placed to deliver services because their proximity to and engagement with communities means they will be able to more effectively design the services that local people want. In other instances – e.g. in BSCC and ABIS – co-production is a strategy or method that has been introduced to improve services. In both illustrations, the key suggestion is that involving citizens in design and delivery of services will make them, in some way, 'better.' As we will see in Chapter 5 and Chapter 6, this provides a contrast to the Lyon and Montreal organizations, where the primary considerations are involvement and collaboration, delegating service provision to a secondary priority or a result of the engagement in co-production.

C. *Co-production focuses primarily on individuals, rather than collective/societal value.*

Another key distinguishing feature of co-production under the Service Delivery Logic is a predilection towards individual co-production with less emphasis on collective co-production (which requires the participation of groups of citizens, but the benefit of the co-production extends to the wider community or society as a whole) (Nabatchi et al., 2017; Brudney & England, 1983). Across the practices and discourses of interviewees in Sheffield, there was limited discussion of aims to undertake activities that could lead to systems-wide change. Instead, co-production approaches focus on individual service users and volunteers (such as one-to-one mentoring and personal support) or small groups (e.g. BSCC parent/toddler groups, Enterprise's mental health social cafe participants, or several of the ABIS group activities).

This focus is most clearly illustrated by ABIS – a programme that, in targeting older people's loneliness, could take an individual (a person's own circumstances), group (loneliness in community context), or collective (loneliness as a societal problem) approach. Throughout ABIS we see a focus on taking a 'person-centred approach,' which thereby prioritizes activities that produce benefit for individuals. This theme links back to the first and second points – because of the need to be business-like and provide outcomes/impact, organizations tend to focus on easily quantifiable successes, such as the number of service users who have gone through a programme.

7 Summary and conclusions

In summary, this chapter explored the co-production between citizens and professionals working for non-profit organizations in Sheffield, England. By applying the institutional logics framework of rules; practices; and values, beliefs, and ideas, we can see that the organizations are by and large shaped by an assimilation of the market, state, and community logics into what I term a Service Delivery Logic. The Service Delivery Logic – informed by restrictions of contracts and grants (rules) and ideas around social enterprise, community development, and pragmatism – creates conditions that promote instrumental approaches to co-production. These approaches include informal community engagement, co-facilitation of group services and activities, and a large focus on personalization rather than collective co-production. Co-production is undertaken and understood as a means to an end, as a utilitarian way to improve local communities.

At the same time, we also see evidence of a Communitarian Logic, where the state logic withdraws and organizations contend primarily with the market and community logics. In these instances, co-production becomes enforced rather than voluntary and pragmatic, and citizens are involved in service delivery as a matter of protecting much-needed services in communities. The Communitarian Logic creates co-production that is more ad hoc and less ambitious, thwarting the more empowering, democratic, and innovative potential of co-production.

Notes

1. The focus of this study is on England specifically, rather than the UK as a whole, because of the differences between the third sectors and certain social service policies between the nations (England, Scotland, Wales, and Northern Ireland) of the United Kingdom (Alcock, 2010). However, I reference the UK in some instances insofar as this is the focus of most institutional typologies.
2. For simplicity, I refer to these organizations as community development organizations.
3. While these programmes have not been anonymized as per agreements with interviewees, the interviewees and the sub-contracted organizations associated with the programmes are anonymized.

4. For those individuals I interviewed at both stages of the research, I have indicated 'interview 1' or 'interview 2' when quoted. Two of the community development organizations had a change of director during the research period, so the original and new directors are indicated by interview date.
5. Formerly called the Big Lottery at the time of the research.
6. Sure Start is a UK government programme that aims to tackle areas of disadvantage for young children, through childcare services, community development, and support for parents and families. See e.g. Pemberton and Mason (2009).
7. Knowing that there was potential to bias interviewees' choice of language, I tried to refrain from using the word *co-production* early in interviews and instead asked questions about the different ways that service users and citizens were involved in services. Towards the end of interviews, I asked, "The word that I'm using in my research is *co-production*; is this a word that you use?"

References

Alcock, P. (2010). A strategic unity: Defining the third sector in the UK. *Voluntary Sector Review*, *1*(1), 5–24. https://doi.org/10.1332/204080510X496984

Alinsky, S. (1989). *Rules for radicals: A practical primer for realistic radicals*. Vintage Books (Original work published 1971).

Beckert, J., & Lutter, M. (2013). Why the poor play the lottery: Sociological approaches to explaining class-based lottery play. *Sociology*, *47*(6), 1152–1170. http://doi.org/10.1177/0038038512457854

Bevir, M., Rhodes, R. A. W., & Weller, P. (2003). Traditions of governance: Interpreting the changing role of the public sector. *Public Administration*, *81*(1), 1–17.

Brandsen, T., Van de Donk, W., & Putters, K. (2005). Griffins or chameleons? Hybridity as a permanent and inevitable characteristic of the third sector. *International Journal of Public Administration*, *28*(9–10), 749–765.

Brudney, J. L., & England, R. E. (1983). Toward a definition of the coproduction concept. *Public Administration Review*, *43*(1), 59–65.

Defourny, J. (2001). From third sector to social enterprise. In C. Borzaga & J. Defourny (Eds.), *The emergence of social enterprise* (pp. 1–28). Routledge.

Esping-Andersen, G. (1990). *The three worlds of welfare capitalism*. Polity Press.

Fotaki, M. (2011). Towards developing new partnerships in public services: Users as consumers, citizens and/or co-producers in health and social care in England and Sweden. *Public Administration*, *89*(3), 933–955. http://doi.org/10.1111/j.1467-9299.2010.01879.x

Freire, P. (2000). *Pedagogy of the oppressed*. Continuum International Publishing Group (Original work published 1970).

Kisby, B. (2010). The big society: Power to the people? *The Political Quarterly*, *81*(4), 484–491. http://doi.org/10.1111/j.1467-923X.2010.02133.x

Lapsley, I. (2008). The NPM agenda: Back to the future. *Financial Accountability & Management*, *24*(1), 77–96.

Lowndes, V., & Roberts, M. (2013). *Why institutions matter: The new institutionalism in political science*. Macmillan International Higher Education.

McLaughlin, H. (2009). What's in a name: "Client", "patient", "customer", "consumer", "expert by experience", "service user" – what's next? *The British Journal of Social Work*, *39*(6), 1101–1117.

McMullin, C. (2021). Challenging the necessity of New Public Governance: Co-production by third sector organizations under different models of public management. *Public Administration*, *99*(1), 5–22. http://doi.org/10.1111/padm.12672

Nabatchi, T., Sancino, A., & Sicilia, M. (2017). Varieties of participation in public services: The who, when, and what of coproduction. *Public Administration Review*, 77(5), 766–776.

Needham, C. (2011). Personalization: From story-line to practice. *Social Policy and Administration*, *45*(1), 54–68.

Nyssens, M. (2006). *Social enterprise: At the crossroads of market, public policies and civil society*. Routledge. Retrieved May 27, 2021, from www.routledge.com/Social-Enterprise-At-the-Crossroads-of-Market-Public-Policies-and-Civil/Nyssens/p/book/9780415378796

Ostrom, E. (2007). Institutional rational choice: An assessment of the institutional analysis and development framework. In P. A. Sabatier (Ed.), *Theories of the policy process* (2nd ed., pp. 21–64). Westview Press.

Pemberton, S., & Mason, J. (2009). Co-production and sure start children's centres: Reflecting upon users', perspectives and implications for service delivery, planning and evaluation. *Social Policy and Society*, *8*(1), 13–24.

Pestoff, V. (2019). *Co-production and public service management: Citizenship, governance and public service management*. Routledge. http://doi.org/10.4324/9781351059671

Salamon, L., & Anheier, H. (1998). Social origins of civil society: Explaining the non-profit sector cross-nationally. *Voluntas*, *9*(3), 213–248.

Skelcher, C., & Smith, S. R. (2015). Theorizing hybridity: Institutional logics, complex organizations, and actor identities: The case of nonprofits. *Public Administration*, *93*(2), 433–448.

Speer, P. W., & Hughey, J. (1995). Community organizing: An ecological route to empowerment and power. *American Journal of Community Psychology*, *23*(5), 729–748. http://doi.org/10.1007/BF02506989

Taylor, M. (2004). The welfare mix in the United Kingdom. In A. Evers & J.-L. Laville (Eds.), *The third sector in Europe* (pp. 122–143). Edward Elgar Publishing.

Thornton, P. H., Ocasio, W., & Lounsbury, M. (2012). *The institutional logics perspective: A new approach to culture, structure, and process*. Oxford University Press.

Vickers, I., et al. (2017). Public service innovation and multiple institutional logics: The case of hybrid social enterprise providers of health and wellbeing. *Research Policy*, *46*(10), 1755–1768.

5 Social Solidarity Logic and formalized co-production in Lyon

While co-production research is being undertaken in many countries worldwide (with a particular concentration in continental Europe), there has been a surprising lack of research on co-production in France, with a few exceptions that include France as part of a larger study (e.g. Parrado et al., 2013). Likewise, the French literature on participatory democracy and other collaborative approaches is comparatively underdeveloped in relation to the Anglo-Saxon interest (Bacqué & Gauthier, 2011; Bacqué & Sintomer, 2020). This raises the important question – is there less research on co-production in France because co-production does not happen there? If not, why not? Or, if it does take place, is it simply understood differently or called something different?

In this chapter, I consider the third sector case studies in Lyon, France, to further explore the impact of institutional logics on organizations' approaches to co-production of services with service users/citizens. I begin the chapter by outlining the context of the third sector in France and in Lyon and by providing an overview of the organizations under study (five 'social centres,' a parent co-operative, and a multi-organization movement to tackle older people's isolation). This is followed by an analysis of the approaches to co-production undertaken by the cases, following the institutional logics framework.

1 Context: the third sector in Lyon

Lyon is a city with a population of about 500,000 (1.3 million in the greater Lyon Metropolitan area). Although France is known for being a highly centralized state, third sector organizations in Lyon have relationships with three levels of local government (the city, the *Métropole de Lyon*, and the Region). The city of Lyon is also subdivided into nine arrondissements, each of which are responsible for managing some local facilities and have an elected mayor and citizen committees, although they do not manage their own budgets. Third sector actors regularly manage policies and grants from the city, the *Département*, the *Métropole de Lyon*, and various national government departments, in particular the Social Security and Family policy branch (*Caisse des*

DOI: 10.4324/9781003245605-5

Allocations Familiales – CAF). Each of these levels of government thus produces rules and regulations to which third sector organizations are subject.

In terms of the national level typologies used to classify countries by welfare and non-profit regimes, France is consistently categorized as corporatist, with welfare benefits based on social insurance and a strong link between professional or occupational status and entitlements (Esping-Andersen, 1990). Its non-profit sector (also in the corporatist category) is large and benefits from a high degree of welfare spending that is focused on funding service delivery organizations (Salamon & Anheier, 1997, 1998). As an illustration of the difference between liberal and corporatist non-profit regimes in practice, in France, 60% of the welfare provision workforce is employed in non-profit organizations compared to 26% in the UK (Archambault et al., 2014). France's third sector developed to a large degree alongside the welfare state as a major provider of services, making it a more corporatist partner in this arena, with some even arguing that the third sector is treated as no more than an arm of the state (Barthélemy, 2000).

The 'third sector' in France is, however, conceived as a broader group than just non-profits, with a more socio-political perspective that defines the sector more by its activities and values basis instead of a legal basis. The French third sector tends to be identified as the 'social economy' or the 'social and solidarity economy,' broadly defined as organizations that aim to benefit the community, are democratically governed, and which privilege people over capital in the distribution of incomes, as discussed in detail in Chapter 2 (Evers & Laville, 2004). Social economy is meant not to classify types of organizations, but rather as an analysis of different modes of exchange and organizational operations, where public and community rationalizations take precedence over market logics. With a strong influence of the co-operative movement, emphasis is put on the democratic international operations of social economy organizations.

French third sector organizations can take several legal forms, with different implications for the involvement of service users. Associations are non-profit organizations, which may be incorporated or unincorporated, thereby encompassing both small, neighbourhood organizations and larger, service-providing non-profits. For co-operatives, there are two legal forms – *société coopérative et participative* and *société coopérative d'intérêt collectif*. The former is a more traditional worker co-operative, where decision-making is entrusted to workers, but the latter has a broader remit of including multiple stakeholders (including service users and representatives from local associations) in the organization's governance. The ethos of internal democracy through voting is a cornerstone for these organizations.

Lyon is known for having a strong social economy and its topography and history have shaped the development and value basis of its associative sector. The city has two main hills that were historically known as the 'hill that prays' and the 'hill that works,' due to the location of the Fourvière Basilica and convents on the former and a concentration of silk workers who inhabited the latter. Silk workers' protests in the 1830s against poor wages and working conditions led to the creation of the first consumer co-operative in France, an *épicerie sociale* (social grocery store), as well as many mutuals and health services. The social and solidarity economy is still shaped by these two strong value traditions – Catholicism on the one hand, and workers' self-organization on the other.

2 Case study organizations and research methods

Mirroring the research in Sheffield, I followed a similar approach of purposive and snowball sampling in Lyon, interviewing stakeholders from local network organizations who acted as key informants to support my selection of case study organizations.

I analysed five organizations called *centres sociaux*, or 'social centres,' which are organizations located in disadvantaged neighbourhoods across France. Social centres (where *social* refers to 'social services' rather that 'social club') provide space for community activities, like community centres, but they also adhere to political aims of social development and active citizenship (McMullin, 2018). The concept of the social centre was developed in France in the early 20th century, modelled on the settlement movement in England, which aimed to reduce inequalities by advocating middle class volunteering alongside poor people in 'settlement houses' that provided services such as education, training, childcare, and healthcare. In France, social centres grew in number with the establishment of the welfare state after the Second World War, and again with further state investment in the social sector in the 1970s and 1980s. Social centres are supported by funding from the family branch of social security (CAF) and local and regional public agencies, with the remit of improving social cohesion and citizen empowerment. I have anonymized these five organizations as Avancé, Mouvement, Équipe, Diversité, and Familles.

I also considered two further case studies – a parents' organization and an association/movement to tackle loneliness and isolation of older people. The parents' organization, ACEPP (*Association des Collectifs Enfants Parents Professionnels*), is a federation of parent co-operative nurseries across the country. The organization has a national level representative body and regional networks that represent local co-operative nurseries. Research was undertaken with the regional organization in Lyon and with parent volunteers active in their local co-operative nursery.

The other case study, Monalisa, is a national movement and network of institutions and associations that sign a pledge to tackle social isolation of older people in their areas. Monalisa was initiated in 2013 by a government minister who established a working group to discuss the issues of older people's isolation, and the association was developed to create and support 'citizen teams' across the country to bring together those with common aims. Associations are encouraged to sign a charter committed to the shared goals, and Monalisa thus acts as a rallying force for associations offering services and support for older people.

I conducted a total of 31 interviews – 19 with staff and volunteers of the case study organizations and 12 with individuals from networks and other local organizations. I also conducted a further interview with a Monalisa representative in 2020. Interviews were conducted in French, aside from those with two respondents who were fluent in English. Like in Sheffield, I transcribed interviews intelligent verbatim. Because French is my second language, I enlisted the help of a native French transcriber for several of the interviews where interviewees spoke particularly quickly, to ensure the integrity of the data. In these instances, I checked the transcripts carefully for accuracy. I have also personally translated the quotes included in this chapter from French to English, with the support of a native French speaker.

I attended and observed the annual general assembly of three of the social centres, a social cafe of one of the organizations associated with Monalisa, and the 30th anniversary of ACEPP, which was both a celebration as well as an opportunity to discuss the work of the organization informally with a number of stakeholders (including staff, volunteers, and local elected officials). Several of the events I observed also included booths, posters, and displays set up to highlight various projects, many of which described specific co-production practices. Finally, I analysed organizational documents. The selection of relevant documents for the Lyon case studies was relatively straightforward because of the French associative norm to produce detailed, publicly available organizational plans, charters, and mission statements. For the five social centre case studies, I examined the four-year 'social plans' (*projets sociaux*), which provide extremely detailed (70- to 80-page) evaluations of the previous plan, strategies for the coming four years, and outlines of the resident involvement and consultation processes that had gone into producing the plans.

3 Institutional logics, co-production, and the third sector in Lyon

The institutional logics framework enables us to better understand some of the unique characteristics of the French cases – in particular, the opportunities for and constraints on co-production by non-profit practitioners and citizens. In this section, I discuss in turn the rules; norms; values, beliefs, and ideas that structure decision-making and actions by the case study organizations in Lyon and how these in turn shape co-production practices.

A. Rules

Charters

The first category of rules that impact third sector organizations are the formal charters or conventions that third sector organizations sign. For the social centres, each association must become a signatory of the National Charter of Social Centres, which defines such an organization as "a centre of initiatives brought by local people, supported by professionals, capable of defining and pursuing a plan of social development for the entire population of a territory" (*Charte fédérale des centres sociaux et socio-culturels de France*, 2000). Signing the charter means agreeing to adhere to the founding values of human dignity, solidarity, and democracy (which are discussed in detail in relation to values) and that the association will take an approach of collaborating with residents.

This essentially means that co-production is formalized as a requirement or rule of being a social centre. The importance of this charter in defining the adherence to values as a rule presents an interesting interconnection between different elements of these organizations' logics. In describing the relationship between rules, narratives, and practices, Lowndes and Roberts suggest that "narratives are often used to justify the existence of rules; [and] rules often formalize well-established practices" (Lowndes & Roberts, 2013, p. 53). In this case, the rules defined by this charter not only provide a formal codification of practices, but they also provide the main defining narratives of social centres, rather than narratives justifying the rules. In these rules, the boundaries between the logic of the state and that of the community are blurred. The existence of a charter to formalize values mirrors the French republican emphasis on constitutionality, while at the same time, the rules themselves are very much indicative of a community ethos of local unity and cooperation.

This importance of rules defined by a charter was also key for Monalisa. The project conceives of itself as a social movement; however, it was initiated by a government minister who established a working group to discuss the issue of older people's isolation across the country. The working group then developed a charter that associations, public institutions, and other actors in the field of older people's services could sign, promising to take part in the movement to tackle loneliness and isolation amongst older people. In a clear manifestation of the state logic, the mobilization was launched to coincide with the preparation of a law on the 'adaptation of society to an ageing population.' The guiding aim of the 'movement' is to increase collaboration and cooperation between associations that work for older people, but the logic guiding its establishment demonstrates a uniquely French understanding of the relationship between civil society and the state: even a social movement, which is typically grassroots-led and characterized by a fluidity of organizing principles, is defined by the rules of a formal, legalistically defined charter.

> So this working group worked for seven or eight months, and they produced a document, a reference to say that faced with an ageing society, faced with the isolation of older people, what was needed was a national mobilization. And Monalisa was created as a result of this working group. . . . So it was created because at the national level, there

> was a whole movement which aimed for the major associations to be signatories around a charter, which also committed to values.
>
> (Senior staff, Monalisa org 4)

At the same time, this charter enables signatory organizations to interpret how they will implement the charter. Signatories agree to "participate in the support and deployment of Monalisa citizen teams, respecting their choice of membership" (Charter, Monalisa). The wording of the agreement allows for flexibility in how associations interpret and translate these rules into practices, which will be discussed in the following section.

Public policy

Third sector organizations are also influenced by rules that stem from government policies. Across the sector, several laws were mentioned by stakeholders as being particularly influential for social economy organizations and associations:

- *Loi du 1er juillet 1901 relative au contrat d'association*: Introduced the right to form non-profit associations. This established the legal framework for the third sector.
- *Loi n° 2002–2 du 2 janvier 2002 rénovant l'action sociale et médico-sociale*: Along with establishing a charter of rights for patients/service users, the Loi 2002–2 requires that certain types of service providers establish service user groups that can be consulted on or involved in decision-making.
- *Loi n° 2014–173 du 21 février 2014 de programmation pour la ville et la cohésion urbaine*: Established the requirement of citizen councils in 'priority' disadvantaged areas.
- *Loi n° 2014–856 du 31 juillet 2014 relative à l'économie sociale et solidaire*: Established a legal framework for organizations of the social and solidarity economy, enabling them to get access to government grants and contracts.

The Loi 1901 was discussed by several interviewees and in organizational documents, and many associations often refer to themselves as being '*une association loi 1901*' ('an association based on the 1901 law'), demonstrating the continuing centrality of this law (rule) in shaping the identity of associations. The *Loi 2002–2* and *Loi février 2014* were discussed in conversations about health and social care services (for the former) and in relation to neighbourhood renewal (for the latter), but both arose as a response to my enquiry about the concept of co-production.

> That's co-production – a movement from both sides. There is a law in France, which is the law 2002–2. This law says that you have to put service users at the centre of the plan. . . . The law required a committee, once a month or once. . . . It depends, where professionals and service

> users meet each other and exchange. It was really something new in 2002. It has revolutionized the associative sector.
>
> (Manager, Other organization 1)

The *politique de la ville* ('city policy'), a national urban renewal programme that targets areas of disadvantage through a process of partnership building between public powers and civil society, is especially significant for the social centres. Three of the social centres suggested that this policy has shaped their rules, especially in relation to policies of involvement and co-production. However, there was also some scepticism about the way the policy is designed and implemented and the degree to which it has been successful at changing practices.

> [*Politique de la ville*] tried to introduce this idea of co-construction, co-constructing the contract which will define the urban renovation, but in practice, it's not done. For example, the new contract which is defining the amount of money that will be put into this suburb for the next five years, they were supposed to be developed with a group of citizens, but it hasn't been done. They have been signed without any consultation.
>
> (Director, Diversité, interview in English)

The director of this social centre expressed some frustration with the government policy and its lack of success in encouraging a new culture of enhanced citizen participation in disadvantaged urban areas. Although the state and community logics are primarily blended within the social centres, this example shows an instance where there is occasionally conflict between the centralized state logic and the fact that the social centres would prioritize the more community-centred logic.

While the *politique de la ville* was primarily discussed in relation to the policies and rules it introduces, it also acts as a source of grant funding, and its guidelines and requirements have created some tensions. Neighbourhoods that are designated as 'priority areas' are allocated grants under the programme, and changes to the policy that determines which areas are priorities have recently impacted Familles. One of the two neighbourhoods covered by this social centre was reclassified as no longer a priority zone and therefore ceased to be eligible for funding and support under the policy (despite, as the chief executive argued at the social centre's annual general assembly, the neighbourhood still being home to many families in difficulty). This issue of the changing rules and boundaries of the *politique de la ville* and its implications on funding, while not mentioned by interviewees from other social centres, is a topic that was considered in the social plans of Diversité and Équipe as well.

The rules imposed by the state also come into conflict with the community logic in other instances where social centres attempt to take a co-productive approach. The director of Familles described an innovative alternative education project that the organization designed to support difficult teenagers by giving them work experience placements at the social centre, rather than allowing them to drop out of school. The aim was to work in partnership between teachers, professionals at the social centre, and the teenagers to co-produce an educative programme for them. The project, however, was met with some resistance by education authorities who were strongly driven by a state-centric logic of national education. The social centre faced considerable barriers in receiving funding and permission to take the project forward, which is evidence of the community logic of collaboration and local small-scale initiatives splintering from the state logic.

Funding

Besides the issue of boundaries for *politique de la ville* funding, contracts and grants generally posed limited constraints on the organizations in Lyon. This is a function of the way many third sector organizations are funded, which also provides a telling indication of the fundamental logics impacting these organizations. The social centres are primarily funded by the CAF, as well as grants from several government departments, the city, and the region, which are tied to specific projects. Likewise, ACEPP receives grant funding from multiple government sources but also earns income by providing back-office support for parent co-operatives and receives specific project funding. Unlike in contexts that have been heavily influenced by the principles of New Public Management (such as the UK), these projects are defined flexibly and with less stringent performance measurement requirements.

> There is a tendency to say that all nurseries should be managed within the framework of public service. However, here we promote instead what comes under the grant agreement, because the idea behind that, from a philosophical point of view is that it's a group of residents who have an initiative, who put forward a project and who will defend this project to the collectivity who will finance the project.
>
> (Project manager, ACEPP)

Interviewees from ACEPP discussed several funding streams that are allocated with the aim of improving parents' political participation, funding to 'develop associative life' and funding from the Rhône Region to support the organization's 'participative approach.' Rather than being funded to deliver quantifiable results, ACEPP puts forward a social and political project, and it receives government funding towards supporting these aims and values. This clearly shows a recombination of the community and state logics, with an absence of the market logic.

Social centres are funded based on their designation as such, i.e. being an organization that is in charge of social service activities (*une association d'animation vie sociale*). This means that funding is received as an overall allocation/grant and is linked with the purpose of the organization, rather than to particular services or the need to deliver specifically defined outcomes.

For us, it's an advantage because we really have this funding for our basic operation and based on that, we've got the opportunity to develop some. . . . It's not the heart of our activities, but because we are funded for the services we are providing, plus we have *subventions* [funding] for our general activities. With this funding, we can really develop activities targeting the issues of empowerment, co-construction, co-development, co- whatever you want with not so much pressure from our funders.

(Director, Diversité, interview conducted in English)

While the other four social centre directors expressed similar experiences of limited rules imposed by funding bodies, this does not mean that these rules are entirely absent. The director of Diversité explained that while grant funding is not restrictive, some funders (particularly the European Union) are beginning to request that recipients of contracts prove results and outcomes – a requirement that is a relatively new and unfamiliar phenomenon in France, a country that has been considerably less influenced by the norms and rules advocated by New Public Management (McMullin, 2021). Aside from this one example, there were virtually no instances that suggested the presence of a market logic (in the broadest sense, as it concerns performance management and business efficiency) defining the organizations.

Governance

Rules also emanate from inside an organization, including governance procedures, constitutions, and other formal policies that define how an organization should undertake its work. As with externally imposed rules, internal rules in Lyon demonstrate a blend between the state and community logics. These types of internal rules appear to be considerably more significant in shaping the logics of the French organizations than was the case in England. As non-profit associations, the Lyon organizations are governed by elected boards of directors/trustees (*conseil d'administration*). For social centres, an important aspect of their governance structure is that these trustees must be residents (as opposed to, for example in the case of many British charities, representatives of other local community organizations who are actually paid staff). The *conseil d'administration* was described by several of the respondents in Lyon as playing an important role in defining the direction of the social centre.

As far as the board of trustees is concerned, the administrators (trustees) are very present and very invested in their role as administrators and volunteers of the social centre. Where we could perhaps improve things as a social centre, it's in linking better with local people – how do we go meet them, and how do we 'construct' with them and propose activities?

(Development officer, Mouvement)

This importance of involving residents in organizational governance was highlighted by the other four social centre directors as well. Social centres are membership associations – in order to use (most) services, take part in activities, or stand for election to the board, residents must join the organization as fee-paying members. Like the adherence to the National Charter of Social Centres, the governance structure of being run by residents forms an important part of social centres' identities, again linking formal rules to values and beliefs, in creating a driving institutional logic. This demonstrates another example where collaboration between paid professionals and residents is institutionalized within social centres, as well as how the state logic is transposed to the local level, with democratic representation playing a key role within each association.

Similar internal rules and governance structures were found for ACEPP. As ACEPP is a representative organization of co-operative nurseries, the involvement of parents is mainstreamed into every level of organizational governance and decision-making as a core tenet. Parents are involved in the governance of individual co-operative nurseries, in the board at the regional level (i.e. ACEPP du Rhône), and finally in the board and decision-making structures of the national level of the network. This widespread involvement in governance is in addition to everyday volunteering and involvement of parents in each nursery's activities, and it shows how the involvement of parents at all levels forms an essential part of how ACEPP is guided by rules.

> The action of ACEPP relies on the collaboration between parents and professionals, the acceptance and respect of diversity, the participation in local and civic life. We propose activities that privilege a participative approach, associative life, the role of parents and the quality of children's services.
>
> (Brochure, ACEPP)

Similar again to the social centres' rules, ACEPP defines itself by its democratic and participative approach. This is defined even more explicitly as a collaboration between parents and professionals – suggesting that co-production is one of the key procedures for decision-making and action. This degree of formality of parental involvement shows a stronger impact of the state logic, as the parent representatives are democratically elected, and decisions are often made through voting.

B. *Norms and practices*

Co-construction

One of the most important areas for the involvement of citizens by French associations is in the 'co-construction' of four yearly 'social plans' (i.e. strategic plans). When asked a general question about how residents and service users are involved in different ways by each organization, the most common response was about these social plans and how they are 'co-constructed' with citizens. This term *co-construction* is frequently employed in French to refer to the involvement of citizens 'up-stream' in policymaking or strategic priority setting (Vaillancourt, 2009). In the English language literature, this is more closely analogous to the notion of co-creation, defined in Chapter 2 (see also Brandsen & Honingh, 2018).

The social plan is a key part of the democratic functioning of social centres, and as a requirement from the national federation and the CAF, social centres are required to design these plans in collaboration with residents and members of the association. This strategic priority-setting was noted by all five social centres as a key area of collaboration between staff and residents. Co-construction of social plans is done using a range of methods by different social centres – all use some sort of traditional survey or consultation, while some also employ more intensive co-design methodologies.

For example, interviewees from Avancé described in detail their process for involving residents in the priority-setting process, which included some innovative methods. Visitors to the community centre building were encouraged to write their "wishes, proposals and requests for the four years to come" (Projet Social, Avancé) on pieces of paper shaped like light bulbs, which were displayed in the lobby. These were subsequently collated, analysed, and developed into priorities within the plan. For the other three organizations that discussed the involvement of residents in the creation of the social plan, the process was more akin to a process of intensive consultation of members through surveys and discussions.

> So we did what we call a diagnosis. We interview our own members. . . . We did a questionnaire. In the neighbourhood, we had two questions about how you feel about your neighbourhood. Are there any good things? Bad things? . . . Do you come to the social centre? We try to work on the strengths and weaknesses of the area. And we went to meet residents. We did a questionnaire in the social centre. Then, we posted ourselves in several places around the social centre – the exit of the school . . . so that there were people we did not know. We took interns, and the trustees participated. The trustees, the people on the board. We also try to get them involved, through things like that, to do the survey.
>
> (Director, Familles)

Notwithstanding the ambiguity between consultation and co-design in these examples of co-construction, this involvement of local people in defining the strategic direction of the social centres in Lyon reflects the importance of the community logic in organizational practices. Here, the informal valuing of community members' views and priorities is privileged above the bureaucratic dominance or regard for democratic voting as the sole legitimate source of decision-making that characterizes the state logic. The social plan provides a platform to develop the concrete activities and actions that will support the value of participation that is established by the national federation, thus formalizing what might otherwise be informal practices.

Involvement in decision-making

The French blending of the state and community logics results in participation being approached as an explicitly political project. Participation in internal decision-making processes – both formally in governance (as discussed regarding rules) and more informally (i.e. a *norm*) is often highlighted by these organizations. Like the adherence to the National Charter of Social Centres, the fact that social centres are membership organizations governed by residents forms an important part of their identities, again linking the existence of formal rules to practices and values in creating a driving institutional logic. This is further extended to the norms of decision-making within the organizations, particularly at the annual general meetings, which are widely publicized as an important function in determining organizational strategy and priorities. This illustrates another example where collaboration between paid professionals and residents is institutionalized within social centres, as well as the way in which the state logic is transposed to the local level, with democratic representation playing a key role within the association.

Social centres' annual general meetings are generally well attended – at the three I observed, there were approximately 30 to 40 members/residents in attendance at two (Mouvement and Familles) and 80 to 90 at the third (Avancé). These meetings involved not only the formal procedures of electing representatives to the board of trustees but also posters and displays of activities and a performance by children from one of the association's programmes (Familles), interactive games and contests (Mouvement), and participative workshops (Avancé). The workshop I attended during the AGM of Avancé was about ideas to introduce more political debate to the activities of the social centre, asking participants to discuss the themes they would be interested in having debates about, and how the social centre should facilitate debates. All three AGMs were followed by a reception or meal, offering an integration between the official, formal, and political aspects of involvement and the solidarity and reciprocity of community.

The influence of the state logic is prevalent across the decision-making practices of French organizations, particularly those described by the social centres. Day-to-day activities are strongly influenced by the formal constraints produced by national laws, the National Charter of Social Centres, and the social centres' own strategic plans, which provide explicit guidelines for the organization's priorities for the coming four years, as well as action plans for achieving each goal. Discussions with directors and staff members reveal that, unlike many cases where actors' practice diverge from or conflict with official rules (Lowndes et al., 2006), social centre staff tend to adhere to the protocols set out in their strategic plan documents.

> Here in our social centre, we have many, many volunteers. I think there are more than 100. So in the social centre, we function with '*commissions de travail*' (work groups). So there is a group for 'associative life.' There is an activities group and there is a group. . . . In the social plan, it's all written.
>
> (Volunteer 1, Avancé)

It is important to note that this quote is from a volunteer at the social centre, rather than a staff member, showing the reach that bureaucracy has within this organization (which is representative of the practices observed at the other Lyon social centres). The 'Napoleonic' administrative tradition, which favours codification of standards and practices means that there is a strong emphasis on ensuring that there are particular rules and procedures in place for many elements of the way that associations operate (Peters, 2008).

Similarly, supporting parents to make decisions is a key norm for ACEPP. In particular, parents are encouraged to decide upon how co-operative nurseries should be run and which activities they would like to develop. Staff then support them to deliver these activities.

> In the day-to-day, we work well together. The professionals do not do the decision-making. That is to say that when a decision has to be made, it's the parents who are managers and who will make the decision. The person in charge, she's there – we'll consult her. We'll ask for her opinion, but on the other hand, she does not have the right to vote. It's the same principle here.
>
> (Frontline staff 2, ACEPP)

This type of more informal co-decision-making is in addition to the formalized role that parents play in the governance of co-operative nurseries and ACEPP. 'Supporting' parents in a process of co-decision in this way is linked to narratives of empowerment and citizenship, which is explicitly elaborated in one of ACEPP's brochures as "Parental involvement: A citizen act." Parent participation in childcare activities is framed as being about parents exercising their rights and developing themselves politically to promote and protect the role of parents. As elaborated in the next section, this practice extends from decision-making to co-delivery of childcare services as part of the network of co-operative nurseries.

Co-operative participation

The social centres and organizations associated with Monalisa are all non-profit membership associations whose core functioning draws upon the formal and informal involvement of members and residents, but this participation is not obligatory. For ACEPP and the nurseries that make up its members, regular involvement of parents is expected as part of a requirement of co-operative membership. Every description of the organization's activities is enmeshed with the ways in which parents are involved, including co-design of services (through e.g. committees) and an expectation that parents volunteer a certain amount of time directly to co-operative nurseries. Familles, which also runs a nursery, similarly attempts to involve parents in the functioning of the nursery, but this is not a requirement as it is for co-operative nurseries.

This approach blends the state logic of democracy with the more localized, relationship basis of the community logic. In many ways like the social centres, co-production is mainstreamed into the definition of ACEPP and as such, it forms an important part of all decision-making, which is always done in collaboration between parents and professionals. One may say that co-production is in fact the primary 'informal rule of the game,' which takes place because it is formally specified by rules.

> Participation being obligatory allows each person to participate, but we focus on participation that makes it possible for each person to participate, because not everyone has the same level of engagement or the desire to do things, or the availability, etc. What we say a lot in the network is that the more participation is diversified – i.e. that one can be president, one can be treasurer, one can lead an outing to a market, run a cooking workshop with children. . . . The more varied the possibilities for participation, and thus the wider the diversity of audience that is reached.
>
> (Project manager, ACEPP)

The formal requirement of parent participation plays out in multiple spaces. These were highlighted during a photo competition at ACEPP's anniversary celebration, where attendees were asked to vote on the best photo that demonstrated 'parent and professional collaboration.' Photos showed people playing music, going on field trips, sharing meals, chatting, etc. Another example of this multi-faceted approach to participation includes a board game developed to identify the needs and desires of parents in different parts of the region. Playing pieces were made by a local artisan, game questions were devised by local people, and game board photos are customized for each local area.

> The nursery that I chose, it's a lot of parental involvement. The parents, each family has to spend four to five hours per week at the nursery doing various tasks – cleaning, helping out the staff and kind of helping out with the children, doing activities with them, changing diapers or helping with their dinners and things like that. And also, you have a role as an employer, so you help run the nursery on the administrative side.
>
> (Frontline staff 1, ACEPP)

Within each co-operative nursery, parents are required to volunteer a certain amount of time each month. Interviewees acknowledged that many parents who place their children in a co-operative nursery do so not because they are attracted to the democratic ethos, but rather because of convenience of location or other factors. As noted in the previous quotes, parents are however encouraged to participate beyond the required minimum of volunteering, in both participating or leading activities as well as in more strategic and decision-making roles. The importance of parent participation and the motivations behind it are a driving democratic and empowerment ethos, which will be discussed further in relation to values.

Citizen-led projects

The norms of involvement in decision-making and co-construction discussed thus far show the vast influence of more formal constraints of rules (governance, charters, etc.) and the infiltration of the French state logic on practices. One area of more informal practices is in the facilitation of citizen-led projects, which was described by Avancé, Mouvement, Familles, and ACEPP (with the related notion of citizen teams also being a core component of Monalisa). These practices have much in common with the notion of the facilitation of citizen or civic initiatives (Igalla et al., 2019; Bakker et al., 2012), but these initiatives are not fully self-organized and independent – the French organizations encourage citizens to propose their ideas to them, but then the organization assumes risk and ownership while realizing the activity in partnership.

At Mouvement, this practice was framed primarily as providing support and expertise to enable residents to set up community groups and to support existing small groups; while for the other organizations, respondents gave examples of small services or projects that were citizen-led but supported by paid professional staff. Respondents from these organizations contended that one main role of staff members was to be available to empower local people to design and actualize their own projects, events, and activities by offering them skills (such as IT and marketing skills) and resources (printing, facilities, event spaces, staff, and volunteer time). ACEPP also described several instances where parents proposed activities or events to their co-operative nursery, such as garage sales and a photography project.

> For each project, the idea is really that we always do it together. For the garage sale project, it's really carried by parents, but it doesn't impact the day-to-day of the crèche. Any projects that impact the day-to-day, they have to be developed with what we call committees or work groups. . . . In each committee there is a professional point of contact and two or three parents, so that the idea is that it's always partly professionals and partly parents.
>
> (Frontline staff 2, ACEPP)

At Avancé social centre, the director and two volunteers who were interviewed described two examples of projects that were initiated by citizens and realized with the support of staff working for the social centre – a *gratiferia* (market where everything is free) and a weekly community picnic during August when the social centre building was closed. This approach reflected one of the key strategic priorities of the social plan to support the initiatives of residents. Both projects were suggested to staff members by residents. Social centre staff supported the residents by designing and distributing flyers, and organizing necessary permits, whilst the residents recruited volunteers and brought food, drinks, and activities to the picnics. These examples represent both co-design and co-delivery – citizens initiated the ideas for the activities, but they were designed through close collaboration with social centre staff and finally realized because of the joint actions of citizens and staff.

The formalized priority of supporting citizen-led projects does not, however, always translate into reality with great ease. The directors of Diversité, Avancé, and Équipe spoke about the barriers the social centres faced in trying to improve their processes of involving local people and indicated that their participation practices fell somewhere short of the rhetoric of their social plans.

> We are trying to say, "We are not here just to develop services, but to be a place where people can come, where we can help them identify the issues they want to develop, help them build projects and put them in the heart of our activities." We are really far from the empowerment issues, but trying just to put co-construction of projects to start with before moving more with empowerment, so just putting the place of the public to be able to construct with us, to build with us the activities, was the first step we have been trying to do.
>
> (Director, Diversité. Interview conducted in English)

Monalisa also promotes practices like these citizen-led projects. One of its primary focuses is on the development of citizen teams to be mobilized to support lonely older people. Monalisa started this process by mapping where services and associations existed already across France in order to identify areas of duplication and gaps in provision. This mapping exercise was framed as a way of valuing the expertise and experience of citizens and local groups that are already working towards the same aims and to support the creation of citizen teams to be supported to develop their own activities. According to an interviewee from the National Network, as of 2020, over 700 such teams had been formed. Unlike the practices of the social centres and ACEPP, however, this promotion of citizen teams is less of a practice of co-production (due to the limited engagement of professionals with the citizens) and more directly about active volunteering.

Citizen-led projects in the French cases are typically more likely to relate to complementary rather than core service provision (Brandsen & Honingh, 2015). Encouraging local people to propose projects and activities that can then be supported with professional help from staff again reflects the strength of the community logic in defining practices. This practice is in fact the most detached from the state logic, in that the support of citizen-led local projects celebrates local differences and does not require formal authorization or democratic representation.

C. *Values, beliefs, and ideas*

Finally, we arrive at the ideational elements that shape organizations' practices of co-production. Through analysing the narratives of interviewees, as well as text from organizational documents, I identify several key themes that encompass organizational values, beliefs, ideas, identities, and stories.

French political culture

Third sector organizations' values, beliefs, and identities that define their co-production practices are not entirely self-determined but are shaped to an extent by other field-level actors such as local government, third sector networks, and representative organizations. Several stakeholders in Lyon and academics elsewhere in France indicated that they believed that one of the biggest barriers to citizen participation and co-production is French administrative and political culture.

> You have some elected officials who think that citizen participation doesn't bring much, that residents don't have enough perspective to have a point of view on what the general interest can be. That they're too attached to their own daily personal problems. And so we're still in a representative democracy, and it's the role of elected officials to make choices, to make decisions.
>
> (Manager, Ville de Lyon)

This appears to be consistent with the literature on administrative traditions, which suggests that France's Napoleonic tradition centres the state in political life, in opposition to the perceived particularist interests of individuals or communities (Peters, 2008; Painter & Peters, 2010). The centralization of power within the French state, as well as the conceptualization of public service and public benefit are thus seen as creating barriers for third sector organizations aiming to engage in more creative and co-productive practices. There seemed to be consensus amongst stakeholders that France, in general, is less innovative when it comes to adopting citizen participation initiatives.

> Today, we're starting to talk to citizens. So that's to say that in the logic, the political logic, even if it's put in practice by an association who defends the service user, who puts them at the forefront, who tries to co-construct with the service user, it's not in the culture, in fact. The culture is really that public policy is constructed by the state and even if it's pushed by associations, it's constructed by the state and then associations are managers of services, in fact.
>
> (Director, Lyon Network 3)

Many respondents argued that French political culture prevents public powers from undertaking citizen involvement initiatives, or it prevents those from being effective. This position echoes findings from Sintomer and De Maillard (2007) on the *politique de la ville*, where there was limited success in implementing participation initiatives because of the tension between representative and participative democracy in France. As an expert interviewee argued, "I would say the political culture could be one barrier. The traditional French republican political culture is very inhospitable to this."

This condemnation of French political culture as a barrier to citizen involvement and co-production was common but not universal. Monalisa, conceived more as a common cause under which associations who are already working to fight older peoples' isolation can unite, convened around an ethos of non-centralization and a lack of dogma about how local associations interpret the mission and operationalize it into concrete practices.

> In fact, Monalisa is not very hierarchical. It's a mobilization, so it means that it's the citizens who must take up the action and who create their team. A team can be, I don't know, five or six people who visit. . . . But each can have their own range of actions. . . . It can be variable. It depends on the people that will mobilize and their time.
>
> (Regional Representative, Monalisa)

This value of flexibility and non-hierarchy contradicts much of the other findings from the French organizations, where the state logic has informed many of the values and beliefs, particularly around the 'general interest.' The French state logic discourages the notion of differentiation between communities, meaning that the 'community' logic appears to be more of a translation of the national state logic into local contexts. French republicanism promotes a uniformity of the values, cultural beliefs, and norms that constitute the narrative aspect of institutional logics. As such, co-production or involvement activities that explicitly accept that a variety of outcomes will arise or that some communities may hold different values than others is generally viewed with suspicion. The description of locally based citizen teams working for Monalisa is therefore uncharacteristic of the typically formalized, hierarchical, and controlled approach that most of the interviewees in Lyon described. However, the fact that Monalisa was initiated from the top-down rather than bottom-up to promote these values and aims of reducing older people's social isolation in local areas is consistent with the French republican state logic.

Solidarity

One of the key guiding values across the organizations in Lyon is the notion of solidarity. This term frequently appears in organizational documents (such as the social plans of all five social centres) as well as at the field level of the National Federation of Social Centres. In interviews, respondents often spoke about solidarity as discursively linked to notions of mutual aid and fraternity as well as to describe projects that would typically be categorized as charity. In the social plans of two social centres, solidarity is described as the following:

> Solidarity: The social centre supports the construction of a space for exchange and sharing, where each local resident has their place. A space where social and intergenerational links are created.
>
> (Projet Social, Mouvement)

> Solidarity: Considering men and women as showing solidarity with one another means being capable of living together [*vivre ensemble*] in society is a continuing conviction of Social Centres since they began.
>
> (Projet Social, Avancé)

In the second quote, solidarity is also linked with the concept of *vivre ensemble*, which translates to English roughly as 'living together,' but it can probably best be understood in English as something akin to 'peaceful coexistence' of different groups in society. Many translations of French texts to English equate *vivre ensemble* to 'diversity,' but diversity and multiculturalism are somewhat at odds with French political culture. *Vivre ensemble* is a uniquely French way of resolving ideas of *fraternité* and *solidarité* with the reality of an increasingly diverse population in France. The idea of multiculturalism conflicts with the French conceptualization of citizenship, where everyone – regardless of religion or ethnicity – is French and French alone, with no space for different communities within this identity. Thus *vivre ensemble* represents an essential element of the logics of social centres as well as ACEPP, as a blend of the state and community logics in a way that self-consciously aims to allow for individuals to be both French and acknowledge their religious or other cultural identities. For example, one of the social centres has as a strategic priority to "promote the '*vivre ensemble*'" in its social plan:

> Reinforcing the act of 'reaching out' to residents, no matter their age or sociocultural origins.

> Adapting our offer to be attentive to different populations (to make cultural mixing [diversity] work, it's necessary that different people share the same service or the same activity). . . .
>
> Paying attention to welcoming vulnerable populations.
>
> (Projet social, Familles)

These complementary values – human dignity, solidarity, and *vivre ensemble* – contribute to the logic that defines social centres' engagement in co-production. In other words, a mainstreamed, fundamental value of social centres is to provide spaces where local people of all backgrounds are welcomed – both just to attend, but also to contribute to decision-making. Like the rules and practices discussed, these values in Lyon exhibit a blending of a state logic that advances a singular notion of nationhood and citizenship with a sense of local belonging that typically characterizes the community logic.

Importantly, however, the values of solidarity and *vivre ensemble* that guide the Lyon organizations are *not* linked with the notion of 'community.' The idea of 'community' is somehow 'not French' (or, as one interviewee jokingly put it, "*C'est pas frenchy, ça*!"). A representative from a regional network of social centres explained:

> In France, talking about 'community' isn't allowed because that refers to the private sphere, and what we share in France in terms of being citizens, that's what must be shared in the public sphere.
>
> (Representative, Social centre network)

Community has a negative connotation in France because it is linked to communitarianism, which the French associate with splintering cultural communities that do not adhere to the values of the Republic. Local difference is typically admonished, rather than celebrated, and the idea of strengthening local communities is viewed as a way to diminish the power of the state. This again recalls the notion of the French state as protector of the general interest and the fact that organized interest groups are conceived as being contradictory to this aim. Solidarity is therefore preferred as a value that emphasizes joining together with other people as fellow citizens.

Values as a rule

One of the key characteristics of the organizations in Lyon is the fact that values are officially recorded in organizational agreements. As discussed in relation to rules and organizational charters, this codification of values was common across the social centres, ACEPP, and Monalisa. For the social centres, the 'benchmark values' defined in the National Charter of Social Centres are: human dignity – referring to being inclusive and respectful of cultural differences; solidarity – building social cohesion and neighbourliness;

and democracy – opting for a governance arrangement that values debate and sharing of power (*Charte Fédérale des Centres Sociaux et Socio-Culturels de France*, 2000).

> So, the social centre, it's a structure that is defined by its plan and by its territory. The two are linked. The objective and the territory go together, rather than the objective being determined by the territory. And the third pillar of the definition of a social centre is the democratic functioning. That is to say, it's an associative structure that is run by a general assembly with volunteers who function under a democratic model. All social centres have these three axes – a plan, a territory, democratic functioning.
>
> (Director, Équipe)

This centralized definition of values is shared by Monalisa, where member organizations sign a charter as a promise to promote shared values of collective action to fight older people's isolation. ACEPP (which, like the social centres, is structured with local organizations belonging to a regional umbrella organization and a national representative body) also creates a shared sense of identity and purpose across the network through a central declaration of values. For this organization, parent participation forms the guiding value.

> At ACEPP we have three fundamental values, which we find in all our projects. The fundamental values are that the parent is the first educator of their child. . . . Our second value is the collaboration between parents and professionals around the child, and by extension, it has turned into activities like this one, that cooperation between citizens and institutions that take into consideration the child in the city. The third value is that family services, the places where children come for day care, these are first and foremost local places for social development – far from being centres for profit, centres that charge. It creates links between people; it creates networks of solidarity; it allows parents to be supported because they are no longer alone with their children but are now in a network. So we try to put that in practice everywhere.
>
> (Project manager, ACEPP)

Across the cases, various interpretations of co-production and citizen participation form a central part of defined organizational values. Indeed, without prompting, all the ACEPP interviewees independently discussed examples of parent and professional collaboration in projects and various aspects of organizational operations. This collaboration is expressed as driven by an ethos of empowering individuals as citizens and as parents to both exercise their democratic rights as well as to join in solidarity – notions that are associated with both the community and state logics. Furthermore, this emphasis on parent participation was framed as a reaction against a 'medicalized' approach to childcare provision, which essentially pitted this community/state logic against the incumbent professional logic of the 1970s and 1980s. Like the social centres, the core values of ACEPP are explicitly codified in organizational documents, effectively meaning that the non-material elements of the logic (values, beliefs) become material rules by which professionals' behaviour is guided.

Citizenship and power

Interviewees in Lyon also employed discourse related to empowerment of residents, employing the English word *empowerment*, because attempts to translate the word into French have been somewhat less effective discursively. *Le pouvoir d'agir* ("the power to act") is used as the closest alternative, but this cannot be eloquently used as a noun, verb, and adjective like *empowerment, to empower*, and *to be empowered*. The way that French third sector organizations use the word *empowerment* and *pouvoir d'agir* reveals some important aspects of the values that inform co-production practices.

> We are very good in providing services, but we wanted to move towards more places where people can come and develop projects, but also developing the idea that the people are also citizens and they have to develop their capacity, their empowerment. That's where we're trying to move.
> (Director, Diversité, interview in English)

Here, empowerment is discursively linked with citizenship – the idea of empowering local people is about enabling them to gain the skills and confidence to exercise their rights as citizens. This then leads to a more overtly political conceptualization of involvement (and hence co-production) where people are involved in activities with the implicit motive of making them able to engage politically. Echoing this perspective, the goal of supporting active citizenship appeared as a priority or objective in all five Lyon social centres' social plans (e.g. "encouraging the citizenship dynamic of residents" and "development of local citizenship"). We also see this value playing out through practices, such as making spaces for political debate, which was discussed by interviewees from Avancé and two of the organizations associated with Monalisa.

One of the defining elements of the values and identities of ACEPP is around helping to give parents a voice and recognizing and challenging traditional power structures. One of ACEPP's projects is around popular education, a collective movement to support groups of parents in disadvantaged areas to join together and research a theme related to parenthood, conducted with the support of an academic researcher. This project allows people and their lived experiences and expertise as parents to be valued as co-researchers. These research projects were used to empower parents and support them to become active citizens and have a voice about the issues that matter to them.

> [In the co-operatives crèches], it's the parents who have the power. And here ACEPP, it's the same – it's the volunteers who have the power. There are a lot of things that are internally managed, but when there's really a decision to be made, it's made by the volunteers. And the staff don't have the right to vote in those cases.
>
> (Frontline staff 2, ACEPP)

> The idea of [popular education project] is how to give a voice on parenthood to parents themselves because we were saying a lot of things, usually produced by researchers, etc. But the voice of parents, we didn't hear it, it was imperceptible. . . . That's the question – how do we support a voice, a position that's sufficiently audible so that politicians and institutions start to recognize something? The [project], at the same time as the parents lead the research, they lead what we call citizen actions – they participate in a certain number of events to talk about their projects, talk about the research that they lead, etc.
>
> (Project manager, ACEPP)

This project again shows the politicized framing of co-production held by ACEPP. Rather than simply viewing nurseries as a place where parents drop their children during the day, childcare and children's services are reconceptualized as a way to bring parents together to assert their rights and responsibilities and gain confidence in this role. While the interviewees at ACEPP did not use the word *empowerment*, this notion was expressed several times in terms such as "capacity-building" and "supporting citizenship" (Project manager, ACEPP). The shared identity and driver of ACEPP staff then is to support parents to gain confidence, skills, and power.

Narratives and discourses of co-production

Unlike the organizations studied in England, in France there was limited familiarity with the term *co-production* (even though the term can technically be directly translated to *co-production* in French). Consistent with the French literature on involvement and participation, *co-construction* appeared to be the preferred term. When specifically asked whether *co-production* was a word they would use to describe their activities, interviewees frequently relayed their perception of co-construction instead.

> For us, co-construction is when we get around the table, like a partnership table. . . . It's a tool for the co-construction of local projects. Behind co-construction, when a resident for example has a project for the area, we can very quickly encourage them to meet other residents,

> to go and connect with institutions, to go and see people affected by the issue so that the project isn't just 'me and my project because I think something,' good or bad, it doesn't matter, that it becomes a project that is co-constructed with the actors of the area.
>
> (Project manager, ACEPP)

Other respondents similarly defined co-construction as having multiple stakeholders at the table to define projects or services and the idea of partnership between institutions, associations, and citizens. As discussed in relation to practice, co-construction is thus more analogous to the way that *co-planning* or *co-governance* are used in England, whereby citizens are involved in setting forth priorities and contributing to policymaking, rather than in the implementation or delivery phase (Vaillancourt, 2009; Jetté & Vaillancourt, 2011). In other words, *co-construction* relates to the *input* side of public policy, whilst *co-production* refers to the *output* (McMullin, 2019). Discursively, the term was typically linked to notions of empowerment and citizen participation, but there was some critique about politicians reappropriating these terms.

> So co-production, we're more in the 'doing,' because there's an element of production. So with co-construction, it's upstream, it's before. It's also just words – I don't know in English – but in any case, in French, sometimes these words are used a lot at one point, without changing anything in practice. So there are words also where you can really put content, but there are people who sometimes say, "Yes. Co-produce, co-construct, is that what they're saying?" The politicians, before every election say, "Listen, we're going to co-design together. You'll see, we'll listen to you. It'll be great. Vote for me."
>
> (Director, Avancé)

This scepticism of *co-construction* as a term was less widespread than in England in relation to co-production, with the only critiques leveraged at a frustration about misappropriation of terminology by politicians or other organizations who do not actually engage in co-construction practices. This is likely due to the perceived ownership or provenance of the respective terms – while co-construction is widely associated with the social centre sector, as it relates to the notions of citizen participation and governance, co-production in the UK is perceived by third sector actors as having been coined elsewhere to describe practices they had conceived using different vocabulary.

The distinction between co-production and co-construction may seem minor, and indeed interviewees frequently assumed the words were interchangeable. However, the distinction between the two terms and the way they are employed exposes a difference in the way that institutional logics are combined in the ideas of French non-profit organizations. Co-construction affords a greater weight to the involvement of local people in governance and decision-making, or the democratic participation aspect of involvement and collaboration – thus applying the state logic to the values and narratives of participation. Co-production, on the other hand, focuses more on the doing – the involvement of community members and service users in producing their services, through contributing time and resources, volunteering, etc. The co-production emphasis on *production* illustrates a greater assimilation of the market logic.

4 Blending of the Napoleonic State and 'local solidarity' (community): a Social Solidarity Logic

Through the rules, norms, values, beliefs, and ideas that shape the practices of co-production in the Lyon organizations, we see the manifestation of a blended type of hybridity. In a blended hybrid, organizations resolve the tensions between competing identities, structures, and/or values espoused by the different logics that drive them by strategically mixing these together (Skelcher & Smith, 2015). While logic blending is often used to describe social enterprises seamlessly blending the market, state, and community logics (e.g. Nyssens, 2006), in Lyon the organizations blend two institutional logics particular to the French case – Napoleonic State and local solidarity logics – into an overarching logic. I term this a 'Social Solidarity Logic,' which helps us to understand the uniquely French narratives and practices of co-production.

The first element of this blended logic – the Napoleonic State Logic – reflects the French governmental and administrative traditions. France is defined by a republican ideology, whereby the State (a proper noun) is a strong central authority that exists to protect the values of the Republic and to promote the general interest. This differs from the Anglo-Saxon, or 'no-state' tradition (Bevir et al., 2003), where there is no legal basis for the state, and it exists only as a result of a contract with society. Furthermore, additional differences between notions of the 'general interest' or 'public benefit' divide the state logics of England and France. The French conception of the general interest is considered to be a theoretical construct protected by the state, which is superior to the individual interests of citizens and transcends partisan preferences (Bacqué & Gauthier, 2011). The Napoleonic State logic, consequently, is heavily influenced by rules and legality to determine appropriate action.

The second element, the community logic, is also interpreted differently in the French context. According to Thornton et al. (2012, p. 52), the community institutional logic is characterized by "the collective relationships between people that emphasize the interpersonal and particularistic." The community as an institutional order draws legitimacy from trust and reciprocity and typically involves individuals in close proximity geographically (although communities of interest and online communities increasingly are included in this definition). However, as discussed in relation to the values and narratives surrounding solidarity, the notion of 'community' contrasts to the French notions of equity, equality, and universalism, and the French are loathe to use the term *community* in a positive light. This presents a curious puzzle when analysing the logics of third sector organizations, which were clearly influenced by a logic beyond that of the state (but which is also not related to the other five institutional orders). In many ways, the state logic defines the community logic in France – in the sense that many of the rules, practices, and values that define traditional community work and associations are the same as those that emanate from the government, but in a way that is locally translated and implemented. I thus term this French version of the community logic a 'local solidarity logic.' This logic rejects identities based on local group membership and the differentiation between values and beliefs of different localities, favouring instead a local application of French Republican values and identities.

Blending two institutional logics does not mean that both have equal influence on organizations' rules, practices, and values. Across the case study organizations in Lyon, evidence suggested that the Napoleonic State logic played an especially strong role in shaping rules. Interviewees frequently cited national laws and charters as playing a large part in defining their identities, mission, and practices. The Napoleonic tradition of bureaucracy and hierarchy also is reflected in the structure of the local case study organizations, which each also had a national umbrella branch or network that represented similar associations in other cities. This appeared to be a relatively common phenomenon across other sub-sectors of the social economy that I researched, with most well-known associations in Lyon being branches of, or associated with, a national organization.

Beyond the direct impact of national laws and regulations on the Lyon associations' activities, the Napoleonic State logic also informs the rules that associations implement internally and the way in which they conceptualize rules versus practices. The local blending between a Napoleonic State logic and the local solidarity logic comes to the fore in an examination of organizational governance and internal rules. All the Lyon case study organizations have produced organizational charters that codify their founding mission and values. This duty to codify values clearly demonstrates the blend of French state ideology with that of local solidarity – i.e. constitutions and formal records are considered valuable and necessary to protect rights and demonstrate an organization's purpose and commitment. Often these charters take a primarily symbolic function, such as Monalisa's charter to which signatories join in a promise to work towards tackling older people's isolation.

The local solidarity aspect of the Social Solidarity Logic reflects the French discomfort with the idea of community because the in-group/out-group sense of community identity conflicts with the source of identity defined by the state. The reality is, however, that there is a real sense of neighbourhood belonging and territorially specific rules and practices in different parts of the country and different parts of Lyon. The narrative that perhaps best explains the translation of these notions into a French phraseology is the concept of *vivre ensemble*, which technically translates as 'living together' but is typically grouped with ideas of diversity and community cohesion. *Vivre ensemble* allows for a recognition of cultural, ethnic, and religious differences of individuals, while remaining true to a French unitary notion of citizenship and identity. Although this notion of *vivre ensemble* is promoted by the state at the national level, in practice it can only truly be understood and pursued at a local level, between individuals.

Despite the expected tensions and obstacles to co-production in the Lyon third sector, multiple compelling examples were found across the case study organizations. This discredited the initial tentative hypothesis that the political and administrative cultures of France would prevent third sector organizations from undertaking co-production activities. Indeed, the existence of a deeply ingrained ethos of co-production in ACEPP and the social centres reveals a paradox between the French state tradition of centralization and unified protection of the general interest of all citizens and the strong evidence of co-production practices supported by values of solidarity. This has gone unnoticed in part because of the siloes in the French research between formal participation initiatives, or co-construction, and informal collaboration and volunteering. Co-production exists at the interstices between these areas.

5 Implications for co-production: Social Solidarity Logic and formalized co-production

The blending of the Napoleonic State and local solidarity logics creates some challenges for co-production in the French third sector, but it also allows for the emergence of space for co-production between citizens and professionals in ways that are at odds with the dominant assumptions of the co-production literature. Three key implications for co-production by nonprofit professionals arise:

A. Co-production as a rule, rather than a norm

Across the case studies in Lyon, co-production practices and the values that motivate these are formalized and codified through official documents. The influence of the Napoleonic State logic deems formalized rules to be indispensable in shaping professional practice. Co-production – which is delineated as "initiatives brought by local people, supported by professionals" by social centres and "cooperation between parents and professionals in both the design of the organizational plan as well as the running of daily activities" by ACEPP – is therefore both formalized into organizational charters and mainstreamed into organizational purposes and strategies. Formalizing co-production practices represents a way that third sector organizations reconcile the competing and conflicting logics of the state and community.

This notion that co-production is formalized as a rule in these cases reveals some of the weaknesses of the co-production literature, where co-production is typically described as more of an informal practice or process by which services can be designed and delivered. The assumption of informality fails to account for logics, like the Social Solidarity Logic, whereby culture and traditions drive organizations to provide formal justification and records of their values and practices. Co-production as a rule rather than a norm also results in certain types of co-production taking place, with a greater emphasis on governance rather than informal day-to-day activities.

B. *A focus on 'co-construction of policy' rather than 'co-production of services'*

The term *co-production*, or an equivalent term to describe the collaboration of professionals and service users/citizens in designing and delivering services, did not form part of the lexicon of third sector actors in France. Instead, interviewees spoke frequently about co-*construction*, which focuses more on the involvement in planning and decision-making, rather than delivery and implementation. This is important because of the impact that discourse and narratives have in shaping the values and beliefs that underscore co-production. In this case, the Social Solidarity Logic delimits the appropriate arena for citizen participation to be the involvement in decision-making, at least insofar as narratives are concerned. While there were indeed numerous examples of citizen involvement in actively delivering services and projects (through volunteering or in projects directly led by citizens themselves), the French respondents rarely grouped citizen-led projects or the involvement of citizens in delivering services in with their discussions of participation initiatives, framing these as outside the scope of 'participation.'

These discourses are significant because of the impact that discourse has on practice. Language and narratives generate meanings for actors and justify particular actions, so the application of a particular concept, or the lack of a word for a concept, shapes what people do. The French cases prioritize discussions of policy and strategy co-construction because this arena for involvement is recognized as valuable and meaningful. The Social Solidarity Logic, which is premised around many of the values of the French State therefore prioritizes these formalized democratic activities in practice as these are more easily described and discussed by participants.

C. *Co-production focuses on collective benefit, rather than individuals*

The notion of individual co-production, where citizens co-produce the services from which they benefit directly as individuals, was almost non-existent within the French case studies. Instead, co-production as a means to include and improve things for the collective was typically the primary way that co-production was understood and promoted. The preference for collective over individual co-production reflects the French notion of *service public*, which defends the notion of public services as underscored by notions of equality and universality of access. This value creates a philosophical tension with the idea of individual co-production, where individual citizens may be given special treatment, access, or benefits that privilege them over others. Likewise, a focus on the collective over the individual reflects a public management model of the Neo-Weberian State, which maintains the centrality of the state as a political actor, thereby retaining control over the design and delivery of public services (McMullin, 2021). In the instance of third sector delivery of services, therefore, there are considerable efforts made to ensure the principles of universalism over particularism. This logic consequently translates into the level of co-production between professionals and citizens as well.

6 Summary and conclusions

In this chapter, I analysed co-production between citizens and professionals working for non-profit organizations in Lyon, France. The guiding institutional logic of these organizations, which I term a Social Solidarity Logic, results from a blend between particularly French interpretations of the state logic (or 'Napoleonic State') and the community logic (or 'local solidarity'). This type of hybrid organization is strongly influenced by rules or formal constraints that result in tendencies towards formalization of practices and values through conventions, charters, and other written documents. Organizations prioritize the involvement of citizens in strategic priority-setting, governance, and decision-making as members, with a greater focus on forms of collective co-production over individual co-production.

The Social Solidarity Logic and formalized co-production represent a distinct contrast to much of the literature on the third sector and co-production. In relation to the third sector, studies tend to posit that non-profits exhibit hybrid characteristics between the state, market, and community, but the French cases diverge from this, with a lack of market logic influence on their rules, practice, and values. Second, the common positioning of co-production within trends towards New Public Governance (where the third sector and citizens play an increasingly important role in designing and implementing public policy) is likewise a mischaracterization of the French cases. While many examples of co-production between citizens and professionals were present, these take place within a framework of constraints and motivations that are unique to the French context, and a public policy environment that remains fairly wedded to traditional bureaucratic policy-making processes.

References

Archambault, E., Priller, E., & Zimmer, A. (2014). European civil societies compared: Typically German-typically French? *Voluntas*, *25*(2), 514–537.

Bacqué, M.-H., & Gauthier, M. (2011). Participation, urbanisme et études urbaines. *Participations*, *1*, 36–66.

Bacqué, M.-H., & Sintomer, Y. (Eds.). (2020). *La démocratie participative*. La Découverte.

Bakker, J., Denters, B., Vrielink, M. O., & Klok, P.-J. (2012). Citizens' initiatives: How local governments fill their facilitative role. *Local Government Studies*, *38*(4), 395–414. https://doi.org/10.1080/03003930.2012.698240

Barthélemy, M. (2000). *Associations: Un nouvel âge de la participation?* Presses de Sciences Po.

Bevir, M., Rhodes, R. A. W., & Weller, P. (2003). Traditions of governance: Interpreting the changing role of the public sector. *Public Administration*, *81*(1), 1–17.

Brandsen, T., & Honingh, M. (2015). Distinguishing different types of coproduction: A conceptual analysis based on the classical definitions. *Public Administration Review*, *76*(3), 427–435.

Brandsen, T., & Honingh, M. (2018). Definitions of co-production and co-creation. In T. Brandsen, T. Steen, & B. Verschuere (Eds.), *Co-production and co-creation: Engaging citizens in public services* (pp. 9–17). Routledge.

Esping-Andersen, G. (1990). *The three worlds of welfare capitalism*. Polity Press.

Evers, A., & Laville, J.-L. (2004). Defining the third sector in Europe. In *The third sector in Europe* (pp. 11–42). Edward Elgar Publishing Ltd.

Igalla, M., Edelenbos, J., & van Meerkerk, I. (2019). Citizens in action, what do they accomplish? A systematic literature review of citizen initiatives, their main characteristics, outcomes, and factors. *Voluntas*, *30*(5), 1176–1194. https://doi.org/10.1007/s11266-019-00129-0

Jetté, C., & Vaillancourt, Y. (2011). Social economy and home care services in Quebec: Co-production or co-construction? *Voluntas*, *22*(1), 48–69.

Lowndes, V., Pratchett, L., & Stoker, G. (2006). Local political participation: The impact of rules-in-use. *Public Administration*, *84*(3), 539–561.

Lowndes, V., & Roberts, M. (2013). *Why institutions matter: The new institutionalism in political science*. Macmillan International Higher Education.

McMullin, C. (2018). Co-production and community development in France. In T. Brandsen, T. Steen, & B. Verschuere (Eds.), *Co-production and co-creation: Engaging citizens in public service delivery* (pp. 208–210). Routledge.

McMullin, C. (2019). Coproduction and the third sector in France: Governmental traditions and the French conceptualization of participation. *Social Policy and Administration*, *53*(2), 295–310.

McMullin, C. (2021). Challenging the necessity of New Public Governance: Co-production by third sector organizations under different models of public management. *Public Administration*, *99*(1), 5–22. https://doi.org/10.1111/padm.12672

Nyssens, M. (2006). *Social enterprise: At the crossroads of market, public policies and civil society*. Routledge. www.routledge.com/Social-Enterprise-At-the-Crossroads-of-Market-Public-Policies-and-Civil/Nyssens/p/book/9780415378796

Painter, M., & Peters, B. G. (2010). Administrative traditions in comparative perspective: Families, groups and hybrids. In *Tradition and public administration* (pp. 19–30). Palgrave Macmillan.

Parrado, S., Ryzin, G. G. V., Bovaird, T., & Löffler, E. (2013). Correlates of co-production: Evidence from a five-nation survey of citizens. *International Public Management Journal*, *16*(1), 85–112.

Peters, B. G. (2008). The Napoleonic tradition. *International Journal of Public Sector Management, 21*(2), 118–132.

Salamon, L., & Anheier, H. (1997). *Defining the nonprofit sector: A cross-national analysis.* Manchester University Press.

Salamon, L., & Anheier, H. (1998). Social origins of civil society: Explaining the non-profit sector cross-nationally. *Voluntas, 9*(3), 213–248.

Sintomer, Y., & De Maillard, J. (2007). The limits to local participation and deliberation in the French "politique de la ville". *European Journal of Political Research, 46*(4), 503–529.

Skelcher, C., & Smith, S. R. (2015). Theorizing hybridity: Institutional logics, complex organizations, and actor identities: The case of nonprofits. *Public Administration, 93*(2), 433–448.

Thornton, P. H., Ocasio, W., & Lounsbury, M. (2012). *The institutional logics perspective: A new approach to culture, structure, and process.* Oxford University Press.

Vaillancourt, Y. (2009). Social economy in the co-construction of public policy. *Annals of Public and Cooperative Economics, 80*(2), 275–313.

6 Social Movement Logic and citizen-led co-production in Montreal

Quebec is a place of paradox – as the only francophone majority province in primarily anglophone Canada, it balances a history of French and English colonization, the subjugation of indigenous populations, and a rich multicultural tapestry issued from inflows of migrants from around the world. This creates a unique backdrop for co-production in a third sector that differs considerably from its broader Canadian context.

In this chapter, I focus on the city of Montreal, where I analyse the community development sector in two neighbourhoods and the ways that these organizations engage citizens in multiple processes of co-production. I begin with an overview of the context, including the development of the third sector in Montreal and a brief discussion of the case studies. I then explore the rules; norms; and values, beliefs, and ideas shown in the case study organizations as these define their approaches to co-production. The chapter finishes with a synthesis of the findings and a discussion of the guiding institutional logics and impact on co-production in the Montreal third sector.

1 Context: the third sector in Montreal

Quebec is the second largest province in Canada by population and with over eight million inhabitants, the province makes up 23% of the population of the country. In Quebec, 85% of residents speak French as their first language, compared to only 3.8% in the rest of Canada, and this linguistic difference along with historical and cultural divisions between Quebec and the rest of Canada underscored a long-time movement for provincial sovereignty. Two independence referenda were conducted in 1980 and 1995, the latter of which failed by less than one percentage point. In part because Canada is a federal country, and in part through devolution of powers that followed these movements for independence, the Government of Quebec maintains responsibility for many policy portfolios, including health, education, training, and welfare services, which is the vast majority of areas in which the third sector is active.

Montreal is the second largest city of Canada, with a diverse population of 1.7 million residents. The Island of Montreal is divided into 19 boroughs

DOI: 10.4324/9781003245605-6

('*arrondissements*') that have responsibility for local services (e.g. parks and recreation, waste removal, snow clearance) and, crucially, local social and community development. Montreal is a city of distinct neighbourhoods with unique identities, and the community development sector is relatively fragmented. Most boroughs of the city have a community development corporation (CDC) that acts as a *Table de quartier*, or 'neighbourhood roundtable' in English. Unlike the community development/community regeneration organizations in Sheffield and the social centres in Lyon, community development corporations in Montreal do not always directly deliver community services. Instead, they act as facilitators of local community networks and citizen participation in each neighbourhood.

While national level typologies are useful at distinguishing the key differences between the welfare systems and non-profit sectors in more centralized and unitary states such as the United Kingdom and France, the categorizations of federal states such as Canada mask some crucial underlying differences between provinces. Canada's third sector is frequently categorized alongside those of the UK, the US, New Zealand, and Australia (see e.g. Phillips & Smith, 2014), with low government spending on social welfare and a large non-profit sector that receives low levels of funding. However, the political, cultural, and historical development in Quebec has differentiated it considerably from the rest of Canada. There, the 'third sector' is further split into three types of organizations – non-profits that provide services (primarily health and social care) for the state but do not engage in advocacy or political activities, 'autonomous community organizations,' and social and solidarity economy (SSE) organizations (McMullin et al., 2021).

Autonomous community organizations are non-profit organizations that are community-rooted and democratically governed and that are "free to determine their missions, orientations, approaches and practices" (MTESS, 2001, p. 21). Social economy organizations, by contrast, are defined as organizations that seek to respond to social/societal needs whilst creating jobs (particularly for those excluded from the workforce) by selling goods or services (Arsenault, 2018). Unlike the broader definition of social enterprise seen elsewhere, social economy organizations in Quebec are also distinguished by collective ownership; that is, they are constituted either as co-operatives or non-profit organizations. Quebec has a long history of co-operatives and mutuals that can be traced to its dual roots with settlers from the United Kingdom and France. The Desjardins group – the first federation of local credit unions and mutual aid societies in North America – was founded in Quebec in the early 20th century.

While the notion of social economy in other countries, such as France, includes *all* non-profit associations, co-operatives, and mutual organizations that are defined by internal democratic operations and societal and/or member benefit, in Quebec the autonomous community sector explicitly rejects inclusion in the category of social economy. The historical development of this situation and implications in terms of policy and funding will be explored in relation to the rules impacting these organizations. Because of the particular categorization of third sector organizations in Quebec, I tend to refer to 'community organizations' in this chapter rather than third sector or non-profit organizations because this is the distinct category to which the case study organizations associate (and thereby separate themselves from other types of non-profit and social economy organizations). In some instances, I compare these community organizations with social economy organizations, but it is important to clarify that the analysis and identification of logics pertains to autonomous community organizations only and cannot be expanded to apply to social economy organizations or some other types of non-profits. As we will see through the analysis of the rules and narratives of these community organizations, there are important distinctions that differentiate these organizations' logics from other types of third sector organizations in Quebec.

2 Case study organizations and research methods

This chapter is based on an in-depth analysis of several projects and services delivered by two community development corporations (CDC) in Montreal. CDC Rosemont and CDC Centre-Sud were selected based on suggestions from local experts who recommended both organizations as engaging in innovative approaches to co-production with residents and service users.[1]

The research involved interviews with key local stakeholders across the community sector and social economy sector (11) to establish a baseline understanding of the scope, focus, and approach of the third sector in the city, followed by in-depth case studies of co-production by CDC Rosemont and CDC Centre-Sud. As CDCs, their purpose is to act as a network and convener of the autonomous community sector in their neighbourhood of the city of Montreal. CDCs act as a link and facilitator for other grassroots organizations to provide community services and provide the structure, opportunities, and support for partnerships and collaborations. CDCs are therefore coalitions or consortia (the term '*regroupements*' is most commonly used in French) of organizations that provide services in the social services, family, employability, literacy, housing, culture, environment, and migrant integration sectors. Their purpose is to provide support, training and a central point for collaboration for these organizations working to fight poverty and social exclusion, as well as acting as a 'catalyst' for the development of community services and projects (MTESS, 2021).

Because services and activities are developed in multi-stakeholder partnerships where each CDC acts more as a facilitator than a service provider, data were collected primarily through observation in meetings, events, and as a participant observer in three 'action groups' facilitated by CDC Rosemont. CDC Rosemont has institutionalized a process of co-production through a six-year process called *Décider Rosemont Ensemble* (Deciding Rosemont

Together), which has spawned the creation of multiple community action groups. The case study research took an approach of in-depth organizational ethnography, through which I conducted participant observation as a member of three community action groups, attending 23 meetings, workshops, and events over the course of a year, for a total of more than 45 hours of observation. Observations in the field also included numerous informal interviews/discussions with both citizen and professional co-producers before and after meetings and during meals at celebration events as well as email conversations between members of the three action groups in which I participated. I also conducted more formal semi-structured interviews with one CDC staff member and three professionals from local organizations that were involved with the action groups. These interviews allowed me to interrogate both the specifics of the co-production case studies as well as the broader institutional logics (particularly the narratives and sector-wide rules) that impact the third sector.

CDC Centre-Sud takes a less structured and systematic approach to co-production, instead providing opportunities for professional support and facilitation for citizen-led and grassroots-community group led initiatives through their Grassroots Collective Intelligence Laboratory (*Laboratoire populaire d'intelligence collective* or LPIC). One of the components of the LPIC is a "support service for the ideation and co-creation of projects." Because *co-creation* is the term employed by this organization, this language is reflected in my analysis.

I conducted interviews with two employees of organizations involved in initiatives where CDC staff were supporting a process of co-creation, and three employees of the CDC (two of whom I informally reinterviewed five months after the first interview to inquire about progress of their initiatives). I also attended/observed four events/workshops where I spoke informally with participants and took detailed fieldnotes. For both case studies, I also analysed documents, including organizational strategies and reports and official minutes of meetings that I was unable to attend.

3 Institutional logics, co-production, and the third sector in Montreal

As in the Sheffield and Lyon cases, I explore the practices of co-production within the third sector in Montreal through the lens of institutional logics. Because of the uniqueness of the Quebec third sector as compared to the rest of Canada, the institutional logics approach enables us to better understand the enablers and constraints that these organizations face.

A. Rules

In this section, I discuss the rules – regulations, laws, and funding instruments – that shape the community sector in Quebec broadly, to illustrate the array of formal constraints that shape the logics of the third sector in Montreal. Here, I draw upon examples both from the case studies as well as from other initiatives in Montreal, which are used to provide a deeper exploration of the context in which the case studies operate.

Government policy

One of the first areas of rules that impact the third sector is the devolution of responsibilities from the federal to the provincial level, including both the regulations relating directly to the sector as well as most of the policy areas in which the third sector is active. The federal government thus has limited interactions with and influence over the community organizations in Quebec. This has an important impact on the institutional logics that shape the sector, because there are important differences in state institutional logics that emanate from different levels or sources. Greenwood et al. (2010), for instance, show how two competing state logics (one centralist and one more regionalist) in Spain during two different time periods differentially impacted businesses' adaptation to market and family logics. In the case of Canada and Quebec, the former has taken on many of the discourses and practices of New Public Management, while the latter has taken a divergent path that provides more support for the community logic rather than putting this in competition with the state and market logics.

Although an in-depth discussion of the history of the third sector in Quebec is beyond the scope of this chapter, it is important to explain several key events that have resulted in public policies that explicitly support the third sector and protect these organizations' ability to engage citizens in co-production. Prior to the 1960s, the Catholic Church was hugely influential in Quebec society, as a major provider of health, social services, and education, but also active in establishing a Catholic labour union movement. The 1960s brought the Quiet Revolution, during which time the provincial government began establishing a public welfare state and taking control of most health and welfare services run by the Church. Leftist activists, suspicious of the growing reach of the state, began to mobilize support for community control of public services and programmes and sowed the seeds for a militant associative sector that strongly advocates for social justice, community control, and local social development.

In the late 1990s, a series of concerted efforts by social movements pressured the provincial government to take action against poverty by increasing investment in social services, housing, and other programmes to alleviate poverty. This movement coincided with the resurgence of the movement for provincial sovereignty (a few months before the second referendum on separation from Canada was to be held), and this political climate meant that the provincial government was especially open to the appeals of this social movement in order to increase popular support. In 1996, a summit was held by the Premier of Quebec, who invited representatives from Quebec businesses, unions, community organizations, and social movements to discuss ways to improve the economy and unemployment. This spurred a long-time approach to policymaking known as the Quebec Model of Social Development (Bourque, 2000; Jetté, 2011), which is based on multi-stakeholder involvement in critical dialogue and consensus-building.

As a result of these developments, the Quebec provincial government has developed framework policies that explicitly delineate the relationship between the government and the autonomous community sector, and the government and social economy (MTESS, 2004; Ministère de l'Économie et de l'Innovation, 2015). As noted in the introduction to this chapter, the social economy relates to collectively owned organizations (NPOs and co-operatives) that seek to both improve the community and create jobs, while the autonomous community sector rejects participation in market activities. The 2013 Social Economy Act formalized the legal framework that defines the organizations that comprise the social economy and outlines the ways that the provincial government will both support and promote the contributions of the SSE to the economy. This was followed by government action plans in 2015 and 2020, which present specific objectives for improving and encouraging the work of the sector (McMullin, 2021b).

In the case of the autonomous community sector, the *Secrétariat à l'action communautaire autonome du Québec* (Secretariat for Autonomous Community Action, SACA) was created to formally institutionalize the Quebec Government's commitment to supporting the community sector. In 2001, the Government Policy on Community Action was adopted, as the culmination of co-construction efforts between the government and the community sector. This policy marks an important point in the development of the relationship between the community sector and the Government of Quebec by recognizing the unique characteristics of the sector and explicitly protecting the independence of the sector from state influence.

> Community organizations represent that portion of our social infrastructure that is distinct from the State's public services and that is citizen-based and whose purpose is to improve the daily lives of Quebecers. These versatile community organizations not only provide insights into new issues, but also foster the development of new approaches and experiments with varied and innovative forms of intervention. To preserve this asset, we must respect their independence and ensure they are sufficiently distanced from the State.
>
> (MTESS, 2001, p. 15)

The policy defines the type of organizations that qualify as 'autonomous' community organizations (i.e. non-profit, community-based, democratically governed organizations that are free to determine their own mission) and stipulates that the difference between the community sector more broadly and *autonomous community action* (ACA) is that ACA relates to organizations that more specifically have been created through the initiative of the community and "use active citizenship practices." Government policy thus creates unique conditions in terms of the rules that inform the institutional logics of the third sector in Quebec. Rather than imposing the state logic on the sector, public policy instead protects the integrity and independence of the community *from* the state logic.

The 2001 policy on community action is significant in shaping the logics that inform community organizations' approaches to co-production. Far from either constraining organizations' abilities to engage in co-production or posing other restrictions, this policy instead creates and protects the conditions that community organizations need to be able to engage citizens in co-production. By stipulating that ACA organizations must be driven by and rooted in the community, as well as prioritizing volunteering and active citizenship alongside efforts for social change, government policy in this instance creates rules that further the community logic, rather than the market or state.

Funding

The 2001 government policy that defines ACA organizations and their relationship to the state also guarantees core funding to support the mission of all organizations that meet the criteria of ACA. This puts these organizations in a unique position in Quebec, where funding for their basic back office functions is guaranteed by the government but they are simultaneously protected in their right to engage in advocacy and criticize government policy. Although the eligibility for this core funding has become more restricted, a 2021 policy specifically protects it for the 66 CDCs across Quebec that are designated as hubs for community organizations, including CDC Rosemont and CDC Centre-Sud (MTESS, 2021). This guaranteed government funding provides an example of the complementarity of the state and community logics, with government explicitly recognizing the key role that the community sector plays in contributing towards public policy objectives.

However, provincial government funding does not suffice for the range of activities and services that community organizations deliver in Quebec. Cuts to the amount of financial support the government offers have been made in recent years, and it is increasingly difficult for a new organization to start up and be granted funding. Organizations generally must therefore seek grant funding (from other public organizations or levels of government, including the City of Montreal and borough councils) or from foundations such as Centraide (United Way) which is a significant funder of services and projects in the sector.

> "How are we going to pay for that?" When people ask the question, you say, "Well, we'll find it afterwards." (Laughs) Because in the end, that's also our 'appreciative approach,' to say, "What do you want? What

> do you dream of?" . . . For a long time we've made people work like that, but it was super important for us to say, "We don't talk about money." But above all, we had the Collective Impact Project. That's nevertheless a reality. We are lucky to have this funding from Centraide, which is significant. We have a little more than a half a million that was invested in the first year in different projects.
>
> (Consultation officer, CDC Centre-Sud)

This lack of significant constraints caused by contract and grant requirements was common across the organizations studied (both CDCs and interviewees from organizations associated with each), and these also did not constrain organizations' abilities to engage in co-production. This was evidenced in instances when an organization had to search out additional funding to support their activities. In general, organizations were often able to quickly find small grants to support particular services and activities to involve citizens.

> If there are different activities of the [action] groups, if it's a $500 project, that's great, I can ask for $500 from the *députés*.[2] And when we get to things like the Social Forum, then we'll seek $10,000 from Centraide; obviously they'll be present. We ask the *Caisse Locale* (credit union), which has a significant community development fund, which will give $2,500 to donate to the Social Forum. In the year of the Social Forum, we can quickly find $50–60,000 to achieve an exceptional year. In the meantime, we have basic organizational funding from the Quebec government, since we're a CDC. If we didn't have this funding from *Table de Quartier*, we could never do that. That's for certain.
>
> (Senior staff, CDC Rosemont)

Because of the government policy that at least guarantees that core functions will be financed, funding rarely creates rules for organizations when designing their activities and whether/how citizens are involved in these. In cases where organizations do need to apply for extra grants for their activities, often there is a great degree of flexibility in deciding what services are needed. This is because of the government's stated commitment to promoting community autonomy and recognition that community organizations know best what is needed, which continually prioritizes the community logic over the state and market logics even in allocations of resources.

Beyond government funding, Centraide is an important funder of the CDCs, particularly its Collective Impact Project (CIP), which is financed by several major foundations. The CIP supported one of the initiatives developed under Décider Rosemont Ensemble (a new community hub) and the entirety of CDC Centre-Sud's collective action approach. Rather than targeting funding at specific programmes or services, the CIP focuses on providing financial assistance for neighbourhoods to "increase the impact of local mobilization to achieve significant results in poverty reduction" (Collective Impact Project website).

> To accomplish this, Centraide brings together dozens of partners (philanthropic foundations and strategic partners) to provide financial support and other contributions to neighbourhoods according to their priorities, including the changes they want to see and the actions needed to bring their vision to fruition. In addition to financial assistance and other contributions, participating neighbourhoods benefit from support, planning assistance, and the structuring and evaluation of their collective processes.
>
> (Collective Impact Project website, www.centraide-mtl.org/en/collective-impact-project/)

It is important to note the wide breadth of the funding remit bestowed by the CIP, which allows complete discretion to be exercised by local neighbourhoods in determining their priorities and approach to engaging citizens in local social development. Unlike, for example, grant funders in the United Kingdom that require quantitative performance management systems, the market logic is absent from this programme, with success measured more through qualitative improvements and storytelling. The CIP funding provides limited rules and locally tailored support to foster the community logic.

Internal organizational rules

One of the key tenets of ACA organizations is internal democratic functioning, which means that third sector organizations in Montreal place an important emphasis on governance, as well as on participative approaches that include staff, members, and residents more broadly. Several interviewees discussed having regular meetings for members to make decisions about the organization (both the CDCs as well as affiliated organizations).

Rules are also used to structure large-scale and formalized processes of strategic planning and project/activity development. CDC Rosemont's Décider Rosemont Ensemble process, which involves residents in consultation, priority setting, idea development, and finally in action groups that bring the most popular and promising ideas to fruition. Three iterations of DRE have taken place (in 2006, 2012, and 2018), with each building upon learning from previous cycles and growing in scale and scope. In 2018, residents and community sector organizations (over 1,500 individuals out of a borough population of 130,000) were first consulted via events and in-person and online surveys about the needs and aspirations of the borough. In-person surveys were conducted by a team composed of trained citizen researchers and CDC Rosemont staff.

Following the consultation stage, a 'social forum' event was held (referenced in a quote in the previous section) where over 300 citizens and community sector staff participated in workshops (co-facilitated by staff and residents) to pinpoint the most important priorities upon which to focus and then to brainstorm concrete activities or 'community actions' that should be developed to support these priorities. The decision to create action groups consisting of *both* professionals and citizens was based on feedback from earlier iterations of DRE, which were originally based on the creation of a 'citizens' committee' and a 'professionals' committee' to determine neighbourhood priorities:

> Over the course of preparing that event [public forum], the citizens said, "What's with this idea to have two separate groups?" It was the classic reproduction of professionals – they're the experts, and citizens express their 'lived experience.' And the citizens said, "No, if we want to have a public forum to choose the priorities of the neighbourhood and we put everyone together, we also need to fuse the two committees."
>
> (Senior staff, CDC Rosemont)

Rules are used to provide a driving purpose and framework of the co-production effort and to ensure the active and continued involvement of different stakeholder groups but stop short of delimiting how the collaborations should subsequently unfold. This process can be seen to canvas all of the stages of co-production (Loeffler & Bovaird, 2021) – co-planning/prioritization/strategic decision-making, co-design (of individual services/interventions), co-delivery/implementation, and co-evaluation. In this case, citizens and service users are not only involved in the services that already exist but are supported to design and create exactly what they believe should exist, with very little prior limitations or instructions on what is possible.

Each action group is required to have a community organization from the borough who is responsible for coordinating the group, along with the involvement of a minimum of three citizens (generally residents of the borough) and two further paid professionals who work for other community organizations from different sub-sectors. Co-production is thus officially required by DRE, but each action group is free to determine its own internal functioning and day-to-day co-production practices.

The extensive DRE process is often upheld as a model for other boroughs of the city. Indeed interviewees from CDC Centre-Sud said they had taken inspiration from DRE when designing their own process of neighbourhood priority-setting and project development. Their approach followed a similar process of neighbourhood forums where a theory of change was developed, a creation of committees and several mapping and co-design workshops. Finally, ideas for collective actions were developed under the priority headings of 'healthy eating,' '*vivre ensemble,*' 'housing,' and 'work-study-thrive.' Like CDC Rosemont, while CDC Centre-Sud provided an overall structure (i.e. general rules) for the process, the actual execution was allowed to be highly flexible and open to the priorities and interests of involved residents.

B. *Norms and practices*

Because each CDC takes a different approach to forming partnerships and facilitating citizen co-production, I employed an approach of engaged organizational ethnography to study the practices, values, and beliefs around co-production. This entailed undertaking interviews with staff of organizations supported through CDC Centre-Sud's co-creation processes, becoming a participant observer in three community action groups formed by CDC Rosemont, as well as attending events for both.

Action groups

As we saw in the previous section, CDC Rosemont employs a loose framework of rules to create a structure for a neighbourhood-wide priority-setting process and co-production of community services/activities. The three action groups that I studied focused on the creation of services/activities in the area of poverty reduction, under the priority heading of being (or becoming) "a neighbourhood that cares for people who are vulnerable, isolated, alone or on the margins."

The first, 'Restopop' (which stands for *restaurant populaire*, or grassroots/community restaurant) aims to establish a restaurant to provide healthy, high-quality but affordable meals in an environment that encourages socializing. This restaurant, staffed by resident volunteers and/or paid apprentices as part of a work integration programme, will be a sort of social enterprise project (rather than a soup kitchen or charity) that aims to help isolated people integrate into the community. The second group, originally called 'Drop-in' and later *Libre espace* ('Free space') was initiated as an idea to create a space where vulnerable or isolated individuals can "drop in" without the requirement to buy anything, take part in specific activities, or access any services. Finally, the third, VIE (standing for *vulnerable, excluded, isolated*), was created to develop a training programme to raise awareness of the precariousness of living in poverty in the neighbourhood.

> Our project aims to intervene on one of these [DRE's] priorities, namely that of making Rosemont a neighbourhood that cares about people who are vulnerable, isolated, alone or on the margins. The following fall, an action group of citizens and frontline staff was formed with the objective of setting up a space for respite for people in very vulnerable situations in Rosemont, to fill a need identified by the community.
>
> (Summary document, Libre Espace)

The rules of DRE require that each group has both professional and citizen members, but the way that this co-production is undertaken is determined by the groups through their norms and practices. Driven by an ethos of equal collaboration, tasks for each action group are distributed between members – both professionals and citizen co-producers – according to their interests, skills, and availability, rather than pre-emptively determining what professionals do and what citizens are involved in. For Restopop, meeting facilitation rotated between group members (although it was usually, though not always, the professionals who took on this task) and planning was broken up into three sub-committees responsible for long-term planning, market scoping, and development of short-term actions to get the project off the ground. As a participant observer, in planning meetings to develop each of the actions, it was often difficult to determine which participants were paid professionals and who the citizen volunteers were because participation of both groups was roughly equal. In fact, in two instances, professionals announced that their work contract was ending or that they were moving to a new role but would continue to participate in the action group as citizens rather than professionals.

> As you all know, lately we have been concentrating within our respective action groups and we have taken the time to get to know each other, to reflect, to analyse and frame what we want to do as actions. This work will necessarily result in actions aimed at the social development of our charming Rosemont. Next Saturday we have the opportunity to have a booth at the Rosemont Family Day to promote our actions and issues. . . . 1. As an action group will we go? 2. Who is interested? 3. How will we present our actions?
>
> (Email communication with all action groups)

While Restopop has benefited from the consistent collaboration between a large number of both citizens and professionals, professional-citizen participation has been less balanced for VIE and *Libre Espace*. *Libre Espace* struggled in its early stages to attract citizen group members, meaning that in addition to participating in planning meetings, professionals have also had to work to recruit more citizen co-producers in order to comply with the requirements of the DRE framework. There were numerous discussions around how to attract potential *Libre Espace* service users as members of the action group, but the group was struggling to do so. VIE conversely was driven more by citizen than professional contributions. While it is not uncommon for co-production initiatives to experience disengagement of citizen/service user participants, VIE also lost professional group members whose expertise was particularly important for the values and mission of the project. However, the involved citizens were key to ensuring that the project continued – one citizen took over the lead and coordination for the project and ensured that the brochure was developed, and this was then printed by the CDC.

The action groups also include co-delivery of services as a key component, but this was again determined based on which group members had the skills and interest to deliver particular activities. For Restopop, which has a long timescale from initiation to the eventual establishment of a permanent location, delivering several one-off 'solidarity meals' has been a way to test out possible locations and meals, get the word out about the project, and attract more citizens to become involved. While funding for these meals was acquired by a CDC Rosemont staff member, the meals themselves were prepared, cooked, and served by citizen group members alongside community sector professionals. During the time of the research, *Libre Espace* had experienced some setbacks in finding a location for the service and had not yet managed to start delivery. The group had not decided what role citizen volunteers would play in running the service, given the desire to balance citizen involvement with the potential need for specialized training (e.g. in health and safety, conflict management, and managing crises, considering that the targeted clientele might be experiencing mental health challenges).

*Co-design (*co-création*)*

Both CDC Rosemont and CDC Centre-Sud included co-design workshops as part of their approach to citizen/resident involvement. In both cases, the term *co-création* is used in French, though its meaning relates more to co-design or co-production more broadly, with a focus on an active participation of citizens throughout the process of developing and delivering new services. This usage is therefore more implementation-focused than the standard academic definition of co-creation that concentrates on policy and strategy (Brandsen & Honingh, 2018). As I discussed in relation to the rules of DRE, CDC Rosemont undertakes co-creation as part of the early stages of strategic priority setting for the neighbourhood through workshops, consultation, and two large neighbourhood forums. For CDC Centre-Sud, its involvement approach centres around providing support and facilitation for co-creation under the heading of their Grassroots Collective Intelligence Laboratory, or LPIC (the acronym in French), a (metaphorical) space that aims to 'encourage innovation and the development of collective intelligence of the area' (CDC Centre-Sud website).

The LPIC translates this aim into reality through three areas of concrete practices. First, '*Soupe Locale*' is a monthly micro-funding initiative (which relates more to the facilitation of citizen initiatives than to co-production) where attendees contribute a nominal amount for a meal, and citizens present initiatives they hope to receive funding for. At the end, all participants vote on the most promising proposal, and that initiative receives all donations. Second, staff organize and run training and development for citizens and community sector professionals, such as workshops on how to include people living in poverty in social movements that fight poverty, and skills development for co-creation (e.g. group moderation/facilitation, public speaking, and moving from idea to action). Finally, the most significant area of activity for the LPIC is in providing a support service to community organizations for the development of ideas and co-creation of projects to benefit the neighbourhood. This support includes working with community sector staff to identify needs and to develop ideas for particular projects or services through a process of co-creation with residents or service users. The aim of these practices is to employ methods that are inclusive and empowering, support knowledge transfer, and mobilize networks of other potential partners (local organizations and/or public bodies).

> We want it to be a space for citizens, but we also want it to be a space that is frequented by [community] organizations, institutional actors, elected officials. We want to mix everyone together so that through these exchanges we can really 'construct'[3] together, co-construct projects that are really promising for the community of Centre-Sud.
>
> (Consultation officer, CDC Centre-Sud)

This co-creation support service supported three projects: a healthcare community of practice (discussed further in relation to networks and partnerships), a pet day care for people experiencing homelessness, and an initiative by an evening centre for people with mental health problems to better meet the needs of younger clients. The director of the evening centre came to the LPIC because she noticed that their clientele was ageing, and they were concerned that the centre was not providing a sufficient offering for younger adults in the neighbourhood who suffer from mental health problems. The centre operates under the principles of democratic functioning (where members vote on services and activities), and the service offer had thus become particularly skewed to the longest-term members who were more likely to vote. The LPIC was then used as a support to help co-create new services to target younger adults.

> She [Consultation officer] approached us and said, "I can help you with this!" So we said, "Okay, let's see where it can go." It really started like that, with small discussions. Following the participation of [Consultation officer] at the CDC, she brought us into a process where we'll consult the other partners, we'll consult the young people. It's really with them that this approach is done – consultations and really reflecting about what we want to do with this project and how it can really respond to the needs that have been identified on the ground.
>
> (Director, CDC Centre-Sud affiliated org 2)

The CDC facilitated several roundtables and workshops between the evening centre staff and representatives from other local organizations serving a similar target population (younger adults with mental health challenges) to determine the need and appetite for particular activities (a "listening phase"), which was followed by more intensive co-creation process with service users and potential service users. The CDC supported co-production by providing a framework for the evening centre to engage service users, facilitating meetings/workshops, recruiting and supporting participants, and providing expertise in co-design methodologies. Like the CDC Rosemont community action groups, these practices have been almost entirely driven by the community logic – the emphasis of these norms is on creating solidarity amongst a target population and better supporting their needs, rather than being constrained by issues of profitability (market logic) or public service provision (state). The focus of these workshops shows the breadth of activity in the community development sector in Montreal – while there is often a focus on the development and implementation of concrete services, the emphasis on social justice, advocacy, and empowerment illustrates the importance of a social movement basis in their activities.

Networks and partnerships

Co-production within the community sector in Montreal is rarely limited by organizational boundaries. The examples of co-production discussed thus far all take a multi-organizational form in that the services are designed not only in co-production between service users/citizens and the staff members of *one* non-profit, but instead via groups that include citizens, staff members from *multiple* non-profits, and occasionally public officials as well. Involving citizens with lived experience and staff from numerous organizations was a cornerstone for both CDC Rosemont and Centre-Sud. As discussed in the rules of DRE and the practices of the DRE action groups, interorganizational partnerships form the backbone of CDC Rosemont's norms of co-production.

Likewise, CDC Centre-Sud subsumed their co-creation approaches under a broader intention of creating and supporting networks in the neighbourhood. Some activities, such as *Soupe Locale*, were promoted for one purpose (facilitating access to small grants for citizen initiatives) but served the more important role of creating new networks between citizens and professionals who might be able to find other ways of working together on shared ideas. For Centre-Sud's youth and mental health project, similarly, while the focus of co-production was on involving service users in designing their own services, the CDC facilitators of the co-production process also brought in other local organizations to share their expertise:

> So with youth organizations, are there possible collaborations? In the sense that if there are young people who attend a facility and who have a space that's theirs, well, it takes professionals as well with the youth.
>
> (Consultation officer, CDC Centre-Sud)

As the interviewee went on to describe, the approach was taken to involve professionals from other organizations to ensure that the new youth focus of the evening centre was indeed filling a gap in provision, as identified both by professionals and by service users from other organizations. A similar approach was taken by the *Libre Espace* action group at CDC Rosemont: during the design/ideation phase, action group members undertook meetings and 'exploratory visits' of similar services in other neighbourhoods, and a focus group with professionals who have an 'expertise with the most vulnerable populations in Rosemont' to help develop the project. The focus group (which was co-facilitated by two of the group members – one professional and one citizen) asked participants for their expertise on what type of population should be targeted, where in the area there was most need for such a service, and what should be offered, among other things.

Another arena where co-design and network formation intersected was in CDC Centre-Sud's support to create a 'Caring community of practice,' with the aim of bringing together healthcare practitioners, non-profit professionals, and citizens (as patient-partners and citizen-partners) to discuss best practice in health and social care and ways to break down siloes, improve the valuing of patients' voice, and create sustainable partnerships. This initiative was brought to the LPIC because the CDC were seen to be "experts in co-creation" (Project officer, CDC Centre-Sud affiliated org 1) and could therefore facilitate the building of links between diverse partners so that this initiative could get off the ground.

> Our first co-creation workshop was really more general to first create a link between all the actors who are involved in the Caring Community: institutional actors, community actors, citizens, patients. . . . There were also people from the CIUSSS [health services], management. So there were people from everywhere. That was the idea. It was to open up the conversation and see if people were interested and to start thinking a little bit about how the Caring Community is going to fit together.
>
> (Project officer, CDC Centre-Sud affiliated org 1)

Networks and partnerships for co-production are also facilitated by a norm of community organizing that is supported within the third sector and by links between the third and public sector. One of the interviewees, a participant in one of the DRE action groups, is employed under the job title of 'community organizer' but works for a government health organization. This role is about supporting community *organizations* rather than the traditional definition of community organizing as mobilizing citizens, acting more as a partnership builder.

> Our role more precisely, as professionals, is to support community organizations that ask for it. It's voluntary. . . . Then also sometimes we offer a service in the community . . . Sometimes conferences or consulting expertise, things like that. Our support role takes different forms – facilitation, putting together a group to draft a report or applying for funding.
>
> (Community organizer, CDC Rosemont affiliated org 3)

This is significant because of the unique manifestation of institutional logics in this perspective – while the interviewee is a public servant, thus representing the state logic to an extent, their role is to support and facilitate community networks in a way that reconciles the state and community logics. This type of open communication between partners and within networks to support and enrich the co-production between professionals and citizens is in part due to a culture within the third sector that prioritizes collaboration and knowledge sharing over competition. Respondents suggested that this happens Montreal-wide (and elsewhere in Quebec), but that some areas suffer from paternalism and clientelism while other neighbourhoods (including Rosemont and Centre-Sud, but also Hochelaga) have developed strong local networks that provide mutual support for organizations to engage in co-production.

This collaborative norm is perhaps the most explicit manifestation of New Public Governance, or an emerging trend in public administration towards partnerships and network governance (Osborne, 2006). In the case of Quebec, these norms of cross-sector collaboration have long been a feature of the Quebec model of social development (McMullin, 2021a). Like the practices of community action groups and co-design previously discussed, partnership working in the third sector similarly follows the community logic, in the sense that these norms are defined by working together with those in a shared local geography.

C. *Values, beliefs, and ideas*

While there are some differences in the norms and co-production practices of CDC Centre-Sud and Rosemont, several common themes arose across interviews with employees and stakeholders that help explain the underlying ideas, motivations, and identities that shape the logics underscoring co-production. These themes also emerged from an analysis of organizational documents and observations of events and meetings.

Autonomy

One of the prevalent values across the community sector in Montreal is the importance of autonomy from the government – in asserting and insisting upon independence, community organizations explicitly reject the intrusion of the state logic into both their practices and identities. As discussed in relation to the rules that structure the sector, autonomy is a value that is also recognized and protected by the state via public policy. Discourse regarding the sector in the Government of Quebec's policy on community action (which was developed in partnership with the sector and therefore reflects its values and beliefs), asserts:

> Respect for the independence of community organizations is based in part on the fact that community action is an internal response to the needs of

> the community itself, a process that includes determining these needs and, in turn, implementing the appropriate means for addressing them.
>
> (MTESS, 2001, p. 17)

Autonomy translates into both organizational practice, by rejecting participation in certain activities that might compromise an organization's independence from the government or the market, as well as organizational values and identities. This value of autonomy leads to some instances where community organizations are reluctant to work with the government. An interviewee (a public servant/community organizer) explained that their position was sometimes treated with suspicion by organizations due to the connection with the public sector:

> There are other neighbourhoods that are more, shall we say, activist, where they are really autonomous. Autonomous community organizations, they could say, "We don't need you." They're not obligated to work with us. Just because we support an autonomous community organization doesn't mean they're not autonomous. That's not it at all. We want to support them according to their needs, their desires. We never force them, "Do this, do this, do this."
>
> (Community organizer, CDC Rosemont affiliated org 3)

Other similar examples of hesitation or outright rejection of the participation of public servants and politicians were described by interviewees as well as observed in meetings. For CDC Rosemont, this was borne out of a history of mixed relationships with the public sector that has led to a cautious distancing from some elected officials who have either been unsupportive of the community initiatives, or conversely, have tried to take credit when things have gone well. When Restopop ran a series of 'solidarity meals' early in the project to raise awareness, this required a small amount of funding to cover the cost of food and supplies. A local councilmember offered to cover the full cost of the event; however, the group decided to turn down half the money to avoid politicization or questions of ownership of the project. Similarly, debates were raised for both Restopop and *Libre Espace* about whether they would be comfortable having a local elected official involved in the groups. In both instances, the politician was welcomed (because they had former experience working directly in the community) but with the proviso that it would be in an advisory capacity rather than as a decision-maker.

The values and identities surrounding the importance of autonomy display the strength of the community logic at the expense of other potential intervening logics. One of the defining characteristics of community action organizations is that they are free to determine their mission and approaches to activities and their services and practices. This autonomy also extends to their protected ability to engage in political actions and advocacy. As the *Réseau Québécois de l'action communautaire autonome* (Quebec

Autonomous Community Action Network) describes, "Although they are funded by the government or by partners, they belong to the community" (RQ-ACA. org). This puts the sector in a unique position of having its autonomy politically and financially guaranteed by the provincial government, whilst it is simultaneously fully protected in its ability to criticize the government and undertake community work that it deems important, in the way that it deems appropriate. This, therefore, allows it to leverage the community logic in a way that mainstreams co-production for the sake of the community.

Collective action and social change

The values, beliefs, and identities expressed by interviewees from Rosemont and Centre-Sud are also strongly influenced by norms and discourses from social movements and collective action, with both neighbourhoods having long-standing histories and reputations of activism. This ethos comes through in the way that many interviewees discussed citizen mobilization for collective *action*, as opposed to more passive approaches of involvement. The co-production literature often takes a position of the need for professionals to 'harness' the skills, expertise, and resources of citizens (e.g. Bovaird & Loeffler, 2012), which places the impetus on the professional. The social movement frame instead showcases the sense of agency that citizen participants share that they can create change through collective action (Polletta & Jasper, 2001). This was evident in the discourse employed by interviewees, who often referred to the *mouvement communautaire* (community movement) or *secteur de l'action communautaire* (community action sector) rather than the third/community/associative sector.

This means that, essentially, there is no community sector without the active participation of citizens in collaboration with professionals. In many ways, the core function of the professionals who work for community development organizations in Montreal *is* to engage in co-production, rather than to deliver a service that they *can* co-produce with citizens. While the assumption in much of the co-production literature is that co-production represents a move from professional delivery of services (and indeed, this was the alternative most commonly put forward by respondents in England and France), in Quebec, co-production was juxtaposed against the idea of "traditional self-organized community provision" (see Bovaird, 2007). The community movement thus brings together traditional service provision with the tradition of self-help organizations.

> This is the basis of autonomous community action. There are no organizations that can function without the citizens being there. That's the basis. Autonomous community action organizations are set up because there are citizens who have identified a problem, got together, and finally created an organization that is sometimes more structured, other times. . . .

> Or they are going to ask, are they going to have a charter, or not. But the idea is to stand up and say, "How do we fix this? What can we do?"
>
> (Research officer, Community sector network org)

> The combination of [practitioners and citizens] is a winner. If it were just practitioners, I would find it a shame because we can speak 'for,' but then we're not speaking 'with.' And just individuals, in my experience, if it's just done by citizens, it unfortunately falls by the wayside.
>
> (Director, CDC Rosemont affiliated org 1)

The logic that shapes the organizations of the third sector in Quebec is centred around the notion of social change, citizenship, and local social development from a community-centred perspective, and thus, citizens are seen to be the central driver for all community action. Unlike citizenship discourses that link involvement with democratic participation (and therefore invoke the state logic), citizen-led co-production conceptualizes the citizen as a member of the community working towards local change.

Within each organization, a key set of priorities or frames are used to organize the actions for social change. For Rosemont, the strategic priorities set through consultation with citizens were to ensure the neighbourhood remains economically accessible; improve the use of public transport; be a neighbourhood that takes care of vulnerable, isolated, and excluded people; make the east of the neighbourhood more dynamic; and create public spaces that facilitate exchanges. In focusing on priorities around action for social change, these organizations draw upon the framing and action repertoire of social movements. As the director of CDC Rosemont reflected on the difference in approach between the first two editions of Décider Rosemont Ensemble and the third (most recent) edition, the process was redesigned to ensure that social change was at the heart of the projects developed.

> After three years we asked ourselves two questions. . . . The monitoring committee got together for the 2nd edition – 2012–2017 – and asked, do our projects really fight against poverty and social exclusion? Because for the 2nd edition, the success stories were the little free libraries, the cleaning service, etc. And strangely, we had invited professionals as experts in the fight against poverty and exclusion, knowing that the projects should all benefit from the expertise of the professionals in the fight against poverty and social exclusion.
>
> (Senior staff, CDC Rosemont)

It is important to note that the creation of a collective identity around social change is not necessarily a unique characteristic of the Quebec third sector, as compared to the English and French cases. Indeed, in many of the organizational documents in France, particularly the social centres' social plans, strategic directions are clearly defined around social goals (such as 'act for the *vivre ensemble,*' 'fight against isolation,' and 'reinforce the link with youths and integrate them into the associative life of the social centre' for Avancé). Similarly, Monalisa defines itself as a social movement. However, the French approach to social change and active citizenship was often framed in a somewhat top-down manner – with a focus on professionals *empowering* citizens, or citizens being encouraged to sign charters, for example to promise to work towards ending older people's loneliness. The Montreal cases represent a more bottom-up approach to social action, with priorities, issues, and actions all defined by citizens (or by collaborations between citizens and professionals).

Community sector versus social economy

One of the significant narratives across the non-profit organizations studied in Montreal is in the clear drawing of a line between community sector organizations and social economy organizations. As previously discussed, historical developments have resulted in a trifurcation of the third sector into three distinct categories of service provision non-profits, the autonomous community sector, and the social economy. The community development organizations studied for the research identify themselves as belonging to the autonomous community sector, and this has a significant impact on their values and identities.

> There is a big distinction – the social economy is often a place for integration of new migrants. That could be into jobs, often poorly paid jobs, and mainly focused on health and social services. . . . By comparison, the community sector, we are really about maintaining the community. We are about empowerment. So we want people to take back power, while they [the social economy] are more about delivering services. That's the big, big distinction, and we find ourselves there. It's in our mission. We're not in the social economy.
>
> (Director, CDC Rosemont affiliated org 1)

> The model is different, the organizational structure is different – a social economy process is still about turnover, productivity, the profit that you reinvest. As a non-profit organization, we're not in these issues. There is an organizational logic and then a financial logic that is completely different.
>
> (Community integration officer, CDC Rosemont affiliated org 2)

As the first interviewee describes, autonomous community organizations see their purpose as being one of empowerment and citizen involvement (and by extension of co-production in the services they deliver) in a way that invokes the community logic. In taking a position to distinguish the ACA from the social economy, there is an explicit and unambiguous rejection of the market logic from interfering in the functioning of these organizations. Interestingly, many individuals from the social economy sector did not perceive there to be a fundamental contrast in values between the social economy and community sector (with both centred around solidarity, democratic participation, and community improvement), but that this was operationalized into different practices in each sector (see McMullin, 2021b).

> So sometimes, you still have some old style ideological blocks. But in most cases, people just do what has to get done and call it whatever you want to a certain extent. It's unfortunate that there are people that keep pushing on the differences as opposed to the similarities, because there are so many of them.
>
> (President, Social economy network org 2)

> For all sorts of reasons in Quebec, autonomous community action did not want to be associated with the social economy, precisely because they were losing grants and the freedom to act, etc. . . . It's principally about the principles of the social economy conceived since 1997, but they added an element that said, 'must aspire for economic viability.' That means that a community organization that says, "I'm very happy, it's 5% of my income and I don't want to grow" – it would not necessarily be a social economy enterprise."
>
> (Director, Social economy organization)

For the autonomous community sector, this value of separation from the social economy is intricately linked to the values of autonomy and collective action, which they aim to protect from the influence of the market logic. At the same time, the necessity to find financial support for services that are not covered by core government grants has meant that community organizations have increasingly begun to venture into activities that are traditionally the domain of social economy organizations. One interviewee associated with CDC Rosemont, before explaining how they saw this distinction between social economy and community sector, mentioned that their organization had to find "other sources of funding, like social economy projects" (Community integration officer, CDC Rosemont affiliated org 2). To reconcile the community sector rejection of the market logic with the periodic shortcomings in finances, professionals discuss market activities as being social economy *projects* that therefore place them outside of the traditional value basis of the organization. This is a classic approach of segmentation within the third sector (Skelcher & Smith, 2015), where an organization reconciles competing logics by compartmentalizing certain activities that are based on a different institutional logic.

Discourses of participation, co-production, and co-creation

As we saw in the analysis and discussion of co-production in Lyon, the term *co-production* is rarely (if ever) used by practitioners in France, but French interviewees often employed the term *co-construction*, which tended to refer more to the involvement of citizens in strategic priority setting or policymaking. While nearly half of the population of Montreal report being fully (English-French) bilingual, French is the default language spoken in Rosemont and Centre-Sud. Montrealers similarly employed the term *co-construction*, which Vaillancourt (2009, p. 277) describes as the involvement 'upstream' in the design of public policy, whilst "co-production lies downstream at the moment of its implementation."

Unlike in France, however, respondents in Montreal also spoke about *co-création*. This word was used to refer to the direct collaboration of citizens/residents/service users along with paid professionals in developing *and* implementing projects or services. Used in this way, *co-création* is in fact more in line with *co-production* in English than with the academic usage of the term *co-creation* – which refers to citizen involvement in service design or strategic planning rather than in implementation (Brandsen & Honingh, 2018). Although there is a great degree of ambiguity and inconsistency across the field of both theory and practice, Table 6.1 aims to provide a comparison of the French and English terminology.

Co-création formed a significant part of the discourses of CDC Centre-Sud, where a main service offered relates to helping local community organizations engage citizens in co-creation.

> We offer a support service in ideation and co-creation of projects. For us it's important to be able to offer support to both organizations as well as citizens who want to develop projects in the neighbourhood – projects that will be at the heart of citizen development but also directly involve the actors concerned by the project.
>
> (Consultation officer, CDC Centre-Sud)

> The idea of co-creation is really to not reinvent things, but to put in place mechanisms that work with what is already here in the neighbourhood. . . . At the level of co-creation, and consultation and consultation/dialogue (*concertation*), it's really 'done by and for.'
>
> (Project officer, CDC Centre-Sud affiliated org 1)

Table 6.1 Co-creation and co-construction discourses in Quebec

Terms used by French-speaking interviewees	*English equivalent*
Co-création	Co-design: involvement in the "content and process of service delivery" (Voorberg et al., 2015, p. 15) And/or co-production: involvement in the implementation phase/delivery of services
Co-construction	Co-creation: involvement in general strategic planning of a service (Brandsen & Honingh, 2018); or co-planning

CDC Centre-Sud distinguishes between 'ideation' and 'co-creation' in a way that is similar to how interviewees from Age Better in Sheffield distinguished between co-design and co-delivery of services. In documents for CDC Centre-Sud, co-creation was described as a way to develop projects that "put citizens and concerned actors at the heart of the process of development." Interviewees from both CDC Centre-Sud and CDC Rosemont talked about 'co-creation workshops' in relation to the Caring Community for the former and as part of the Social Forum for the latter, where ideas were developed for community actions. This usage would most commonly be equated to co-design, as a forum where different stakeholder groups come together to solve a common problem.

While the term *co-creation* was enthusiastically adopted by CDC Centre-Sud, it was less prevalent in the discourse of interviewees associated with CDC Rosemont (though it was well understood if I employed the term in an interview or meeting setting). There, narratives revolved more commonly around citizen participation and mobilization.

> Since 2006, the Décider Rosemont Ensemble initiative has mobilized a large number of citizens and stakeholders around neighbourhood priorities defined collectively during social forums in order to guide the actions to be taken in the neighbourhood.
>
> (Décider Rosemont Ensemble website)

The discourses of co-*creation* and *mobilization* put a distinctly active spin on the involvement of citizens – rather than 'getting involved' or 'professionals involving citizens in co-production,' we see much more of an emphasis on citizens as a motor for social change (supported by professionals). Regardless of the vocabulary that interviewees employed, there was a near universal focus on their role as a facilitator of citizen involvement, rather than on a provider of services first, and involver of citizens second.

4 Community logic and a rejection of the state and market logics: a Social Movement Logic

In terms of the institutional logics of the community sector in Quebec, a striking picture emerged – rather than exhibiting characteristics of hybrid organizations that manage some combination of the state, market, and community logics, the Quebec organizations' rules, norms, values, and beliefs were almost exclusively defined by the community logic. When the state or market logic did arise, it was through an explicit *rejection* of the market logic and intentional distancing from the state logic. I term this driving logic a Social Movement Logic. It is important to reiterate that the organizations investigated in Montreal operate in the same sub-sector of community development activities as the Lyon and Sheffield organizations – they therefore provide equivalent types of services and are not therefore strictly civil society or advocacy organizations where one would indeed expect a Social Movement Logic to predominate. Instead, the Quebec community sector harnesses this logic to shape the service-providing portion of the sector as well.

While social movements and the community sector are typically loosely connected under the heading of civil society, social movements are characterized as collective action that is mobilized against a political opponent in order to articulate a shared grievance or claim (Tarrow, 2011). Being driven by the Social Movement Logic as I have defined it does not necessarily make an organization a 'social movement organization,' which is defined as a "complex, or formal, organization which identifies its goals with the preferences of a social movement or a countermovement and attempts to implement those goals" (McCarthy & Zald, 1977, p. 1218). Social movement organizations' purpose is to mobilize resources and recruit adherents to engage in collective actions such as protests and campaigns. Community organizations, by contrast, may exist for broader reasons than advocacy and the defence of rights including mutual aid, charity, and service provision (Frumkin, 2002). Thus, community organizations need not necessarily be involved in sustained collective action (protest) that characterizes a social movement. In Quebec, we can observe how an extended process of contention and collaboration between the state and civil society has continued to shape the autonomous community sector. These organizations now leverage a logic of claims-making, advocacy, and mobilization to support their approach to *implementation* and service provision. This has important implications for what the sector does and how.

In terms of rules, government policy, funding arrangements, and internal organizational rules all reflect the elevation of the community logic over those of the state and market. Quebec provincial government policy protects both the values of the sector as well as their basic financial stability, offering guaranteed core grant funding to organizations that officially meet the definition of autonomous community action. These organizations are therefore recognized in both their advocacy and service delivery functions. This creates a unique environment where government policy (which in other cases serves to regulate and enforce the state logic within the third sector) instead *withdraws* the state logic and creates a funding and regulatory environment in which the community logic can dominate. Internally, organizations' rules likewise revolve around the community logic. CDC Centre-Sud's Grassroots Collective Intelligence Laboratory and CDC Rosemont's Décider Rosemont Ensemble involved rules to ensure the widest possible community participation and representation (residents, potential service users, and staff of multiple local non-profits) throughout processes of co-creation/co-production.

The Social Movement Logic is also characterized by values and beliefs of social justice and change that motivate organizations' core activities, whether in advocacy or in service delivery. This is thus a clear evocation of the community logic – based on shared local identity and values, solidarity, and reciprocity. Interviewees often spoke more of 'community action' and the 'community movement' rather than the community *sector*, signalling the centrality of activism to the identity of these organizations. The narratives of interviewees from the sector centred around the importance of autonomy of the sector from government as well as in contrasting the community sector against the social economy or other non-profit organizations that provide similar services but that choose to participate in the market to do so.

CDC Centre-Sud and CDC Rosemont also both exhibited a preference for norms that similarly reflect the community logic, with both organizations regularly collaborating with citizens and other community organizations in networks and communities of practice to design and implement new services and programmes. These practices of multi-stakeholder collaborations illustrated much of what has been described under the heading of New Public Governance (NPG), which is posited to reflect a shift towards network governance, multi-stakeholder partnerships, and the increasing involvement of citizens in co-production (Pestoff et al., 2012). While the Social Movement Logic reflects the logic of the autonomous community sector organizations studied, this logic is not indicative of the third sector *as a whole* in Quebec, and indeed, social economy organizations and other types of non-profits are more likely to exhibit a blend or assimilation of the market, state, and community, similar to the Service Delivery Logic explained in Chapter 5. It is perhaps indicative of the prevalence of NPG values and norms that has enabled the existence of a multiplicity of organizational forms – and thus logics – within the broader third sector (McMullin, 2021a).

Finally, it is important to stress that although both the Social Movement Logic and the Communitarian Logic introduced in Chapter 5 are both primarily a reflection of the community logic, they differ in several fundamental ways. Under the Communitarian Logic, the dominant community logic is the result of the state withdrawing and transferring the risks and responsibilities of service provision onto citizens and the third sector, a move that is perhaps best illustrated by the cuts to public services in the UK that have resulted in the transfer of public libraries to being managed by third sector organizations and run by volunteers. The Social Movement Logic, by contrast, is a result of the state *supporting* the primacy of the community logic through public policy and funding mechanisms that enable the sector's independent approach to co-production with citizens without seeking to define or control them. The community sector under the Social Movement Logic is strengthened, rather than 'responsibilized.'

5 Implications for co-production: Social Movement Logic and citizen-led co-production

Considering the apparent accordance between theories of New Public Governance and the model of public management evidenced in Quebec, we might also expect there to be a similar correspondence between co-production theory and co-production within the Quebec community sector. However, the Social Movement Logic produces a context in which co-production between non-profit professionals and citizens does not universally comply with broader co-production theory, which is heavily influenced by a public management/Service Delivery Logic. Instead, in Quebec we see several important implications of the Social Movement Logic, as an interpretation of the community logic, on the way that co-production is undertaken:

A. Co-production is driven by citizens, supported by professionals.

While the literature tends to position co-production as a change in practice for professionals, within the Quebec community sector, citizens take a strong leadership position, and the role of the professional is often to support and facilitate rather than drive the process. The Social Movement Logic creates values and norms based around social action and citizen mobilization that foster an environment in which citizens feel empowered and supported to take ownership over services, rather than acting as passive beneficiaries. Co-production therefore tends to be citizen-led, and professionals take a facilitation role rather than a primary service delivery role (McMullin, 2020). This means that the logics that would typically be promoted by more professional practice (i.e. the state or professional logics) are less pronounced.

This type of practice therefore creates a grey area between co-production (tending to refer to services that are provided under the responsibility of a public or third sector organizations) and citizen initiatives where ownership and responsibility remain with unaffiliated and unpaid citizens (Igalla et al., 2019). This means that the professional/citizen dichotomy is less clear-cut, and therefore there are less pronounced power imbalances in these relationships. Citizen-led co-production under the Social Movement Logic is less constrained by some of the primary obstacles previously identified in the co-production literature, such as risk aversion or closed professional culture (e.g. Tuurnas, 2015). This is made possible by designing organizational cultures and structures around co-production norms and practices, and by focusing professionals' job descriptions around co-production.

B. There is no community sector without co-production.

Co-production in this instance is essentially see as the default, rather than a change, innovation, or new way of working. The notion of studying co-production between non-profit professionals and citizens/service users within the community sector in Quebec is almost nonsensical because there essentially is no community sector without co-production. All services, projects, and activities of community organizations take place through active, ongoing, and more or less equal, collaborative relationships between different stakeholder groups – nearly always including professionals from multiple non-profit organizations alongside citizens. This inherent nature of co-production in the Quebec community sector is created and supported by both rules and practices. At the outset, the autonomous community sector has been recognized by the provincial government and explicitly defined as derived from community action and driven by active citizenship approaches. Government policy also recognizes and protects the complete autonomy to determine an organization's mission and approach, thereby nullifying the impact of the state logic. Defining the community sector in this way is also a distinct effort to distinguish it from other types of third sector organizations, namely the social economy, in order to refuse participation in the market.

C. Co-production is undertaken and supported by multi-stakeholder partnerships.

Co-production in Quebec is also undertaken through collaborations between citizens with professionals from *multiple* non-profit organizations. The importance of networks as a means to facilitate professional/citizen co-production is one of the core tenets of the theory of New Public Governance, and this is evidenced in the Quebec context considerably more than in England or France where the Service Delivery and Social Solidarity Logics shape third sector organizations. However, contradicting the claims of the literature that NPG is a 'new' form of governance since the waning popularity of NPM, an NPG type of governance characterized by multi-stakeholder partnerships and a significant role for citizen co-producers has long been a part of the Quebec culture of politics and policymaking, which scholars have called the 'Quebec model of social development' (Klein et al., 2013).

Supported by the Social Movement Logic, non-profit organizations undertake co-production as a matter of collective action. The rejection of the market logic (and a supportive provincial government that retreats the state logic) facilitates co-production across organizational boundaries. Because there is less competition between community organizations for funding, collaboration and cooperation are part of the culture of the community sector. This means that co-production of new services and activities is often undertaken by multi-stakeholder groups (both the CDC Rosemont action groups and CDC Centre-Sud approach to supporting the co-creation of citizen/community sector projects). We can therefore see a type of co-production that is not simply service users + public servants, or service users + non-profit professionals, but in fact public servants + professionals from multiple non-profits + service users + other members of the community.

6 Summary and conclusions

The autonomous community sector in Montreal provides a distinctive case to deepen our understanding of the potential breadth of co-production approaches between professionals and citizens. While non-profit organizations in Sheffield and Lyon exhibited characteristics of hybridity between multiple institutional logics, the Montreal community organizations reject the market logic and have developed a strategic entente with the government that limits the influence of the state logic on their rules, practices, and values. This overall guiding logic is what I term a Social Movement Logic, which facilitates co-production that is citizen-led, focused on social and community change, and embedded in multi-organizational networks and partnerships.

The implications of the Social Movement Logic and citizen-led co-production for our understanding of the collaboration between citizens and non-profit professionals are significant. Citizen-led co-production blurs the boundaries between what we traditionally conceive as co-production (services initiated by formal organizations, where citizens are brought into the process) and the facilitation of citizen initiatives (where professionals support projects that are started by citizens). This also shows that there is potential for widespread, sustainable collaboration between citizens and professionals in service design and delivery, but this necessitates a policy context that supports the operational and financial independence of community organizations. The key factor distinguishing the Social Movement Logic from a Communitarian Logic is that the state does not *withdraw* from supporting public services and the third sector but rather maintains financial support and protects organizations' autonomy in policy and practice.

Notes

1. At the request of interviewees, these organizations have not been anonymized, but all respondents are fully anonymized.
2. Members of the Quebec National Assembly
3. The French word *construire* is translated directly to 'construct' to reflect the parallels between the discourse of 'co-constructing'/'*co-construire.*'

References

Arsenault, G. (2018). *L'économie sociale au Québec: Une perspective politique*. PUQ.

Bourque, G. (2000). *Le modèle québécois de développement. De l'émergence au renouvellement*. Presses de l'Université du Québec.

Bovaird, T. (2007). Beyond engagement and participation: User and community coproduction of public services. *Public Administration Review, 67*(5), 846–860.

Bovaird, T., & Loeffler, E. (2012). From engagement to co-production: The contribution of users and communities to outcomes and public value. *Voluntas, 23*(4), 1119–1138.

Brandsen, T., & Honingh, M. (2018). Definitions of co-production and co-creation. In T. Brandsen, T. Steen, & B. Verschuere (Eds.), *Co-production and co-creation: Engaging citizens in public services* (pp. 9–17). Routledge.

Frumkin, P. (2002). *On being nonprofit: A conceptual policy primer*. Harvard University Press.

Greenwood, R., Díaz, A. M., Li, S. X., & Lorente, J. C. (2010). The multiplicity of institutional logics and the heterogeneity of organizational responses. *Organization Science, 21*(2), 521–539.

Igalla, M., Edelenbos, J., & van Meerkerk, I. (2019). Citizens in action, what do they accomplish? A systematic literature review of citizen initiatives, their main characteristics, outcomes, and factors. *Voluntas*, *30*(5), 1176–1194. http://doi.org/10.1007/s11266-019-00129-0

Jetté, C. (2011). The role of community organizations in the transformation of the social development model in Quebec. *Canadian Journal of Nonprofit and Social Economy Research*, *2*(1). http://doi.org/10.22230/cjnser.2011v2n1a65

Klein, J.-L., Fontan, J.-M., & Harrisson, D. (2013). The Quebec model: A social innovation system founded on cooperation and consensus building. In *The international handbook on social innovation: Collective action, social learning and transdisciplinary research* (p. 371). Edward Elgar Publishing.

Loeffler, E., & Bovaird, T. (2021). User and community co-production of public value. In *The Palgrave handbook of co-production of public services and outcomes* (pp. 31–57). Palgrave Macmillan.

McCarthy, J. D., & Zald, M. N. (1977). Resource mobilization and social movements: A partial theory. *American Journal of Sociology*, *82*(6), 1212–1241. http://doi.org/10.1086/226464

McMullin, C. (2020). Co-production of public services: Institutional barriers to the involvement of citizens in policy implementation. In H. Sullivan, H. Dickinson, & H. Henderson (Eds.), *The Palgrave handbook of the public servant* (pp. 1–17). Springer International Publishing. http://doi.org/10.1007/978-3-030-03008-7_26-1

McMullin, C. (2021a). Challenging the necessity of New Public Governance: Co-production by third sector organizations under different models of public management. *Public Administration*, *99*(1), 5–22. http://doi.org/10.1111/padm.12672

McMullin, C. (2021b). *Financial mechanisms for innovative social and solidarity economy ecosystems: The case of Quebec*. International Labour Organization. www.ilo.org/global/topics/cooperatives/sse/WCMS_829908/lang-en/index.htm

McMullin, C., Roy, M. J., & Curtin, M. (2021). Institutional logics as a framework for understanding third sector development: An analysis of Quebec and Scotland. *Policy & Politics*, *49*(4), 615–632. https://doi.org/10.1332/030557321X16239357875918

Ministère de l'Économie et de l'Innovation. (2015). *L'économie sociale, des valeurs qui nous enrichissent: Plan d'action gouvernemental en économie sociale 2015–2020*. Gouvernement du Québec. www.economie.gouv.qc.ca/fileadmin/contenu/publications/administratives/plans_action/plan_action_economie_sociale_2015-2020.pdf

Ministère du Travail, de l'Emploi et de la Solidarité sociale (MTESS). (2001). *Community action: A crucial contribution to the exercise of citizenship and the social development of Quebec*. Gouvernement du Quebec. www.mtess.gouv.qc.ca/sacais/action-communautaire/politique-reconnaissance-soutien_en.asp

Ministère du Travail, de l'Emploi et de la Solidarité sociale (MTESS). (2004). *Cadre de référence en matière d'action communautaire*. Gouvernement du Québec. www.mtess.gouv.qc.ca/sacais/action-communautaire/cadre-reference.asp

Ministère du Travail, de l'Emploi et de la Solidarité sociale (MTESS). (2021). *Cadre normatif du Programme de soutien financier des Corporations de développement communautaire (CDC)*. Gouvernement du Québec. www.mtess.gouv.qc.ca/sacais/soutien-financier/CDC/index.asp

Osborne, S. P. (2006). The New Public Governance. *Public Management Review*, *8*(3), 377–387.

Pestoff, V., Brandsen, T., & Verschuere, B. (Eds.). (2012). *New Public Governance, the third sector and co-production*. Routledge.

Phillips, S., & Smith, S. R. (2014). A dawn of convergence?: Third sector policy regimes in the "Anglo-Saxon" cluster. *Public Management Review*, *16*(8), 1141–1163.

Polletta, F., & Jasper, J. M. (2001). Collective identity and social movements. *Annual Review of Sociology*, *27*(1), 283–305. http://doi.org/10.1146/annurev.soc.27.1.283

Skelcher, C., & Smith, S. R. (2015). Theorizing hybridity: Institutional logics, complex organizations, and actor identities: The case of nonprofits. *Public Administration*, *93*(2), 433–448.

Tarrow, S. G. (2011). *Power in movement: Social movements and contentious politics*. Cambridge University Press.

Tuurnas, S. (2015). Learning to co-produce? The perspective of public service professionals. *International Journal of Public Sector Management*, *28*(7), 583–598.

Vaillancourt, Y. (2009). Social economy in the co-construction of public policy. *Annals of Public and Cooperative Economics*, *80*(2), 275–313.

Voorberg, W. H., Bekkers, V. J. J. M., & Tummers, L. G. (2015). A systematic review of co-creation and co-production: Embarking on the social innovation journey. *Public Management Review*, *17*(9), 1333–1357.

7 Non-profits, institutional logics, and co-production

A conceptual model

The analyses presented in Chapter 4, 5, and 6 contribute to two key areas of the inquiry: first, the study of third sector organizations as different hybrids of multiple institutional logics, and second, through the application of these hybrid types to illustrate different types of co-production that emerge under each. In this chapter, I synthesize and compare the findings in relation to these two themes. The chapter precedes first with a discussion and comparison of the three models of hybrid organization – the Service Delivery Logic, Social Solidarity Logic, and Social Movement Logic – as evidenced in England, France, and Quebec. The various similarities and differences of the logic combinations are explored and discussed before turning to the implications for co-production with citizens/service users. I explore the conceptual basis for co-production under each logic and the prevalent types of co-production that result.

Building upon these findings, I propose some descriptions of other types of hybrid organizations that are likely to characterize other third sector organizations and propositions of how these will therefore shape organizations' approaches to co-production. Finally, I return to some of the key themes of the co-production literature, particularly in relation to the perceived benefits of, opportunities for, and barriers to co-production, and reflect upon the implications of the models for our understanding of whether, why, and how co-production takes place in different contexts.

1 Models of third sector hybrid organization

Through the analysis of community development organizations (in England, France, and Quebec), programmes to reduce loneliness and isolation of older people (England and France), and parent/toddler programmes (England and France), we arrive at three distinct combinations of institutional logics that shape the rules; practices; values, beliefs and ideas of organizations and form the basis of their approach to co-production. The institutional logics approach allows us to go beyond existing international typologies of the third sector (which primarily focus on public policy, employment, and sources of funding) to more deeply interrogate how these contextual

DOI: 10.4324/9781003245605-7

differences shape the day-to-day practices of professionals who work for these organizations and the service users and citizens they work with.

In the following section, I briefly summarize the three models before turning to a comparison of the implications for approaches to co-production. Many have often noted the difficulty in pinning down a single definition or domain of the third sector (see e.g. Brandsen et al., 2018), and this typology does not aim to further convolute an already complex web of definitions. Rather, this typology is presented as an instrument to better predict, explain, and compare organizational practices, connecting macro, meso and micro level analyses.

A. *Service Delivery Logic (SDL)*

The SDL as presented in England reflects an assimilation of the market, state, and community. In this configuration, organizations are driven primarily by values and beliefs stemming from the community logic but must reconcile these with rules associated with the market (performance management and efficiency) and the state (redistribution and democratic accountability). This assimilation can be seen as a strategic attempt to manage priorities, tools, and values that stem from the imposition of challenger or conflicting logics (McMullin & Skelcher, 2018). As a result, the SDL is characterized by an emphasis on the functional or instrumental purpose as non-profits rather than democratic and expressive functions.

B. *Communitarian Logic*

The Communitarian Logic can be seen as a sort of sub-logic of the SDL, where organizations are shaped by only the community and market logics when the state more or less abandons service provision and leaves the third sector on its own to fill gaps. Pestoff (2018, 2019) contends that a communitarian public administration regime has become more prominent in recent years, which is the result of outsourcing responsibility – without policy and financial support – of public services to communities and the third sector. Under this logic, third sector organizations maintain their community (logic) roots, but without state support, their rules and practices must contend with participation in a competitive marketplace against each other and private businesses. As a result of public sector austerity and the 'hollowing out' of the state in England, the weak impact of the state logic in many cases has challenged the SDL and increased in the prominence of the Communitarian Logic in its stead.

C. *Social Solidarity Logic (SSL)*

In France, the dominant logic combination exhibited, the SSL, reflects a blend of the (Napoleonic) state logic with the French interpretation of a community logic, where the strong influence of the state in terms of representative democracy, universality, and redistribution must be translated into the local context by non-profit organizations. This therefore results in a primacy of formal and recorded rules over more informal practices in shaping the logics of organizations, while their values and narratives reflect a translation of French Republican values (i.e. liberty, equality, fraternity, solidarity, and *vivre ensemble*) into a local context.

D. *Social Movement Logic (SML)*

Finally, the SML in Quebec results as a rejection of the market and separation from – and at times opposition to – the state, elevating the community logic (promoting collective action, networks, and partnership building). While both the Communitarian Logic and SML have in common the primary influence of the community institutional order and limited impacts of the market and state, there are significant differences between these two logics and their impacts on organizations. In Quebec, the SML exists because of an accord between the provincial government and the community sector that permits the withdrawal of government influence over the sector but importantly maintains financial support. The Communitarian Logic contrasts clearly to this, as the state has *withdrawn* both policy control as well as financial support of the sector, leaving third sector organizations to essentially pick up the pieces as a matter of survival.

E. *Generalization of the guiding institutional logics*

These distinct combinations of institutional logics that drive and shape third sector organizations are highly contingent upon the cultural, institutional, and historical contexts in which the organizations operate. It is important to note that these logics may not be indicative of *all* third sector organizations in each of these contexts. However, in the case of England, other research has drawn similar conclusions about the assimilation of the state, market, and community and how this impacts organizational practices (see e.g. Vickers et al., 2017). Likewise in France, interviews undertaken with numerous academics and third sector stakeholders in Paris, Marseille, and Lyon as well as a working group on the notion of 'shared public services' in France corroborate the findings regarding the Social Solidarity Logic in France.

Quebec is perhaps a unique case, because the heterogeneity of the 'third sector' makes it impossible to draw conclusions about other types of non-profit organizations that exist in this context, especially when it comes to traditional non-profit organizations and social economy organizations. The Social Movement Logic can in fact only be said to characterize autonomous community organizations, which are a particular form of non-profit that receive guaranteed core government funding to support a mission of autonomy from the state, community empowerment, and social development.

These organizations are therefore highly unique in their rejection of both the market and state logics, which distinguish them from other social economy organizations that embrace hybrid characteristics and assimilate the state, market, and community (in ways we might expect to mirror the SDL). This example indicates how an identified combination of logics may in fact not be universally applicable across the third sector in a given context.

Quebec also provides a contrasting case in the fact that the third sector ecosystem, and therefore the institutional logics that shape it, vary considerably from the rest of Canada. As discussed in McMullin et al. (2021), historical, cultural, and linguistic factors in Quebec have coalesced in a way that creates a third sector ecosystem that has little in common with the other provinces of Canada. Because the logics discussed are therefore unique to the Quebec context, the findings of a Social Movement Logic are less likely to characterize organizations in the other provinces of Canada, where there is considerably more evidence of the market logic shaping the third sector and an absence of the type of policy frameworks that support the community sector like in Quebec (White, 2012).

2 Implications for co-production

These distinctive logic combinations create conditions that enable and constrain co-production in different ways. As a result, the citizen and professional collaborations in each instance form different types of co-production:

The ***Service Delivery Logic*** supports ***pragmatic co-production***, which is premised on using co-production methods instrumentally to improve the lives of individuals or small groups of individuals. Pragmatic co-production focuses on incremental rather than radical changes and improvements. This pragmatic approach generally aligns well with the dominant theories of co-production, i.e. as a way to make better use of the resources of different stakeholder groups (Bovaird & Loeffler, 2012) and to value the lived experience of citizens and service users (Trischler et al., 2019). What is often under-emphasized under this perspective is the impact on democracy and the potential for broader societal and systems change.

The ***Communitarian Logic***, when the state is withdrawn from the SDL, results in ***enforced co-production*** rather than co-production that is voluntary and pragmatic. In these instances, co-production becomes a matter of survival, as opposed to an ambitious or innovative way to collaborate to make things better. Enforced co-production occurs when citizens/service users are included in service delivery because the service would cease to be delivered otherwise. In this sense, the role of citizens substitutes that of professionals, rather than complementing their contributions, thereby calling into question the degree to which this type of arrangement can still be considered co-production.

The ***Social Solidarity Logic*** reflects a generally more rules-based society where the inconsistency and the informality of co-production conflicts with expectations of universal public service provision and equity. This creates a type of ***formalized co-production***, where the collaboration between citizens and non-profit professionals is codified and required by organizations rather than emerging organically or through employing 'test and learn' approaches. In this instance, co-*construction* (of policy or strategies) serves perhaps an even more crucial function as organizations view citizen involvement in strategic priority setting as being as (if not more) important than involvement in implementation/delivery. Co-production is thus linked to other traditional conceptions of citizen participation, such as participatory democracy.

Finally, the ***Social Movement Logic*** fosters ***citizen-led co-production***, where the role of non-profit professionals is to support and facilitate the process rather than to act as 'traditional' service providers who seek to bring citizens into service delivery. In some ways citizen-led co-production inverts the notion of co-production – while the focus is still on professionals and citizens working together to provide services, the starting point of the exercise is from the community and citizens rather than from professionals and/or the state. The SML also creates coalitions of organizations around shared missions of societal change, which enables co-production between citizens and professionals from multiple organizations and stakeholder groups.

From one perspective, one could argue that the approaches to co-production under each of these models are *different*, but that none is inherently *better* than another, that instead each approach adapts to its particular cultural, institutional, ideological, and normative context, and serves to achieve the aims appropriate to that context. However, taking this perspective means that we also limit the true potential for co-production to have broader and longer lasting impacts on the welfare state and the ability of social services to adapt to evolving citizen needs. Not all approaches to co-production will be able to achieve the ambitious aims of empowering service users, democratizing the welfare state and improving public service outcomes.

As Pestoff (2021) argues, 'transformative co-production' creates systems reform through social innovation and more ambitious changes to organizing and ways of working. Transformative co-production is argued to be based on participatory, inclusive, and collective approaches and involves citizens in a broader reach of the activities. Pestoff contrasts this type of co-production against 'aspirational' approaches, which are more ad hoc and uncoordinated, focusing on individuals and the ways that they can co-create value in the service chain. This type of co-production leaves little space for democratic improvements or broader societal change and there is more 'lip service' paid to true reform than actual action.

Table 7.1 builds upon this perspective in light of the SDL, SSL, and SML in the three contexts. The Service Delivery Logic (SDL) in England most closely aligns with Pestoff's description of 'aspirational' co-production, though I term the prevalent approach in this context 'pragmatic co-production.' With this logic, NPM tools and values have created a conceptual basis for co-production that is based on service management, where co-production is conceived as a way of creating or adding value as part of

Table 7.1 Third sector logics and types of co-production

Third sector logic	*Conceptual basis for co-production*	*Prevalent types of co-production*
Service Delivery Logic (market, state, and community)	Service management	**Pragmatic:** personalization, individual and group approaches, ad hoc, some enforced
Social Solidarity Logic (state and community)	Participatory democracy	**Formalized:** involvement in governance, strategic priority setting, collective
Social Movement Logic (community and a rejection of market and state interference)	Collective action	**Citizen-led:** mainstreamed, empowered, collective

a service chain or ecosystem (Osborne, 2020). This type of co-production is more likely to concentrate on ad hoc or peripheral contributions of citizens, rather than integrating them into genuine public service reform. As outlined in the previous section, when the state logic withdraws entirely from the SDL and results in a Communitarian Logic, the ad hoc nature of co-production is reinforced.

Neither the formalized co-production under the SSL nor citizen-led co-production under the SML directly reflect Pestoff's notion of transformative co-production. The conceptual bases underscoring co-production reflect the unique combinations of logics in the French and Quebec contexts. The former is based on participatory democracy as a guiding concept or value, leading to co-production that is mainstreamed and collective but highly formalized and standardized in a way that limits the creative potential that transformative co-production aims to achieve. The overabundance of rules and a Napoleonic State logic that stifles long-term structural changes and flexible approaches hinders the kind of broader cross-sector partnerships, networks, and bottom-up innovation required for transformative co-production. Opportunities for citizen participation are generally controlled; thus, while co-production occurs in the spaces in which it is permitted, the overall structure of the welfare state and state-society relations remain somewhat impermeable to reform.

By contrast, citizen-led co-production under the SML, as evidenced in Quebec, has most in common with New Public Governance regimes; however, this type of co-production relates to interactions in service delivery that are driven by citizens more or less outside of the broader public service architecture. Citizen-led co-production is supported by a conceptual basis of collective action, rather than a service-dominant or traditional democratic participation approach. While citizen-led co-production under the SML demonstrates perhaps the most significant potential for transformative co-production, it also differs from Pestoff's conception in important ways. Because of the rejection of state influence in community sector provision of services, there is a degree of disconnect with the welfare state, meaning that there is a threat to key principles of equitable redistribution and universal access to public services. This type of co-production represents a mid-point between traditional co-production and the facilitation of citizen initiatives, where paid professionals support the development of community services and projects that are instigated by citizens. This creates the potential for fragmentation and clientelism at the expense of broader democratically determined priorities.

3 Other proposed types of non-profits logics and implications for co-production

The SDL, SSL, and SML are by no means a comprehensive typology for the universe of non-profit hybrids and types of co-production that they undertake. Given the range of cultural, historical, linguistic, and political traditions, the combination of institutional logics shaping the non-profit sector will be highly contingent upon an organization's location and point in time. In this section, I present propositions about two other potential forms of non-profit hybrid organization and the implications of these for co-production with citizens/service users. Because the basis of the third sector is that of civil society, the community logic (or a locally specific interpretation of the community logic) is a necessary component of these types of organizations, but there is a great degree of variation of the influence of other logics, as we have seen in the analysis of France, England, and Quebec.

The SDL, SSL, SML, and the two logic variations discussed in the following section are indicative of broad, multi-purpose non-profit organizations, rather than more specialized organizational types, such as faith-based organizations or organizations providing highly specialized services, such as health care. These types of organizations would integrate further institutional logics – a religious logic in the former and a professional logic in the latter – but these are beyond the scope of this analysis. I conjecture that we can predict the likely predominating blends or assimilations of institutional logics in a given context by considering existing typologies of non-profit regimes (Salamon & Anheier, 1997), administrative traditions (Painter & Peters, 2010), and public management models (Pollitt & Bouckaert, 2011). Given the Western-centric focus of these typologies, the proposed hybrid types are more likely to describe the non-profit organizations in Western democracies with well-developed welfare states and non-profit sectors.

A. Weak (or absent) state + weak community + strong market logic = Social Business Logic and calculated co-production

Like the SDL, another type of state/market/community logic assimilation involves a much weaker influence of the state and stronger influence of the market logic on third sector organizations. This type of hybrid assimilation might characterize non-profit organizations under Liberal welfare regimes and non-profit regimes in contexts or sectors in which public provision of services is weak. These types of organizations are more likely to associate with the notion of social enterprise or social businesses in the Anglo-Saxon perspective, meaning an organization that sells goods and services but also operates for social benefit, or in other words, works towards a double (or triple) bottom line (Cornelius et al., 2008).

There are several potential implications of this logic on how and why professionals might engage citizens in co-production. Because of the substitution of the market logic for the state logic, organizations driven by this type of Social Business Logic are likely to conceive of their service users as customers, rather than citizens. While some previous studies argue that New Public Management approaches to service users as customers are inherently incompatible with co-production (e.g. Pestoff, 2012), others describe different types of co-production that recognize different modes of co-production. Osborne and Strokosch (2013), for example, discuss 'consumer co-production' as an interaction between the service user and provider that is a natural part of the service production process. From this perspective, co-production is about empowering service users as customers.

The Social Business Logic thus underscores an approach to co-production that is almost exclusively focused on individual service users and their needs, rather than on broader community benefit or societal change. Professionals may be driven or constrained by the financial implications of co-production – in other words, co-production may be undertaken only if it is financially feasible and beneficial to the organization – effectively deepening the SDL implication that co-production is undertaken for *pragmatic* reasons to the point that co-production is undertaken for *calculated* reasons – in this instance, if it is deemed that involving service users/citizens in service delivery will not directly benefit the financial bottom line (or the more nebulously defined social/ethical bottom line).

B. Social Democratic state + community logic = collective community logic and public-voluntary **sector** *co-production*

A variation of the state and community hybrid that differs from the French SSL is the form of organization characterized by a strong Social Democratic state logic assimilated with a community logic. This type of 'collective community' logic is representative of third sector organizations in the Nordic countries, where the third sector is comparatively small when measured in terms of paid employment but extremely large and active when considering the number of voluntary organizations and volunteers (Henriksen et al., 2019). This is because with the extent of welfare services provided by the state, the third sector has traditionally played more of an expressive rather than instrumental role, meaning that the focus of non-profit organizations is heavily skewed towards civic and political engagement instead of service delivery (Frumkin, 2002).

In this instance, the state and community logics both shape the third sector, but through different impacts on organizational rules, norms, and values than the SSL. The state logic comes through in relation to values and practices around public services – unlike Liberal and Corporatist contexts, the assumption under the collective community logic is that the state is responsible for public service provision, and therefore the third sector is an *additional* resource rather than a substitute, arm of the state, or contractor. This shapes the expectations of what the sector is and what it is for. Like the SML in Quebec, the community logic is the most defining force for these organizations, but unlike Quebec, this does not result in practices of community control over public services. The establishment of vast welfare states in the Scandinavian countries created a logic of appropriateness specifying the state as the universal provider of social services (Ibsen et al., 2021).[1] The state logic remains strong because of the argument that the community on its own, without the protection of the state, results in a postcode lottery where people who live in some locations have access to high-quality, affordable, and effective public services while others do not.

The collective community logic has important implications for the study of co-production by third sector organizations in Social Democratic countries. In Danish, for instance, the term *samskabelse* is often translated as *co-production* or *co-creation*, but it is understood broadly to encompass the involvement of citizens *and* community groups in public service provision (Mortensen, 2020). Because the third sector is composed more of voluntary groups rather than professionalized service providing organizations, an analysis of co-production between citizens/service users and paid non-profit employees has less applicability in this context. Under this logic, co-production relates to the contributions of the third sector as organized groups of citizens to the delivery of public services provided by the state, which Frederiksen et al. (2021) refer to as 'community co-production.' Co-production is therefore framed as a complement to the work of government service providers, as a way to increase community connections and capitalize upon volunteer efforts without curtailing the responsibility of the state.

4 Challenges and opportunities for co-production

One of the important areas for co-production research is to better understand how and under what conditions co-production can be facilitated. Thus far, co-production theory has primarily focused on identifying opportunities and constraints for co-production from a general and universal perspective. However, as we have seen, each institutional logic poses particular opportunities for and constraints to co-production, and therefore when non-profits blend or assimilate multiple logics, they are faced with the potential consequence of the competing or conflicting rules, norms, and values from each of these (see McMullin, 2020). The institutional logics that guide organizations in context shape the challenges and opportunities for co-production in different ways.

These challenges can be categorized as follows: the role of the state vis-a-vis the third sector, getting citizen co-producers involved, the design of co-production processes/activities, and the challenge of ad hoc versus enduring co-production. Some challenges and opportunities were common across the cases, while others experienced obstacles in different ways due to the inherent contradictions between their guiding institutional logics.

A. Role of the state – control, scepticism, and austerity

One of the key areas when considering the co-production between non-profit professionals and citizens/service users is the role that the state plays vis-a-vis the third sector. For instance, the state logic is associated with bureaucracy, hierarchy, and standardization that create obstacles for co-production, while conversely the values of democracy and equality would be seen to bolster co-production. The state logic has significantly different impacts under the three hybrid logics evidenced. France, England, and Quebec can be characterized as operating under different models of public management – Neo-Weberian State, NPM, and NPG, respectively – which create different relationships between the state and civil society and employ different tools and values to manage these relationships (McMullin, 2021).

First, the case of Quebec is perhaps unique in that the outright rejection of state influence and insistence upon autonomy and rich community involvement is one of the defining features of the community sector. The government supports this separation through public policy and funding to the sector, thereby facilitating an approach to co-production that has little influence of the state logic. While this has the benefit of allowing the sector complete flexibility and agency in determining how best to work with service users and citizens, the lack of state influence risks the potential to endanger universal access to necessary local services.

For the French cases, the Napoleonic State is the most important source of constraints or obstacles to co-production. Because of the emphasis on the state as protector of the general interest as well as the particularly French notion of *service public*, based on the notions of continuity, equality, and mutability (Gilbert, 2006; Chevallier, 2015), the state comes in direct conflict with community-oriented approaches to co-production. The state – whether directly through policies and regulations, or indirectly through the norms and values that trickle down into the third sector – therefore acts as a barrier to co-production in France in ways that were not evidenced in the English and Quebec cases. This has posed a significant challenge to the promotion of co-production both within the third sector and by the public sector in France. A French working group on the idea of '*Services publics partagés*' (shared public services) was convened in 2021 to promote the notion of co-production and explore ways to facilitate the involvement of citizens and communities in public service provision. It has found the greatest obstacle to be the lack of a supportive legal framework.

Finally, in England, the state constrains co-production in other ways, primarily in the access to funds – or lack thereof. Cuts to public services in the UK have created barriers for co-production in many ways. Government contracts for services (from the local authority or health service) are often restrictive and prescriptive in their expectations, which prevents organizations from taking more holistic and long-term collaborative approaches. In addition, the temporality of funding creates constraints on co-production. Organizations rarely receive funding for more than a few years at a time, and both grants and contracts are constantly at risk of not being renewed. This means that even when co-production works well, once it ends, the gains achieved often fall by the wayside. The state logic also creates normative barriers to co-production – whether officially required by contracts or not, the NPM norms of performance management and measurement have created a culture within the third sector of box ticking and of measuring success based on, for example, 'number of individuals engaged with.' This creates adverse incentives to spend extended periods of time supporting and facilitating co-production with a smaller number of (perhaps 'harder to reach') individuals and therefore limits co-production to quantifiable actions rather than qualitative improvements.

B. Getting people involved

The challenge of attracting and retaining citizens and service users as co-producers took different forms under the three logics. In Sheffield, encouraging citizens to engage in co-production was a challenge experienced by all the case studies, no matter the service area. This was often framed as being due to service users' own characteristics – i.e. that they lack the skills, confidence, or desire to engage in co-production. For Best Start Communities Count, this identification of a lack of parent volunteers' skills and capacity to co-produce parent groups led to a reconfiguration of the programme to ensure that professionals took a greater leadership role and would be available to take on facilitation duties if a parent was unable.

In some instances, interviewees in Sheffield indicated that engaging service users in co-production was difficult (or impossible) because service users simply were not interested in being more involved beyond receiving the service. One of Age Better in Sheffield's projects that aimed to target people 'at risk' of social isolation (i.e. approaching retirement) found that these potential service users did not want to be beneficiaries because they did not perceive themselves as being in need of support, but they instead wanted to become volunteers, challenging the overall focus and approach of the programme.

Similarly, while it was generally recognized in Sheffield that co-production is a 'good' thing to do (i.e. a valence issue), several respondents were sceptical about the degree to which it is necessary for certain types of services and certain types of service users. For example, directors from Aspire (the original director in 2015 and their successor in 2019) discussed how they did not believe that service users *wanted* to get more involved.

> On a day-to-day basis, it's a little bit harder to get local people involved. That's largely because most people have such busy, hectic and very often chaotic lives, that they're struggling with their own day-to-day matters, let alone us saying, "What do you want from [Aspire]?" and so on. So people prefer to come and be told what we're going to give them.
>
> (Director [2015], Aspire)

> Our clients on specific projects are generally in financial crisis for whatever reason, for whatever circumstances, and they are quite understandably interested in getting support to help them out of that crisis. They are not interested in engaging, in being involved, in a learning, co-production, a research aspect, activity.
>
> (Director [2019], Aspire)

This sentiment was echoed by others, such as the director of Develop, who lamented that the organization struggled to co-produce a community clean-up day with residents because residents "wanted somebody else to do it (for them)" (Director, Develop, interview 2), or as the director of Enterprise expressed when asked what the barriers to involvement were, "Sometimes I think the clients themselves, because they're not used to thinking for themselves, really. They see themselves as passive recipients" (Director, Enterprise, interview 1).

The challenges of engaging citizen co-producers in Sheffield reflect some of the assumptions about service users and the nature of service delivery by these organizations. Service delivery is perceived as the primary overall purpose of the organization, with co-production being but one (generally positive, beneficial, and preferred) way of working with service users. However, the NPM context of the UK has created a culture of customerization of public services, with the dominant narrative being one of 'choice or exit' as options. This means that both professionals and service users are sometimes challenged to articulate the purpose of co-production if there isn't a direct and immediate benefit for the individual involved.

In Lyon, many of the interviewees expressed few challenges in getting residents involved in governance bodies as trustees or in formal membership activities (for instance, annual general assemblies attract the participation of a large proportion of members, especially when compared to the AGMs of the Sheffield organizations), but other types of involvement faced more obstacles. Some organizations, such as Avancé and ACEPP, discussed many instances when citizens were supported to develop their own initiatives, while other organizations found that involving residents in the day-to-day co-production of activities was more challenging.

> As far as the board is concerned, the trustees are very present and very invested in their role as trustees and volunteers of the social centre.

> Where we have to maybe still improve things as a social centre, it's more in the role with residents: how do we reach them, and how do we propose and create actions?
>
> (Development officer, Mouvement)

An interviewee from Diversité expressed similar concerns about the difficulty of engaging residents in co-production but found the organization's culture and professionalism to be a particular barrier to this – staff were seen to be good at delivering services but were not yet accustomed to changing their way of working to focus more on welcoming the proposals of citizens. Also mentioned were restrictions imposed by government as barriers to getting people involved, such as a tendency for all consultations to be very top-down, allowing little space for bottom-up initiatives. These barriers are generally reflective of how the Social Solidarity Logic creates conditions for formalized co-production: because rules form a significant element of organizations' logics, the opportunity space for informal approaches to co-production is often restricted.

For the Montreal organizations, most arenas (CDC Rosemont action groups and CDC Centre-Sud's various collective actions) struggled less in getting some – often very active – citizens involved in co-production. Because the Social Movement Logic favours active citizenship as a means to solve local problems, the community sector in Montreal is based on a foundation of citizen co-production and culture of involvement.

> It's currently easy to mobilize citizens around an issue. Very, very easy. Here I'm not talking about Rosemont – I'm talking about Montreal. Very easy – give a small budget, simple steps, it's easy, not complicated. A co-creation roundtable, co-decision, co-implementation. . . . Then it's done, you do the communication. It's great.
>
> (Senior staff, CDC Rosemont)

Where involvement becomes difficult, as several Montreal respondents described, is in involving people with lived experience (i.e. vulnerable, isolated, excluded individuals). The citizen co-producers involved in the CDC Rosemont action groups in particular tend to be relatively educated, articulate, and actively involved in the community. Drawing in the involvement of those who might more realistically be service users/beneficiaries of the services developed proved to be more of difficult. This was a challenge similarly raised by respondents from CDC Centre-Sud, especially in relation to the 'young adults and mental health' project and another project that explored the idea of a 'pet day care' for people experiencing homelessness (so that they could attend medical appointments, etc.) For both projects, finding a way to involve individuals in precarious situations was a constant source of discussion. In both instances, staff members of organizations working with target populations were tasked to act as representatives of their clientele in planning/design meetings rather than the citizens themselves.

C. *Designing co-production processes effectively*

Regardless of the logics driving co-production, ensuring that co-production activities are fit for purpose, meet citizen co-producers' needs and desires, and are effectively designed to maximize the benefits for all involved are challenges faced across the board. Because of the variation in motivations driving professionals in different locations, professionals raised different issues regarding the design of co-production. The issue of time and resources was, in some way or another, often a barrier for co-production. This means that the way that resources are employed is especially crucial for ensuring that co-production is effective. For the Lyon organizations, the design of co-production was a smaller part of the discussion because citizen involvement was typically written into organizational plans and structures rather than seen as something intermittent or tied to a particular service. Thus, in the instances where interviewees discussed ways to improve co-production, this generally involved conversations around improving organizational culture and professional practice to become more open to involving citizens more effectively, as a broader organizational project.

In Quebec, the non-profit organizations put a lot of consideration into the way that co-design workshops and the co-creation action groups were organized and run, including the timing of events (in the evenings or weekends, how long events would last) as a means to attract the maximum amount of participation. This was a topic of some debate across both CDC Rosemont and CDC Centre-Sud. For CDC Rosemont, each iteration of the Décider Rosemont Ensemble (DRE) process was adjusted to best facilitate the collaboration between non-profit professionals and citizens in developing new projects and creating social change. The first round of DRE was organized around separate working groups of community sector professionals and citizens, but this was later adapted to combine the groups. The focus of the process was also updated from organizing around sectors (i.e. youth, older people, health, etc.) to organizing around concrete and concerted interventions to ensure that co-production would have a broader collective benefit rather than attention being focused on particular segments of the resident population.

Timing and design of meetings, events, and activities was also a preoccupation for the Quebec and Sheffield organizations. ABIS focused co-design activities around sub-sets of the older population in particular neighbourhoods, for instance with separate men's and women's groups in one area with a large Muslim population. For the CDC Rosemont action groups studied for the research, numerous discussions and debates were had about the timing and location of meetings to best suit citizens' availabilities. This was a matter of some contention for one of the groups when one of its meetings was moved to 4:00 p.m., prompting criticism that this would prevent any of the citizen co-producer group members who work full-time from attending. Also considered as part of the design of co-production was the length of meetings. As one interviewee described, "People will say, 'I don't have a day to waste discussing DRE. *Pff.* That's too long. A half-day? Ah, yes, I'll be there!'" (Senior staff, CDC Rosemont). Likewise, the staff at CDC Centre-Sud discussed the reality of working in the community sector and the idea that focusing on citizen involvement meant that staff members would have to be flexible about their workday. According to one senior staff member at CDC Centre-Sud, "If you do citizen participation, it's certain that you can't have a 9–5 job."

Both CDC Centre-Sud and CDC Rosemont also took great care to ensure that co-production is social, welcoming, and fun for citizens. To launch a 'collective evaluation report' of its activities to support for collective action in the community, CDC Centre-Sud put on a 'Fest-Éval' event (a play on *festival* and *evaluation*), which was a drinks reception in a bar with music and graphic representations of different initiatives decorating the walls. Stakeholders at the event presented outcomes and lessons learned from their projects. CDC Rosemont also focused on providing a convivial atmosphere to solicit citizen involvement in co-production and maintain enthusiasm, including a similar 'neighbourhood meeting' event that included drinks and a buffet.

In Sheffield, ABIS and BSCC both experienced tensions between the way co-production was designed into programmes and the reality of how it worked in practice, sometimes with strict requirements of how co-production should be undertaken (the activities in which citizens should be involved and who was targeted to participate) proving to be unrealistic or unworkable. As noted in relation to the challenges of getting people involved, BSCC adapted its programme design to reduce the expectations on parent volunteers to be responsible for a broad range of aspects of the programme to allowing parents to contribute more to complementary tasks so as not to overburden them.

In other cases in Sheffield, programme designs that were focused on co-producing everything led to some instances of stretching the definition of who was a 'person with lived experience' in order to become a citizen co-producer. For example, most of the interventions by ABIS required that 'older people' (defined as anyone over the age of 50) needed to be involved in designing and delivering all services. However, some interviewees expressed scepticism about all older people as 'peers' in practice – for instance, some citizen co-producers were in their early 50s (and still in the workforce), while many of the actual service users were in their 80s, in poor health, or otherwise quite vulnerable. This meant that while the older 'co-producers' technically ticked the box of being "older," they otherwise had little in the way of shared life experience with the people they were meant to be representing.

D. Balancing service delivery and democratic civil society functions

Co-production confronts third sector practitioners with the challenges of balancing the functions of being a non-profit organization. As discussed in Chapter 2, non-profits serve both instrumental (service delivery) and expressive (civic/political engagement) functions (Frumkin, 2002). The purpose of co-production extends across these functions – contributing both to service delivery improvement and citizen mobilization/engagement, yet the focus on one of these areas over another is more common in certain types of organizations.

Given the name, it is perhaps no surprise that organizations driven by the SDL prioritize their instrumental function as non-profits. Indeed, Frumkin's (2002) typology of non-profit and voluntary action functions contains service delivery (on the demand-side) and social entrepreneurship (on the supply-side) as the two elements of the instrumental rationale. When it comes to co-production by organizations under this logic, the pragmatic approach to co-production wins out over considerations of citizenship and democracy. As non-profit organizations become more and more drawn into service provision as part of a competitive marketplace, their role as part of the democratic fabric of society becomes increasingly devalued. One of the ways we see this play out for the organizations in Sheffield is through their descriptions of organizational purpose – when asked to describe the organization, the directors of all the organizations studied described the history of the organization and the services they provide.

For organizations under the SSL, service delivery is seen as contributing to involvement and collaboration (or co-production), rather than the assumed inverse of co-production contributing to service delivery. This is based on an overall identity of third sector actors that is expressed through narratives about 'what we believe' rather than 'what we do' or 'what we deliver' – often structured around three or four founding values, such as human dignity, solidarity, and democracy in the case of the social centres. One interviewee suggested that this is perhaps a particularly French phenomenon that reflects the importance of '*liberté, égalité, fraternité*' to the French political consciousness. With the prioritization of co-construction and values-driven motivation, the French organizations do not frame co-production practices as being about service improvement. Rather, services are conceived to contribute to the overall values and aims of the organization of supporting solidarity, *vivre ensemble*, and citizenship. This was demonstrated most strongly in the social centres and ACEPP, where clear and successful examples of co-production were identified. In these instances, the services were conceived as pragmatically contributing to the value goals of the organization rather than the other way around.

The SML creates conditions that frame co-production as straddling the expressive and instrumental functions of non-profits. While narratives express values of social change and citizen mobilization, these are harnessed for concrete direct action and the creation of much-needed services and activities in the community. The expressive and instrumental functions are thus merged in the organizations in Montreal. This is because while the community development organizations studied are indeed practical and action-based (i.e. focusing on collaborating directly to solve problems), their values basis and norms are strongly influenced by social movement norms of collective action, mobilization, and (to an extent) protest as repertoires for creating social change. Co-production is therefore a way to leverage the values and practices of a democratic civil society to support and improve service delivery.

E. Ad hoc versus enduring co-production

Scholars have suggested that for co-production to have the greatest chance of creating long-term benefits and broader changes to public service systems, citizens need to be involved in co-producing enduring social services rather than simply ad hoc activities. Ad hoc co-production is also less likely to be sustainable over the long term, because citizens' sense of efficacy and connection to a programme will be challenged if their contributions seem trivial to them (Pestoff, 2014). Indeed, Joshi and Moore (2004) and Bovaird (2007) go so far as to specifically define co-production as the "*long-term* relationships" between professionals and citizens. The extent of involvement in ad hoc activities versus enduring co-production is another of the areas that varied between the three contexts because of their guiding logics.

For the organizations in Sheffield, examples of long-term or enduring co-production were less common than ad hoc, time-limited co-production. This is due almost exclusively to the reliance on short-term grants and contracts that organizations faced. Ad hoc co-production, where citizens participate in a limited scope of activities, included involvement in one-off events (such as co-design workshops or delivering a community clean-up day) or in limited-term services that wrapped up at the end of a grant (such as many of the services and projects delivered under ABIS). The way that these organizations have been shaped by the SDL, strongly influenced by a UK government focus on short-term cost savings, means that sustainability of these programmes and the citizen-professional collaborations that underpin them has often been side-lined.

When co-production was framed as part of community development in Sheffield, organizations were more likely to engage citizens in co-producing enduring services to build capacity and empowerment. For example, BSCC's approach of co-producing parent/toddler groups and family activities with parents was a key effort to ensure the lasting impact of the programme. The challenge for organizations to develop these types of enduring services and co-production practices prompted several interviewees from the community development case studies to express criticism towards the short-term orientation of many funders as well as other organizations working in the city, especially larger, sometimes national organizations who receive contracts to deliver services in Sheffield for the first time without having developed relationships with local organizations and citizens.

In Montreal, the tension between short-term and long-term co-production became a topic of significant debate and contestation for the DRE programme at CDC Rosemont. At an event celebrating successes of the action groups over the previous year, it was suggested that a 'second round' of action groups should be convened, each focusing on new *short-term* actions rather than the development of large, long-term ambitious projects (such as the community restaurant, which would take several years to develop), while still maintaining the requirement that these actions be co-produced between citizens and community sector professionals. The idea of a wave of short-term action groups was proposed to reignite enthusiasm for the process and to bring in new citizen co-producers who might find it difficult to engage in groups that had already been working together for some time.

However, this suggestion was met with considerable opposition on the part of the citizen participants present at the event. Several individuals objected to the requirement that these actions be limited to short-term interventions, because of the lack of potential to create long-lasting connections, solutions, and change to the neighbourhood. This episode of contention shows another example of the logics at play in Montreal and how they shape co-production. Because co-production is primarily led by citizens and focused on local social development and change, the suggestion to change focus to less-ambitious projects and ad hoc co-production was met with resistance because citizens perceived this as being counter to the ethos of DRE.

In general, there was a balance between ad hoc and long-term co-production for the French organizations. Like most of the themes around co-production under the SSL, the French organizations' long/short-term orientation to co-production was shaped by an overall influence of rules, most notably the rules that clarify how and when citizens should be involved. This therefore codified an approach of co-production into the enduring services provided by the non-profit organizations, particularly in childcare, social support, and wellbeing. Long-term engagement was centred around membership in the associations with citizens playing a continued role in setting the strategic direction of the organization and making decisions about the types of services to provide.

At the same time, however, supporting citizen initiatives was an important area for professional and citizen collaboration, and these initiatives generally had a limited duration with more of a focus on events and one-off activities than on enduring relationships. This included, for instance, the community picnics and free market (Avancé) or the many one-off events and activities developed by parent volunteers as part of the co-operative nurseries. Unlike the SDL, where ad hoc co-production occurs as organizations move from one limited-time project funding to another, the French citizen-led projects (and, similarly, Quebec's shorter-term collective actions) were of limited duration by design and not forced to be short-term by financial necessity.

5 Summary and conclusions

This chapter presented a model of institutional logics driving third sector organizations in England, France, and Quebec and the way that these logics in turn help to explain differences in co-production between non-profit professionals and citizens/service users. The Service Delivery Logic, Social Solidarity Logic, and Social Movement Logic are each based on different combinations of the state, market, and/or community. These create different conceptual bases for co-production that thereby privilege different types of co-production approaches: service management and pragmatic co-production, participatory democracy and formalized co-production, and collective action and citizen-led co-production, respectively. I also posit that other types of non-profit organization, outside of the scope of this empirical study, are likely to predominate in other contexts. These include a Social Business Logic that preferences calculated approaches to co-production and a Collective Community Logic that operates co-production between public organizations and voluntary groups, the latter of which may be more prevalent in the Scandinavian context.

Understanding how institutional logics create varieties of non-profit hybrid organization in different contexts is important for our understanding of whether, how, and why non-profit organizations engage citizens in co-production. First, as noted earlier, different guiding logics will tend to preference different approaches to co-production. Second, the opportunities and constraints for co-production will present differently because of these guiding logics. In taking forward the research agenda on co-production and the third sector, employing the institutional logics approach can help us to better anticipate why, for example, professionals may struggle to engage citizens in co-production in one context but not another, or why one approach to co-production may be more successful in one case but may come up against obstacles in another.

Note

1. This may apply less to the Swedish case, where the government has long adopted an NPM-style approach to privatization of many key social services.

References

Bovaird, T. (2007). Beyond engagement and participation: User and community coproduction of public services. *Public Administration Review*, *67*(5), 846–860.

Bovaird, T., & Loeffler, E. (2012). From engagement to co-production: The contribution of users and communities to outcomes and public value. *Voluntas*, *23*(4), 1119–1138.

Brandsen, T., Steen, T., & Verschuere, B. (Eds.). (2018). *Co-production and co-creation: Engaging citizens in public service delivery*. Routledge. www.taylorfrancis.com/books/9781351792578

Chevallier, J. (2015). *Le service public* (10th ed.). Presses Universitaires de France.

Cornelius, N., Todres, M., Janjuha-Jivraj, S., Woods, A., & Wallace, J. (2008). Corporate social responsibility and the social enterprise. *Journal of Business Ethics*, *81*(2), 355–370. http://doi.org/10.1007/s10551-007-9500-7

Frederiksen, M., Henriksen, L. S., & Grubb, A. (2021). Innovation without participation? The counterfactuals of community co-production. In B. Ibsen (Ed.), *Voluntary and public sector collaboration in Scandinavia* (pp. 195–224). Palgrave Macmillan (Palgrave Studies in Third Sector Research). https://doi.org/10.1007/978-3-030-72315-6_8

Frumkin, P. (2002). *On being nonprofit: A conceptual policy primer*. Harvard University Press.

Gilbert, T. (2006). Evolution du service public et principe de subsidiarité. *Revue française d'économie, 21*(1), 3–36.

Henriksen, L. S., Strømsnes, K., & Svedberg, L. (2019). Understanding civic engagement in the scandinavian context. In *Civic engagement in Scandinavia: Volunteering, informal help and giving in Denmark, Norway and Sweden* (pp. 1–32). Springer.

Ibsen, B., Levinsen, K., Fehsenfeld, M., & Iversen, E. B. (2021). Voluntary-public sector co-production in Denmark: Why differences between Welfare areas? In *Voluntary and public sector collaboration in Scandinavia* (pp. 101–136). Palgrave Macmillan (Palgrave Studies in Third Sector Research).

Joshi, A., & Moore, M. (2004). Institutionalised co-production: Unorthodox public service delivery in challenging environments. *Journal of Development Studies, 40*(4), 31–49.

McMullin, C. (2020). Co-production of public services: Institutional barriers to the involvement of citizens in policy implementation. In H. Sullivan, H. Dickinson, & H. Henderson (Eds.), *The Palgrave handbook of the public servant* (pp. 1–17). Springer International Publishing. http://doi.org/10.1007/978-3-030-03008-7_26-1

McMullin, C. (2021). Challenging the necessity of New Public Governance: Co-production by third sector organizations under different models of public management. *Public Administration, 99*(1), 5–22. http://doi.org/10.1111/padm.12672

McMullin, C., Roy, M. J., & Curtin, M. (2021). Institutional logics as a framework for understanding third sector development: An analysis of Quebec and Scotland. *Policy & Politics, 49*(4), 615–632. https://doi.org/10.1332/030557321X16239357875918

McMullin, C., & Skelcher, C. (2018). The impact of societal-level institutional logics on hybridity: Evidence from nonprofit organizations in England and France. *Voluntas, 29*(5), 911–924. http://doi.org/10.1007/s11266-018-9996-8

Mortensen, N. M. (2020). *The challenges of translating and implementing co-production in care services: A Danish case study*. Aalborg Universitetsforlag.

Osborne, S. P. (2020). *Public service logic: Creating value for public service users, citizens, and society through public service delivery*. Routledge. http://doi.org/10.4324/9781003009153

Osborne, S. P., & Strokosch, K. (2013). It takes two to tango? Understanding the co-production of public services by integrating the services management and public administration perspectives. *British Journal of Management, 24*(S1), S31–S47.

Painter, M., & Peters, B. G. (2010). Administrative traditions in comparative perspective: Families, groups and hybrids. In *Tradition and public administration* (pp. 19–30). Palgrave Macmillan.

Pestoff, V. (2012). New public governance, co-production and third sector social services in Europe: Crowding in and crowding out. In V. Pestoff, T. Brandsen, & B. Verschuere (Eds.), *New public goverannce, the third sector and co-production* (pp. 361–380). Routledge.

Pestoff, V. (2014). Collective action and the sustainability of co-production. *Public Management Review, 16*(3), 383–401.

Pestoff, V. (2018). Co-production at the crossroads of public administration regimes. In T. Brandsen, T. Steen, & B. Verschuere (Eds.), *Co-production and co-creation: Engaging citizens in public services* (pp. 27–36). Routledge.

Pestoff, V. (2019). *Co-production and public service management: Citizenship, governance and public service management*. Routledge. http://doi.org/10.4324/9781351059671

Pestoff, V. (2021). *Co-production and Japanese healthcare: Work environment, governance, service quality and social values*. Routledge.

Pollitt, C., & Bouckaert, G. (2011). *Public management reform: A comparative analysis: New public management, governance, and the neo-Weberian state* (3rd ed.). Oxford University Press.

Salamon, L., & Anheier, H. (1997). *Defining the nonprofit sector: A cross-national analysis.* Manchester University Press.

Trischler, J., Dietrich, T., & Rundle-Thiele, S. (2019). Co-design: From expert- to user-driven ideas in public service design. *Public Management Review, 21*(11), 1595–1619. http://doi.org/10.1080/14719037.2019.1619810

Vickers, I., Lyon, F., Sepulveda, L., & McMullin, C. (2017). Public service innovation and multiple institutional logics: The case of hybrid social enterprise providers of health and wellbeing. *Research Policy, 46*(10), 1755–1768.

White, D. (2012). Interest representation and organisation in civil society: Ontario and Quebec compared. *British Journal of Canadian Studies, 25*(2), 199–229.

8 Conclusions and implications for the study of non-profits and co-production

Co-production is a complex and sometimes messy practice – any time multiple groups are brought together to collaborate, there is the possibility of misunderstandings, mismatched goals, and most importantly, the risk of failure. When non-profit professionals and citizens co-produce services, we see further complications arise as professionals balance competing logics that shape how they interact with citizens. Staff may face pressures to be community-rooted yet business savvy, give fair and equal treatment yet respond to unique needs in different communities, or focus on fighting for social change while maintaining core service provision. These competing demands – logics – vary considerably between non-profit organizations operating in different places, sectors, and time periods. A comparative research approach allows us to better understand co-production in context.

In this final chapter, I provide a summary of the findings from the research and implications for the literature on co-production, the third sector, and institutional logics. This book has endeavoured to bridge these streams of research to better explain whether, why, and how co-production is done in different contexts, so that we may be more sensitive to the opportunities and constraints that are present in different locations. The book concludes by reflecting on the limitations of this study and by discussing avenues for future research.

1 Summary

Chapter 2 presented theories and evidence on the co-production of public services and how co-production is understood in relation to the third sector. The notion of co-production stems from public administration traditions centred on understanding how bringing citizens into the process of service design and delivery can improve public services. As the third sector, or non-profit organizations, are drawn into welfare service provision in many contexts, this has become an increasingly important area of inquiry. The chapter also explores our understanding of what the third sector is and how it differs in various countries. Typologies of non-profit regimes and conceptions of the social economy provide a basis upon which to develop

DOI: 10.4324/9781003245605-8

important comparative insights into how and why professionals within these organizations engage citizens in different ways.

Chapter 3 presented the framework for analysis of co-production within the non-profit sector. Institutional logics, or the rules; practices; values, beliefs, and ideas that characterize the market, state, and community institutional orders, variably shape non-profit organizations in different contexts in ways that inform their approaches to co-producing services with citizens/service users. This framework provides a new way of looking at the enablers of and obstacles to co-production, giving us an insight into the macro-, meso-, and micro-level constraints that organizations and individuals face.

Chapter 4 examined case studies in Sheffield, England, of community development organizations, a parent and toddler group programme, and a programme to address loneliness and isolation of older people. While there are some differences in the approaches to co-production and the logics that shape these organizations, there are also some shared lessons across the cases. The analysis showed that organizations in Sheffield are most constrained by the conflicts they experience between the need to be more business-like and engage in performance measurement (market logic) with their traditional practices and narratives of community rootedness (community logic), which makes co-production challenging. A pragmatic focus on co-production as instrumentally improving service delivery also predisposed organizations to shorter-term and ad hoc approaches to co-production, with difficulty in establishing enduring co-production practices due to the short-term nature of grants and contracts.

In Chapter 5, I presented cases from Lyon, France, including five 'social centres,' a parent co-operative, and a coalition to tackle older people's loneliness and isolation. The logics that shaped non-profits in Lyon involved a blend of the state and community (with little evidence of the market logic), which created a focus on formalized processes of involvement (in governance and other decision-making processes) and more focus on co-production as a value rather than an instrumental approach to service improvement. In being linked more to values of participation and democracy, co-production was more about what the organizations believe, rather than what they do or produce. Rather than being constrained by funding and business values, the French non-profits find tensions with the restrictiveness of the French state logic and a strictly delimited notion of what 'public service' and the protection of the 'general interest' mean in contrast to the participation of citizens.

Chapter 6 provided an analysis of ethnographic fieldwork with two community development organizations in Montreal, Quebec, Canada, and their specific approaches to co-producing collective actions between non-profit professionals and citizens in two neighbourhoods of the city. The Quebec organizations were driven by the community logic and a deliberate rejection of the market and state logics. Unlike the French and English organizations, in Quebec, co-production is more driven by citizens, with professional and citizen collaborations occurring in designing and delivering services and projects through multi-organizational partnerships. The autonomous community sector, a particular type of organizations under the heading of the third sector in Quebec, is facilitated in this approach of being community-led through agreements with the provincial government to respect the autonomy of the sector and provide core grant funding.

Chapter 7 reflected on the findings from Sheffield, Lyon, and Montreal, presenting and comparing the three models of institutional logics and types of co-production – a Service Delivery Logic and pragmatic co-production, Social Solidarity Logic and formalized co-production, and Social Movement Logic and citizen-led co-production, respectively. These three models have important implications for our understanding of co-production as a situated practice that is informed by the cultural, linguistic, historical, and institutional context in which organizations exist. These guiding logics impact the challenges faced by organizations, including the relationships with the state, challenges and opportunities in getting citizen co-producers involved, and striking a balance between service delivery and democratic functions and ad hoc versus enduring services.

2 Implications for theory

Co-production offers significant potential to improve public services, but decontextualized studies of the opportunities for and barriers to co-production prevent us from making best use of empirical findings in practice. The lack of research from a comparative perspective has meant that each study tends to adopt one perspective on co-production that is assumed to be understood in and applicable to all contexts. For many years, theorists have been calling for a greater attention to institutions to the study of co-production, as well as the comparison of cases in different countries.

In this volume, I have attempted to respond to both calls. I have applied an institutional logics framework to assess the nuances in the rules; practices; values, beliefs, and ideas that shape non-profit professionals' collaborations with citizens in service delivery. The evidence in France and Quebec challenges some of the principal assumptions of co-production theory, particularly theories situated in a service management approach. In these two contexts, co-production is grounded more on a value basis of participatory democracy and collective action, respectively, which predispose organizations towards co-production approaches that do not necessarily align with theories that position co-production as part of a chain of value creation.

The study also contributes to our understanding of the motivations for co-production. Previous studies have demonstrated the drivers of co-production at the individual level of citizens/service users and professionals (Bovaird et al., 2015; Van Eijk & Steen, 2014, 2016; Tuurnas, 2015) and the organizational level, comparing the public and third sectors (Pestoff, 2009). This study extends this analysis of why and how co-production takes place by identifying factors at the broader field (meso) level and national (macro) level that impact local organizations. While it is important to recognize the agency of individuals and organizations in their own decision-making and behaviour, an analysis of higher-level institutions provides a previously lacking element to interpret why and how co-production happens and what factors enable and constrain actors.

The research also expands the attention of co-production theory primarily on what actors *do* to a focus on the narratives and discourses of co-production. The narratives and stories told by third sector actors relating to their perspectives on co-production reveal more than just the explicit motivations for doing so (e.g. to improve services, etc.) but also the values and beliefs that are linked and help to provide a more nuanced picture of the complex relationships between the factors that impact individuals' and organizations' justifications for behaviour. Taking discourse as a component of social practice (Fairclough, 1995), the study demonstrates how the language that actors use and the concepts that they discursively link to the concept of co-production contribute to the overall production of meaning and practice.

Finally, the research broadens our understanding of co-production within the non-profit/third sector, which has until recently been given less attention in the study of co-production in comparison to public organizations as service providers. The analysis of organizations in three contexts provides new evidence both of co-production by non-profit organizations, as well as deepening our understanding of the different types of hybridity that exist within the non-profit sector(s).

3 Implications for practice

The contribution of this work is both theoretical as well as practical, with concrete applications for public servants and non-profit practitioners who aim to engage citizens and service users more effectively in co-production. The institutional logics approach helps us to better explore the potential for co-production in contexts where the concept is less widely part of the public discourse. While co-production has long been on the public policy agenda in the UK and other countries, in France this notion is only recently gaining public attention as a potential mode of improving public provision. For example, in 2021 a working group convened to discuss how to promote the notion of 'shared public services' in France. Though this group was founded around the ideas of co-production, its debates about the benefits of and barriers to co-production and shared public services have differed considerably from similar discussions in the UK. In an editorial in *L'Obs* news magazine, the group notes that the greatest obstacle to co-production is the state:

> Today, the approach of shared public services suffers from a lack of recognition, cultural difficulties linked to the absence of a real legal

> framework, and a total lack of means to allow initiatives to emerge and spread. These framework gaps potentially expose this approach to abuses: it must not be a way to allow the abandonment or disengagement of the State, or even be perceived as such.
>
> (L'Obs, 2021)

Understanding the logics embedded within particular types of organizations can help: (a) identify the types and sources of barriers and constraints that organizations face in engaging in co-production (e.g. laws, internal governance, and/or funding and contract requirements), (b) explain the drivers and motivations that actors cite for engaging in co-production (e.g. to improve services, or because the organization sees its overall purpose as supporting democratic engagement), and (c) provide insight into the values and beliefs of third sector actors and how these relate to co-production.

The institutional logics approach can thus be used as both a theoretical/analytical framework as well as a practical tool to help practitioners better understand their organization and the opportunities and constraints that it faces in undertaking particular activities. Outlining rules; practices; and values, beliefs, and ideas can help to identify the under-the-radar barriers to facilitating co-production that is empowering, effective, and sustainable. This type of approach or reflection might look like the following:

***Rules*:** What are the formal regulations, procedures, and policies that impact the organization? For example, these might include public policies, contracts, internal policies, and official procedures.

***Practices*:** How do we normally 'do things around here'? This can be determined by observing professionals or having them describe a normal day in their work, including processes, informal procedures, and ways of working.

***Values, beliefs, and ideas*:** Why do we do the things that we do? What motivates us to work in the ways that we work? What do we believe about the work that we do? These values are described by people who work for the organization, as well as in organizational mission statements, strategic plans, and annual reports.

Identifying the rules that shape an organization will help to pinpoint any formal conditions that may inhibit (or in some cases require) professionals to engage citizens in co-production. If these are public policies or funding arrangements, an organization may therefore be expected to adapt its practices accordingly. Alternatively, they may seek out other sources of funding, negotiate with funders, or engage in advocacy with public powers to promote or support co-production practices. Typically, rules are the one area of institutional logics that non-profit professionals can easily identify, and indeed, in many cases this is the area that is most commonly blamed as an obstacle to co-production.

Outlining organizational norms can help to ascertain whether there is a disconnect between official expectations and practice. Discussing and reflecting upon 'how we do things around here' can also reveal how organizational culture and ways of working might obstruct seemingly well-designed co-production approaches. For instance, this might include how professionals communicate with one another and with service users, or the way that meetings are facilitated. Finally, interrogating the values, beliefs, and ideas within the organization presents a way of evaluating the motivations for engaging in co-production, what drives professionals and citizens to take part, and what they believe will be achieved.

4 Limitations and future research

As with any qualitative case study analysis, there are limitations to the research. The case selection may be the first limitation – by focusing primarily on organizations that were suggested as 'best practice' examples of co-production, it is impossible to assess the extent to which these organizations are like others in their areas. The research also only focused on community development organizations, programmes to reduce loneliness and isolation of older people, and parents' organizations/programmes. Studying multiple organizations in each context was an aim to minimize these shortcomings, but the findings represent an interpretation only of the organizations under study and cannot be generalized to a broader population of organizations. Indeed, we are likely to see an existence of other logics in other service areas, especially health and social care, where a professional logic is likely to influence co-production practices.

While the models of a Social Solidarity Logic and Service Delivery Logic appear to describe the cases across the three service areas within Lyon and Sheffield, it is not possible to say with certainty whether these findings are representative of third sector organizations in these two cities, or France and England more broadly. In Quebec, we would be very likely to see a different combination of logics and approaches to co-production in other sub-sectors and possibly in other cities, given the heterogeneity of the third sector in the province.

The methods of data collection may be a second limitation to the research. The identification of practices, because they are "demonstrated through conduct" (Lowndes & Roberts, 2013, p. 52), is naturally best done through observation. While this was the approach taken for the Quebec fieldwork, in England and France it was necessary to sacrifice some of the depth that would have been attained through longer-term immersion for observation in the case study organizations in order to study multiple organizations within the timescale available for fieldwork.

Practices were identified through triangulating interview data with organizational documents and a limited number of observations in some of the case studies, but I appreciate there may be discrepancies between the way practices are described by actors (and in official documentation) and how they are undertaken in day-to-day work. The research also encountered challenges in relation to studying narratives and discourse in two languages. The use of discourse and conceptualization of certain terms are extremely nuanced, both within and between languages. My ability, as a native English speaker, to interpret semantics in French is limited by my own linguistic and cultural subjectivities. I assume full responsibility for any mistakes, misinterpretations, or shortcomings of the research.

These caveats aside, my hope is for this study to open the possibilities for more comparative research on co-production. There is significant scope to take this research agenda forward. The institutional logics approach provides a new and important framework to study non-profit practices in any context, allowing us to understand the nuanced impacts of the state, market, and community on organizations' ways of working, their constraints, and drivers. Further studies are needed that explore whether, how, and why non-profit organizations engage citizens in co-production in contexts beyond the three studied for this project. Compelling questions remain about the co-production practices employed by non-profit organizations in other contexts. Taking this approach also allows us to better extend the geographic focus of co-production research – as Sicilia et al. (2019) demonstrate in a systematic review of the literature, over half of the recent articles on co-production focus on individual European countries. With this geographic prejudice, we take the risk of drawing conclusions and lessons about how and why co-production works that are biased by the institutional and cultural context in which studies were undertaken.

There is a particular need for more research on co-production in other types of non-profit and welfare regimes, particularly Southern European, post-Socialist countries and most importantly, countries of the Global South, where there is less history of public service provision by the state but important traditions of provision by third sector organizations. Studying co-production by non-profits in these other contexts would help us to identify further logic combinations beyond the Service Delivery, Social Solidarity, and Social Movement Logics that shape non-profits' approaches to co-production, enhancing the hybridity literature as well.

More research is needed that explores the similarities and differences between the approaches of public and third sector organizations. The inconsistencies in the unit of analysis when studying co-production and the third sector – i.e. whether we are studying third sector *organizations* co-producing public services *with the state*, or whether instead the focus is on the professionals who work for TSOs and how they engage service users in co-producing the services delivered by the organization – has often impeded clear development of this area of research, and there is significant scope for further work in this area.

Furthermore, the institutional logics framework developed in this manuscript can be employed to study other types of non-profit organizational practices, such as advocacy approaches, internal organizational cultures, and human resources. There is a need for more comparative non-profit/third sector research that goes beyond the macro level and delves deeper into the micro-level day-to-day of third sector work. For instance, Knutsen (2012) explores the expressive and instrumental functions of non-profit organizations from an institutional logics perspective. Expanding this type of approach (where the logics of organizations are identified inductively rather than taken as a given based on indicators such as a particular government policy) to explore organizations from an international comparative perspective could provide important insights.

The value of international comparative research is that it provides a window into the experiences of people and organizations who may have different assumptions, motivations, and expectations about the role of citizens and professionals in service provision. If co-production is to achieve the ambitious aims of democratizing welfare services, improving communities, and addressing wicked challenges, then it is important to take inspiration from experiences from across international borders as well as those in our own backyards.

References

Bovaird, T., Ryzin, G. G. V., Loeffler, E., & Parrado, S. (2015). Activating citizens to participate in collective co-production of public services. *Journal of Social Policy*, *44*(1), 1–23.

Fairclough, N. (1995). *Critical discourse analysis: The critical study of language*. Longman.

Knutsen, W. L. (2012). Adapted institutional logics of contemporary nonprofit organizations. *Administration & Society*, *44*(8), 985–1013. https://doi.org/10.1177/0095399712438371

La France doit passer à l'heure des Services Publics Partagés. (2021, September 27). *L'Obs*. www.nouvelobs.com/ecologie/20210927.OBS49148/la-france-doit-passer-a-l-heure-des-services-publics-partages.html

Lowndes, V., & Roberts, M. (2013). *Why institutions matter: The new institutionalism in political science*. Macmillan International Higher Education.

Pestoff, V. (2009). Towards a paradigm of democratic participation: Citizen participation and co-production of personal social services in Sweden. *Annals of Public and Cooperative Economics*, *80*(2), 197–224.

Sicilia, M., Sancino, A., Nabatchi, T., & Guarini, E. (2019). Facilitating co-production in public services: Management implications from a systematic literature review. *Public Money & Management*, *39*(4), 233–240. https://doi.org/10.1080/09540962.2019.1592904

Tuurnas, S. (2015). Learning to co-produce? The perspective of public service professionals. *International Journal of Public Sector Management*, *28*(7), 583–598.

Van Eijk, C. J. A., & Steen, T. P. S. (2014). Why people co-produce: Analysing citizens' perceptions on co-planning engagement in health care services. *Public Management Review*, *16*(3), 358–382.

Van Eijk, C. J. A., & Steen, T. P. S. (2016). Why engage in co-production of public services? Mixing theory and empirical evidence. *International Review of Administrative Sciences*, *82*(1), 28–46. https://doi.org/10.1177/0020852314566007

Appendix A
Sheffield interviews

Number	*Role*	*Organization*	*Interview date*	*Interview date (follow-up fieldwork)*
1	Director (2015)	Aspire	15 Oct 2015	
2	Project manager	Aspire	27 Jan 2016	
3	Director (2019)	Aspire		30 Oct 2019
4	Director	Develop	22 Oct 2015	16 Oct 2019
5	Community development officer	Develop	26 Nov 2015	
6	Director	Enterprise	27 May 2015	22 Oct 2019
7	ABIS project coordinator	Enterprise	15 Oct 2015	17 Oct 2019
8	Director (2015)	Leisure	03 Jul 2015	
9	Programme officer 1	Leisure	22 Sep 2015	
10	Programme officer 2	Leisure	05 May 2016	
11	Director (2016)	Leisure	02 Nov 2016	
12	Director	Recreation	02 Apr 2016	
13	Senior staff 1	ABIS	02 Jul 2015	
14	Board member 1 (volunteer)	ABIS	15 Jul 2015*	22 Oct 2019
15	Board member 2 (volunteer)	ABIS	15 Jul 2015*	
16	Frontline staff 1	ABIS	15 July 2015*	
17	Frontline staff 2	ABIS	15 July 2015*	
18	Senior staff 2	ABIS		14 Oct 2019
19	Senior staff 3	ABIS		16 Oct 2019
20	Volunteer 1	ABIS		17 Oct 2019*
21	Frontline staff – associated organization	ABIS		17 Oct 2019*

Number	*Role*	*Organization*	*Interview date*	*Interview date (follow-up fieldwork)*
22	Board member (from external organization)	ABIS		22 Oct 2019
23	Staff member 3	ABIS		24 Oct 2019
24	Volunteer 2	ABIS		05 Nov 2019
25	Staff member 4	ABIS		13 Nov 2019
26	Volunteer 3	ABIS		13 Nov 2019
27	Programme manager	BSCC	09 Mar 2016	14 Oct 2019*
28	Community development officer	BSCC	05 May 2016	14 Oct 2019*
29	Early years practitioner 1	BSCC		14 Oct 2019*
30	Early years practitioner 2	BSCC		14 Oct 2019*
31	Staff member	Other organization 1	09 Mar 2016	
32	Director	Other organization 2	15 Jul 2015	
33	Project coordinator	Other organization 3	07 Oct 2015	
34	Project coordinator	Other organization 4	15 Jan 2015	
35	Project coordinator	Other organization 5	21 Aug 2015	
36	Staff member	Other organization 6	11 Feb 2015	
37	Director	Sheffield Network 1	09 Nov 2015	
38	Assistant director	Sheffield Network 2	15 Jan 2015	

* Group interviews (Number 14 & 15, number 16 & 17, number 20 & 21, and number 27, 28, 29 & 30)

Appendix B
Lyon interviews

Number	*Role*	*Organization*	*Interview date*
1	Regional representative	Social centre network	28 Sep 2015
2	Volunteer 1	Centre social Avancé	15 Dec 2015
3	Director	Centre social Avancé	15 Dec 2015
4	Volunteer 2	Centre social Avancé	15 Dec 2015
5	Assistant director	Centre social Avancé	06 Jun 2016
6	Director	Centre social Diversité	01 Oct 2015
7	Director	Centre social Équipe	15 Dec 2015
8	Director	Centre social Familles	01 Jun 2016
9	Development officer	Centre social Mouvement	14 Dec 2015
10	Project manager	ACEPP	12 May 2015
11	Frontline staff 1	ACEPP	12 May 2015
12	Frontline staff 2	ACEPP	13 May 2015*
13	Board member	ACEPP	13 May 2015*
14	Regional representative	Monalisa	17 Dec 2015
15	Senior staff – Monalisa org 1	Monalisa	25 Sep 2015
16	Frontline staff – Monalisa org 2	Monalisa	30 Sep 2015*
17	Director – Monalisa org 2	Monalisa	30 Sep 2015*
18	Project manager – Monalisa org 3	Monalisa	12 May 2016
19	Senior staff – Monalisa org 4	Monalisa	01 Jun 2016
20	National representative	Monalisa	15 May 2020
21	Director	Network organization 1	04 Feb 2015

Number	*Role*	*Organization*	*Interview date*
22	Senior staff	Network organization 2	16 Dec 2015
23	Director	Network organization 3	02 Feb 2015
24	Manager	Other organization 1	05 Feb 2015
25	Director	Other organization 2	06 May 2015
26	Director	Other organization 3	07 May 2015*
27	Board member 1	Other organization 3	07 May 2015*
28	Board member 2	Other organization 3	07 May 2015*
29	Director	Other organization 4	11 May 2015
30	Assistant director	Other organization 5	12 May 2015
31	Development officer	Other organization 6	29 Sep 2015
32	Manager	Ville de Lyon	18 Dec 2015

* Group interviews (Number 12 & 13, number 16 & 17, and number 26, 27 & 28)

Appendix C

Montreal interviews

Number	*Role*	*Organization*	*Interview date*
1	Director	CDC Centre-Sud	18 Oct 2018
2	Consultation officer	CDC Centre-Sud	10 Jan 2019*
3	Senior staff	CDC Centre-Sud	10 Jan 2019*
4	Project officer	CDC Centre-Sud affiliated org 1	26 Jun 2019
5	Director	CDC Centre-Sud affiliated org 2	27 Jun 2019
6	Senior staff	CDC Rosemont	25 Jun 2019
7	Director	CDC Rosemont affiliated org 1	05 Feb 2019
8	Community integration officer	CDC Rosemont affiliated org 2	06 Mar 2019
9	Community organizer	CDC Rosemont affiliated org 3	07 Mar 2019
10	Research officer	Autonomous community sector network org	13 Feb 2019
11	Staff member 1	Government of Quebec	06 Dec 2018*
12	Staff member 2	Government of Quebec	06 Dec 2018*
13	Staff member	Other organization	20 Mar 2019
14	Research officer	Rosemont – La Petite-Patrie borough council	22 Mar 2019
15	Director	Social economy network org 1	27 Nov 2018
16	President	Social economy network org 2	04 Dec 2018
17	Director	Social economy network org 2	13 Dec 2018
18	Director	Social economy network org 3	05 Dec 2018
19	Staff member	Social economy network org 4	11 Dec 2018
20	Director	Social economy organization	04 Dec 2018

* Group interviews (Number 2 & 3, and number 11 & 12)

Index